# HESSE COMPANION

# HESSE COMPANION

Edited by Anna Otten

UNIVERSITY OF NEW MEXICO PRESS

Albuquerque

*First American edition*

This volume contains the complete text of the edition published by Suhrkamp Verlag in 1970 as a companion to the twelve-volume set of Hesse's *Gesammelte Schriften* (*Collected Works*) published in 1970 by Suhrkamp Verlag.

To the Hesse students

# CONTENTS

# ACKNOWLEDGMENTS

Chapter 2, "*Siddhartha*: The Landscape of the Soul," is reprinted by permission of Princeton University Press from *The Novels of Hermann Hesse: A Study in Theme and Structure*, by Theodore Ziolkowski, © 1965 by Princeton University Press, pp. 146–77.

Chapter 3, "*The Steppenwolf*," is reprinted by permission of Cornell University Press from *Hermann Hesse: His Mind and Art*, by Mark Boulby, © 1967 by Cornell University Press, pp. 159–205.

Chapter 4, "The Fulness of Art," is reprinted by permission of New York University Press from *Faith from the Abyss* by Ernst A. Rose, © 1965 by New York University.

Chapter 5, "Hermann Hesse's *Morgenlandfahrt*," is reprinted by permission from *The Germanic Review* 32(1957):299–310.

Chapter 6, "*Das Glasperlenspiel*: Genesis, Manuscripts, and History of Publication," is reprinted by permission from *The German Quarterly* 43 (1970):55–83.

Chapter 7, "Hermann Hesse's *Glasperlenspiel*: Genesis, Structure, Interpretation," by Christian I. Schneider, is reprinted by permission of the author.

Chapter 8, "The Poetry of Hermann Hesse," is reprinted by permission of the University of Wisconsin Press from Joseph Mileck, "The Poetry of Hermann Hesse," *Monatshefte*, Volume XLVI (© 1954 by the Regents of the University of Wisconsin), pp. 192–198.

# PREFACE

The *Hesse Companion* is written for the reader who wants an introduction to Hermann Hesse's writings.

In the first essay, Hesse's life and works are outlined to give an overall view without going into detail. The following essays, affording a closer examination, deal with specific major novels and the poetry. Written by different scholars, they offer various perspectives.

Vocabulary and glossary are compiled to serve as reading aids for those who wish to read Hesse in German. They have been tested at Antioch College. They translate words and expressions—including some from dialects and foreign languages not found in standard dictionaries (such as *The New Cassell's German Dictionary*) frequently used by advanced students. Translations of longer passages in a foreign language are given only when their content is needed for comprehension of the text. They are listed under the first word of the sentence.

Readers who wish to pursue certain ideas further are encouraged to turn to the last section of the book, the selected bibliography. Should this prove insufficient, they can embark on a study of *Hermann Hesse and His Critics*, by Joseph Mileck, the best analysis in English of the secondary literature and the most comprehensive bibliography in English of works by and about Hesse.

Although I have consulted various translations of Hesse's works available in English, I have in many instances foregone the temptation to use smoother English in the quotations for the sake of a translation that is more literal and closer to the German.

While working on the book, I have enjoyed encouragement and help from fellow Hesse students, friends, and colleagues. Thanks are due to my consultants: Dr. Siegfried Unseld, Suhrkamp Verlag, and Professor Viktor Lange, Princeton University, as well as Professors Joseph Mileck of the University of California at Berkeley and Mark Boulby of Case-Western Reserve University, with whom I spoke about the project. I am indebted also to Professor Larry Porter of Antioch College for editorial guidance, and to Mrs. Tonie Bredemeyr, Mrs. Jean Hope, and Mrs. Gerda Oldham for help in preparation of the manuscript.

I should like also to thank all librarians and archivists who have helped me secure books, pamphlets, manuscripts, articles, and letters, in Europe as well as in the United States. Since the list of names would be too long if I included them all, let me mention the most important: Dr. Bernhard Zeller, Director of the Schiller National Museum at Marbach, and his assistant, Mr. W. Schürmann; Miss Helen Thurnheer, Stadtbibliothek Vanadiana, and Dr. L. Matzig, St. Gallen; Dr. Bourquin, Schweizerische Landesbibliothek, Bern; Mr. Zängli, Eidgenössische Technische Hochschule at Zurich; Mrs. Mary Virginia Reecker, Rare Books Department, Library of the University of California at Berkeley; and last, most certainly not least, the highly active and ingenious Joe Cali, of the Antioch College Library, who succeeded in securing interlibrary loans everywhere, defying anyone's gloomy predictions, including his own.

Gratefully, I acknowledge the financial support from the Ford Foundation Faculty Development Fund that made the book possible.

However, my warmest thanks go to the Antioch students who with great enthusiasm, unmatched by equally overwhelming knowledge of German, ploughed their way through the seven volumes of the *Gesammelte Schriften*. Thus it is only fitting that it be dedicated to Stephen, Arno, Pete, Grita, Cathy, Elisabeth, Betsy, Dave, Larry, Ron, James,

Ellen, Bob, Sarah, Grace, Jocelyn, Nelson, Janet, George, Klaus, and all those who share their interest: the Hesse students.

A. O.

Note: References to Hesse's works are to Hermann Hesse, *Gesammelte Schriften,* 7 volumes (Frankfurt: Suhrkamp Verlag, 1957), unless otherwise indicated.

## A NOTE TO THE STUDENT:
## HESSE IS YOUR MIRROR!

It is a hoary wisdom of the ages that man imposes his thoughts on the world, seeing what he wishes to see and what is akin to his thinking. Such has been the case with Hermann Hesse, who has been «canonized« at least three times in this century by cults which have formed around him: twice in Germany, following World Wars I and II, and at present in the United States. In each instance it would seem that the cults were formed of young people who, profoundly dissatisfied with the world created by their elders, set out to seek new values.

Many American youths are displeased with the way of life of their elders and, by extension, with authority and society in general. They resent restrictions imposed on them, be they enforced by the economic, military, or educational system. Feeling that man is in danger of becoming dehumanized in the stifling world of money and machines, they emphasize the individual's freedom to be himself and to move toward a new humanism. Many of these young people have chosen Hesse as their idol, admiring his rugged individualism and society-defying self-estrangement, his uncompromising commitment to change and movement toward a better mankind, his courageous plunges into the subconscious to wrestle with archetypal images and the mystical experience of Unity behind the phenomenal world.

It is only natural that, since they find so many of their own innermost thoughts confirmed in Hesse's writings, they turn to him for guidance. But they should be looking, not for a guide, but for a mirror which will allow them to see themselves more clearly.

Perhaps it might be helpful to tell my own experiences

as a Hesse student who—after looking for confirmation—finally learned that she had found a mirror. Hesse himself did quite a bit to bring this about when I visited him on a sunny summer day in 1959.

The ideas I had become familiar with in reading his works were given an added force and warmth by the personality of the speaker. He was really Siddharta, the Music Master, and the Elder Brother; and a few steps from the terrace, standing out against the sky, was the bamboo thicket from *The Glass Bead Game*!

First, the discussion centered on serious ideas—among them the role and vocation of the writer and the teacher. Then we had an amusing chat about American education, with Hesse trying to see it in terms of his Tübingen at the turn of the century. Words like Castalia and Magic Theater got tossed around considerably. It was clear that Hesse was opposed to any educational system that subscribed to authoritarian rule by the teacher. He advocated a student-centered Socratic dialogue and experiential education. Telling me that his youthful correspondents had been asking him for guidance for years, he said that he did not want to be a counselor, a physician, or a leader, and if there was anything he ever intended to teach, it was that young people should become themselves. He only wanted to help them see themselves more clearly, like an older brother would who found his Way. «The problem is,» he confided, «that the Hesse whom they read, love, or blame is an image of their own Self. They recognize in him only what is akin to their own thinking and ask him for confirmation of these thoughts, and guidance. This I cannot do. They have to find their Way themselves. I am only their mirror!»

# 1

ANNA OTTEN
HERMANN HESSE, HIS LIFE AND HIS ART.
AN INWARD JOURNEY

Hermann Hesse's works, like Goethe's, are all «fragments of a long confession,» reflecting «a single human being and his relation to the world and to his own self» (VII, 303). Yet, although the author's primary concerns are self-recognition and self-realization, these spiritual autobiographies deal not only with his personal life–which would limit and certainly date them–but the human condition in general. They have a supratemporal, almost mystical quality, tracing a man's quest for identity in a universe that is at best indifferent, at worst hostile. Hesse perceives empathically that man is placed between the confusion of matter and the profusion of the stars, in loneliness. It is with this human condition that he grapples.

Since Hesse sees the world and all living creatures as «a manifestation of the Divine» (VII, 497), it is not surprising that he considers the religious impulse as the central characteristic of his life and his work. But it is not within the dogma of an established religion that he posits his search, for then obedience to an established law would suffice. His is an uncompromising will to find his own Way according to his own inner Law.

Hesse's work reflects his life transformed into art. As art, rather than merely copying (i. e., photographing) life, it transforms life into meaning by following aesthetic laws. Thus it affords a much richer panorama than would narrow focus on a personal life, in its fullness revealing much of the intellectual and literary history of Europe during the first half of the twentieth century. We find not only the themes and moods of the first four decades of our century, but also anticipation of many of those that preoccupy us now, at the beginning of the eighth decade. Indeed, Hermann Hesse, whose life began almost a hundred years ago, and whose personal conflict coincided with a crisis in the Western world, is as relevant today as he has ever been.

Reading Hesse, we move in literary history from Romanticism and Neo-Romanticism to realism, from influences of oriental religions to Expressionism, from the great impact of depth psychology to the Existential problem. In cultural history we find that, after initial withdrawal, Hesse strives with courage and commitment to find a way out of crisis—at times sounding a prophetic note of warning (for instance, in «The Brothers Karamazow, or the End of Europe») that is still justified.

Under close study, as individual fragments, Hesse's works offer a confusing wealth of themes and allusions, embracing both Western and Eastern thought. Seen more comprehensively, however, his writings form an organic, multi-faceted whole, which traces the successive stages of the author's evolution or, more appropriately, of his inward journey, leading first to individuation and then to depersonalization (*Entwerden*).

It was a difficult and unharmonious journey, not at all the balanced classical composition he wished it to be.

My life as I visualized it (he tells us) was to transcend. It was to move from step to step. I was to pass through and leave behind one stage after the other in a way in which a piece of music treats one them after the other and various tempi—by playing them, completing them, and leaving them, never to grow tired or to fall asleep; on the contrary, forever awake, forever entirely alert (VI, 511).

When Hesse wrote these lines at the age of 63, he was aware of the futility of trying to plan a life that would be a work of art. One can, of course, discover some harmonious passages, some moments of bliss, when there is some «music of the spheres» (V, 755) approaching the «divine» (V, 760). But there are other sequences, brutal like the smell of «raw meat» or (on the radio) as horrible sounding as «chewed rubber» (IV, 408). We learn that one must have the wisdom to accept even the most distorted music (or disharmonious life), because through it the original spirit can still be comprehended. Hesse-Haller is told that he has no right to criticize the radio or life in general, but that he must learn to listen carefully. Then he will perceive the original music behind the distorted sound and the divine and eternal behind the human and temporal. This «listening,» then, leading first to an awareness of polarities (such as disharmony and harmony, personal and super-personal), but culminating in the perception of an all-embracing unity of being, is the content of Hesse's life and works. Through his writings we can follow his life, as he «leaves behind one stage after the other.»

When Hermann Hesse was born in 1877, the German bourgeoisie was living in pleasant security following their victory in the Franco-Prussian War. Otto von Bismarck, the Empire's able chancellor, made himself heard in world politics; the German Empire was a respected power. Business life flourished as the machine led to industrial development. The time also marked the beginnings of rapid transportation by rail and communication by telephone. All seemed well, particulary at Calw, the picturesque town in the Black Forest where Hesse was born.

His parents, Johannes and Marie Hesse, were fervent Pietists who had spent years of their lives at missions in India. Because of poor health, his father–of German descent, born in Estonia–had come to work for the Calw publishing house of the Basel Mission Society.

Hesse's maternal grandfather also had done missionary work in India; he was a renowned authority on some Indian dialects and spoke several European languages. His rich library, to which young Hermann had access, contained books on Eastern und Western theology and many volumes of eighteenth century literature and works by the Romantics, particularly Jean Paul and Novalis. Such elements were largely consistent with the world represented by Hesse's mother, filled as it was with Christian and Indian legends and dark mysteries. His father's world was a different matter—a stern world of deeply ingrained Pietism, characterized by constant preoccupation with individual conscience, in which all was to be Christian, pure and rational. The child's soul was in a sense divided by these two worlds, and they—and the tension between them—were to be reflected later in most of Hesse's works.

The boy's parents led a humble Christian life, full of «enthusiastic heroism» (VII, 372) and concern for the heathen. They considered their life as a loan of God, to be spent not in «egotistical pursuits» (VII, 371), but in God's service. To the end of his life, Hesse's roots were set in his parents' Pietism; while he considered Kung Fu Tse, Lao Tse, and Socrates as kindred spirits, he saw them as providing only «addition and evolution» (VII, 372) and was never converted to any other religion.

Young Hermann was an intelligent, strongheaded child, bent on having his own way. Formal education did not interest him too much. He preferred to browse in his grandfather's library or to roam through the countryside. Nevertheless, he passed the entrance examination to the seminary of Maulbronn, a famous Protestant school in the classical tradition, described in several Hesse works, particularly in *Beneath the Wheel* and in *Narcissus and Goldmund*. He soon fled from Maulbronn's discipline (as does the central figure in *Narcissus and Goldmund*). Under parental pressure, he returned to Maulbronn, but soon dropped out permanently. At another school he succeeded in obtaining a diploma that corresponds roughly to a terminal certificate at the end of the Gymnasium. This marked the end of Hesse's formal education.

At the request of his father, who was determined to

make him a useful member of society, Hesse became an apprentice mechanic at a clock shop in Calw. The labor exhausted him physically and frustrated him spiritually and mentally, an agony described subsequently in *Beneath the Wheel*. Finally, after sixteen months of work that he loathed, Hesse persuaded his family that he was going to be a writer, and found employment at a bookstore at Tübingen. There, seated on an old chair in a room decorated with photographs of men he admired, he read voraciously, especially Goethe, Nietzsche, and the Romantics. He also wrote melancholy poetry that was published at his expense in 1899 as *Romantic Songs*. In the same year followed *An Hour Beyond Midnight*, a collection of tales and vignettes for which he had found a publisher. Both works reflect the literary modes of the times, Neo-Romanticism and Symbolism, with particular indebtedness to Maeterlinck.

In *An Hour Beyond Midnight*, Hesse withdraws into an imaginary world. In the style of *La Décadence*, the work overflows with sentiment, rhetorical effusions, and romantic clichés. Like Chateaubriand's René, Goethe's Werther and, particularly, Novalis's Heinrich von Ofterdingen, a noble youth is driven by boundless longing. Unable to accept presentday reality, he dreams of far away islands, mysterious temples, beautiful castles, and dark cypress groves–all full of colors, scents, melodies, and lovely maidens. Like Rousseau's Saint Preux (in *La Nouvelle Héloise*), the youth projects his feelings into nature, seeing «lonely» trees and «weary» streams. Indulging in poses, he gazes longingly into the starry skies.

This romantic confessional style–replete with posturing, with effusive prose, with languishing despair–is not to be characteristic of Hesse's subsequent writings. In his next prose work he uses a technique which enables him to reduce sentimentality and bathos: he introduces a confessor who is also observer. The work is *The Posthumous*

*Papers and Poems of Hermann Lauscher*, published in 1901. (In that year Hesse, who had left Tübingen in 1899 to work at a bookshop in Basel, returned to Calw where he had found a similar position that gave him more time for writing.)

Despite his name, Hermann Lauscher is not only a listener, but a profuse talker, as well. Like the protagonist of *An Hour Beyond Midnight*, he is a poet and an aesthete; but Lauscher is superior to him in having a capacity for self-observation. He sees himself as both a keen observer, animated by a self-tormenting love for rational truth, and as a Romantic. This split personality, pulled at by both subjective and objective modes, is in fact two personalities: Hermann and the Listener. This initiates the long line of friendpairs so typical in Hesse's work, all of whom show the divided personality at different levels of self-realization.

A few years later Hesse was very critical of his early prose, terming it sick and incomprehensible. But he referred only to its decadent romantic excesses, for he was and remained very much a Romantic, in fact never denied his affiliation with the Romantic tradition, and it is with good reason that his friend and biographer Hugo Ball called him «the last of the knights of Romanticism.»[1]

Hesse described his approach to fiction as lyrical and as an attempt to convey his *Ich und Weltgefühl* (VII, 252). He called this attitude specifically «German and Romantic» (VII, 252). Thus, although it is clear that Hesse is a Romantic, it is obvious that he underwent an evolution in his life and his art that exposed him to and immersed him in currents of thinking beyond his initial Romanticism, which had been based primarily on the influence of Novalis, Hölderlin, Jean Paul, Eichendorff, and E. T. A. Hoffmann.

1 Ball, *Hermann Hesse: Sein Leben und Werk* (Berlin: S. Fischer, 1927), p. 27.

It is in the *form* of his writings that the evolution from traditional «borrowed» Romanticism to individualized and personalized expression can be most readily observed. From the spontaneous, effusive outpourings of emotions and the Romantic clichés of the early works there is a change to more restrained expression and a struggle for form. In the early work, Hesse wished to express the multiplicity of impressions in a loose form; the mature writings seek a reconciliation of the polarities of life, and the form is controlled. His approach becomes that of a musician who wishes to express the «two-voicedness of the melody of life» (IV, 115) and consequently has to restrain himself and work at his craft. When Hesse says of *The Steppenwolf* that it is »as austere and concise as a sonata« (VII, 495), he affirms this evolution from looseness to control, from spontaneity for its own sake to craftsmanship.

Though mainly characterized by effusiveness and an overly ornate vocabulary, the early works contain many of the themes which prevail in Hesse's later writings. The author as confessor-observer is early in evidence in *Hermann Lauscher*. Following Schiller and the Romantics, Hesse advocates that the poet look at life from a distance and see polarities in a higher synthesis. In this perspective, life appears to be a game. A closely allied theme is the child's view of the world. Poets and children know about the world's oneness. Hesse speaks of the child's *«heile Welt»* (IV, 99) as «innocent» (VI, 675) and beyond polarities. Into his soul «God writes poetry» (I, 219). All is eternal present for the child, who lives, unaware of time's passage, as in a paradise. Yet childhood must be lost, for it is «like a treasure which slips out of playing hands and falls over the edge of a deep well» (I, 98).[1] Other themes are «the mirrored image» (I, 9) and the outsider.

[1] This is reminiscent of Maeterlinck's *Pelléas et Mélisande,* in which a similar symbol is used which may be interpreted in the same way.

It would be ill-advised to ascribe any of these themes simply to Hesse's imitation of literary models. The portrayal of the outsider, for example, arose from deeply felt personal agony. Likewise, the love of nature felt by the hero of *Peter Camenzind* (1904), his next major novel, was not inspired by literary epigones so much as by Hesse's own love for the Swiss Alps which he came to know when he moved to Basel in 1899.

Peter, a farmer's son, is part of nature: rocks, trees, lake, and sun are his teachers. Trees, for instance, live the secret of their seed, unconcerned about anything else. Peter, too, wishes to obey his own inner law. In an ahistorical society, where life is regulated by nature's laws, all is simple–all seems to speak the language of God, the unity behind the phenomenal world. One day, however, Peter leaves the village to study in the city and become a writer (in effect, to lose his childhood). Lured into social life, he discovers only the unnaturalness of men, their pursuit of material gain and their obsession with technological «rubbish». Gradually, he feels that he has a mission: he wants to lead men back to «God-Nature».

This concept is reminiscent of Goethe's *Gott-Natur*, of Hindu and Christian mysticism, of Jung's collective unconscious, and of the Romantics' union of opposites. Peter is, in fact, a Romantic poet. Like his author, he is an aesthetic individualist who seeks the infinite in the finite and who is convinced (like Schleiermacher) that the religious impulse is the root of all true art. Peter wants to write transcendental poetry. In the fabric of real life he perceives magic thread–like premonitions, longings, dreams, and the sensation of «awakening»–that seem to him proof of a second, higher life. These are the same feelings that Novalis had expressed. Also like Novalis, Peter thinks that only the poet can feel what nature can be for man and reveal the secrets disclosed to him by its divine power. Peter's goal is to «help mute nature find expression in poetry» (I, 268). In this pursuit he fails.

The frustrated poet is also unlucky in his love affairs, because he tends to worship women as strange, beautiful, and mysterious creatures who are closer than are men to God. His attitude is like a priest's toward a goddess or a boy's toward a revered mother. He is unfortunate in his friendships too. Lonely at times, he considers suicide, but settles instead for the momentary relief of drunkenness.

Peter venerates St. Francis of Assisi, the childlike saint, and in St. Francis's spirit of universal love he takes upon himself the care of a cripple, whom he loves like a brother. When the cripple dies, Peter returns to his native village. Having discovered the joy of helping others, he takes up a life of service to the community. St. Francis resembles very much Novalis's awakened, childlike student of nature, who confidently receives his inspiration from a higher power and who loves the whole world. Hesse accepted from both models the ideal of love and service. Throughout his work we can follow this ideal of the artist-saint as it takes various forms. In 1950 he still adheres to this ideal:

> I am a poet; I seek and profess. I have the task of serving truth and sincerity (and the beautiful is part of truth; it is one of the forms under which truth appears). I have a mission: I must help those who also search to understand and endure life. (VII, 773).

In *Peter Camenzind* we find another of Hesse's central themes—a moment of «awakening» when a deep insight comes in a flash of inspiration, blending intuition and intelligence before a «suddenly opened inward eye» (I, 251). This event always marks the climax of a Hesse hero's life, revealing to him a world transfigured, which he experiences with childlike wonder and happiness. For Peter the occasion is his mother's death, which causes him to take stock of his existence and realize that he wants to learn, to see, to experience the fullness of life. Such visions, when for a fleeting instant the world is whole in all its magnificence, are described by Hesse in considerable detail, carefully and with the reverence he reserves for what is dearest to him.

The changed mood was well received and the book a great success, establishing Hesse as a writer. He was now financially independent and able to marry Marie Bernoulli, a quiet, music-loving young woman. With her he settled down for a life of rustic happiness (fashionable at the time, due to Tolstoy's influence) at Gaienhofen on Lake Constance.

Eight very productive years followed. Hesse edited and reviewed books, co-edited the liberal magazine *März*. He also wrote stories and poems for various magazines, which were subsequently published in *In This World* (1907), *Neighbors* (1908), *On the Road* (1911), *By-Ways* (1912), *Small World* (1933), and *Gerbersau* (1949). (In most of these short works Hesse lovingly described the humble small town people whom he had known in Calw, fictionalized as Gerbersau. Stylistically and thematically the stories reflect Keller's influence.) The Gaienhofen period shows Hesse's efforts to settle down and conclude an uneasy truce (based on compromise) with bourgeois society. He had become the father of three sons; his *Wanderlust* had been temporarily subdued (reflecting this mood, the characters of his stories usually wander away from their hometown, but come back to it again).

The most interesting work published at the beginning of the Gaienhofen years was *Beneath the Wheel* (1906). Like Hesse's earlier works, it follows a trend of the time, the school novel, but also contains genuine personal experience. In writing it, Hesse hoped to liberate himself from the traumatic experience of his own youth when he «almost became the victim of education, theology, tradition and authoritarianism» (VII, 874).

The novel's central characters are seminarians: Hans Giebenrath and Hermann Heilner. Hans's father is a small town bourgeois who has infinite respect for God, property, and money—though not necessarily in that order. He and the teachers—and by implication also the state and particularly the army—represent the stern masculine world of discipline and intellect. Completely suppressed is the feminine world of the emotions. Seminarians are trained to fit a mold: good clergyman and good citizen. They are to be obedient creatures without self-will. Taught much about Greece and Rome, very little about their own world, the student is never considered as an individual with needs of his own. Nonetheless, few students rebel and fewer actually break out.

Hans is a good student and a docile victim of this system until he befriends the willful and headstrong Hermann. Of weak character and needing a leader, Hans is easily influenced by Hermann's attitude of rebellion against the repressive life they are forced to lead. But only Hermann has the courage to escape. Hans, left behind, retreats into a world of schizophrenic hallucinations, and is sent home. Forced by his practical father to work at a mechanic's shop (as Hesse had been), Hans leads a miserable existence. One day, after a drinking party, he walks into the river and drowns.

Our sympathy goes out to this poor youth, whose joy had been wandering the woods in nature adoration, but whose life is sacrificed to a brutal educational system whose chief function is to produce a type useful to middle-class society. Nonetheless, Hans the non-conformist *is* sacrificed by his author, who in those years was trying to live within the bourgeois order. Hermann gets away and we hear that he has become a «man». In view of his successors, Veraguth and Goldmund, we can assume that be becomes an artist, a subtle way of showing that the artist in Hesse never submitted to society. But it will be a number of years until he makes a complete (and more open) break.

In *Beneath the Wheel,* we have the first detailed description of a mental disease, schizophrenia, though both Lauscher and Camenzind were neurotic. Like his Romantic models and a number of his contemporaries (Thomas Mann, for example), Hesse found psychosis very interesting. In *The Steppenwolf* he stated openly that he was a «schizophrene» (IV, 269) and that «insanity in a higher sense was the beginning of all wisdom, just as schizophrenia was the beginning of all art, all imagination» (IV, 389). The man who has a split personality «can reconstruct it as he likes and thereby achieve an infinite variety in the game of life» (IV, 387–388). (This view is supported, interestingly enough, by Jung, who believed that such men may be artists and educators.) At the time he wrote *Beneath the Wheel,* however, Hesse was much less «playing the game of life» than he was trying to come to grips with existence. It was a time of crisis, when «catharsis by means of *The Steppenwolf*» (VII, 932) hat not yet occurred.

In his next novel, *Gertrud* (1910), an inaccessible woman is worshipped by the musician Kuhn, but marries the singer Muoth. She reminds us of the woman-goddess of *Inseltraum,* of *Peter Camenzind's* Elizabeth, and of the unattainable, far away cloud in Hesse's poetry to which she is compared. Certainly, the inaccessible woman is a familiar figure with the Romantics. Romantic, too, is Kuhn's attitude toward Gertrud: like Peter Camenzind's, that of a worshipful priest.

Outwardly, life at Gaienhofen ran its peaceful course, but inwardly the wanderer in Hesse became restless. Gaienhofen proved to be too secluded; even occasional trips to Switzerland and Italy did not help. Therefore, in 1911

Hesse embarked on a longer trip—to India, Malaya, Sumatra, and Ceylon. As son and grandson of missionaries to India, he had been exposed to its spirit, had idealized it. Now he could drink of that spirit more directly. But the reality was different. He returned from his five month journey without having found the spiritual paradise he had anticipated. He concluded that it existed only as an idea within him.

Convinced that he could not reach self-fulfillment at Gaienhofen, which had become a prison without visible walls, he moved with his family to Bern. In his next novel, *Rosshalde* (1914), the painter Veraguth, committed entirely to his art, is «walled in of his own free will» at first, but then breaks loose (II, 534). The book foreshadows events that will occur in Hesse's life a little later.

Next in publication, though prior in concept, was *Three Tales From the Life of Knulp* (1915). Knulp, a pleasant vagabond, is unmarried. Childlike and fatalistic, he lives in the emotional World of the Mother. Though hostile to the values of middle-class society, he keeps in contact with his bourgeois friends—suggesting that while Hesse worked on this book (from 1907 on), he was still at peace with the bourgeoisie. At the end of his life, however, Knulp confesses that he has a bad conscience—indicating perhaps some Pietism in his background—a Pietism which would judge his life a waste and which saw all waste as sin. But God, addressing the tramp in gentle words, reassures him, and Knulp dies in the snow with a smile.

In contrast to this serenity, Hesse was soon to reach an intolerable state of crisis, which had developed out of mounting discontent over a period of some six years and climaxed in 1916. The Gaienhofen idyll brought him boredom and doubt as to whether an artist could settle down to a bourgeois family life without giving up his art. Actually, the conflict between artist and bourgeois had been present since the earliest works, but after 1916 it took on a strident tone of urgency. In his pre-1916 work, Hesse seems to stand behind (and separate from) his hero, or even to fashion him according to Romantic models. After 1916, he fuses with the protagonist and his art becomes distinctly his own, urgent and dramatic. We find no longer the desire to escape into dream and illusion; instead there is a wish to confront the crisis and find his own identity.

Clearly, the conflict between bourgeois and artist is just another expression of basic antinomies in Hesse's mind, to which he gave various names: spirit and soul, order and chaos, reason and anti-reason, World of the Father and World of the Mother, mind and senses. His great struggle was to achieve a synthesis that would obliterate the polarization. The agonizing difficulty of this endeavor often led him close to suicide. In *The Conjectural Biography* (1925) he calls his time of crisis his «journey through hell» (IV, 481). But in the same essay he also refers to it as «the second great turning point of my life» (IV, 477).[1]

Outer events also contributed to his anguish. For Hesse, the pacifist and cosmopolitan humanist, the outbreak of World War I meant deep agony. Later, in a letter written in 1933, he says that it was in 1914 that he developed a very «sensitive conscience and feeling of responsibility» (VII, 551). He felt that World War I revealed the moral and spiritual bankruptcy of the western world. Trying to sound a voice of reason, he declared his opposition to violence, which he abhorred no matter who used it (a thought he explains at some length in «Thou Shalt Not Kill,» 1918). This explains why he did not join any of the revolutionary groups in 1918, even though–like many of the intellectuals of his time–he sympathized

[1] The first turning point was when Hesse, at the age of twelve, chose to become a poet.

with the German left. More a follower of St. Francis of Assisi than a revolutionary, he preached «love and human brotherhood» (VII, 551). Joining an army or a revolutionary unit deprives the individual of the freedom to make personal, individual decisions. Hesse–too much an outsider and individualist to function within a formal group–had proven before that his response to imposed discipline was rebellion. As he had defied the imposed monastic discipline at Maulbronn, so he now rebelled against imposed German political views.

During the war, Hesse worked very actively as editor of journals and books which were sent to German prisoners of war, devoting all of his time to the task. Despite this, because of his focus on the «inner man» and on supratemporal rather than immediate «practical» issues, his countrymen no longer supported him, and he was branded a traitor and attacked even by former friends.

Extremely discouraged, he finally gave up his German citizenship, stayed in Switzerland, and became a Swiss citizen in 1923. He continued advocating a humanitarianism based on brotherhood, which would lead to a better humanity. The way to it, he claimed, was from within the individual: it was each man's duty to come one step closer to the realization of a new, better mankind by beginning the spiritual renewal in his own heart.

While he was under attack from the outside, his family was breaking up. His wife became mentally deranged and had to be put in a sanatorium; his son Martin was stricken by a serious disease; in 1916 his father died. Hesse tried to «overcome his suffering by understanding, to master it by saintliness» (VII, 143). To no avail. In despair, he consulted Dr. Josef B. Lang, a Jungian psychoanalyst, with whom he had about sixty sessions at the sanatorium at Sonmatt, near Luzern, in 1916 and 1917. The encounter with psychoanalysis proved to be «an encounter with real powers» (VII, 802). Hesse emerged from it a new man, ready to face chaos within and without. The psychic experience took on the significance of a spiritual rebirth, altering Hesse the man and Hesse the artist.

The artistic reflection of the rebirth is Hesse's novel *Demian*. Although he introduces material from psychoanalysis—makes, for instance, conscious use of dreams, memories, and associations—the novel is by no means simply a case history. It is art, the creation of intuition, not of analysis. Characteristically, Hesse found that psychoanalysis had not really taught him anything new. (In «Artists and Psychoanalysis», he claims that Freud, Jung, and Stekel only confirm the poet's intuitive understanding of the unconscious.) For Hesse, the poet is a *Seelendeuter* (VII, 139), whose importance is confirmed by analysis. The very foundation of art, as he perceives it, is the artist's quest for a more intimate relationship with the unconscious. He must relentlessly pursue the Inward Way; he must find his inner law. This is his quest for identity. Since he foregoes the easy solution of conformity, his lot is loneliness. Like the analyst, he must «listen to the hidden sources» only, as Lauscher—animated by a «self-tormenting love for truth»—had done. But Lauscher had avoided confronting himself. The «new note» (VII, 514) that makes itself felt in Hesse's writings after psychoanalysis is precisely the opposite: Hesse now faces himself.

*Demian: The Story of Emil Sinclair's Youth* was published in 1919 under the pseudonym of Emil Sinclair. Hesse chose to write under a pseudonym (using the name of Hölderlin's friend) because he wished to express the change of personality he had experienced with psychoanalysis, and because he wished to appeal to a different kind of reader than formerly. He considered himself to have been a popular writer (he used the derogatory term, *Literat*) before the First World War. Now he wanted to appeal to the generation of young intellectuals, the generation of the Expressionists. *Demian* was a success, even winning the Fontane prize for a best first novel, which Hesse returned after the pseudonym was lifted. It also impressed the new audience he had in mind.

Like *Hermann Lauscher*, the book begins with an introduction. We learn that we are about to hear the story of «a real, unique, living man« (III, 101). We also soon understand, however, that *Demian* has larger implications, pointing on the one hand to the concerns of the Expressionists, and on the other to youth's eternal quest for identity. Hesse's intention is to show how one man «lives the secret of his seed» (III, 406). Hesse-Sinclair searches for the inner law which he also calls the God Within or the Divine. He does not seek self-knowledge for selfish reasons. Since he believes that mankind can advance only by being reborn within the individual, the personal quest becomes a «divine duty» (III, 406), or a suprapersonal task undertaken for the betterment of the human condition. Thus it reflects Hesse's belief in an individualism out of which a «new humanity» will grow.

While pointing back to Kierkegaard and Nietzsche, the belief in the need for a «new man» was also very much a part of the fervent credo of the Expressionists. He spoke for a generation of angry young intellectuals in his belief that the new humanity would only be born after «the twilight of mankind.» Annihilation of tradition—after that, something new, something higher: the millennium! This generation wanted lucid, determined leaders who were willing to go their way in loneliness (as envisioned by Nietzsche) and as outsiders, living far from the herd. Such a breed of men are those Hesse calls «the stigmatized» in *Demian*. They are brothers of Camus' rebel as well as of Jesus.

*Demian* abounds in Old and New Testament terminology, motifs, and figures such as the Prodigal Son, Cain,

Jacob, and particularly Christ. But *Demian* is, nonetheless, not a Christian book. Hesse uses Christian terms primarily as frames of reference. For him, man is not only «spirit become flesh,» but he is also «a thrust of nature». Jesus, we are told by Pistorius, is not a divinity but rather only a mythical hero. Clearly, to Hesse, Jesus and Nietzsche do not represent contradictions, for he also uses many Nietzschean terms. Both Jesus and Nietzsche are seen as men who had the courage to be themselves, to follow their inner law. «What nature has in mind for humanity,» Hesse writes, «is written in the individual . . . It was in Jesus, it was in Nietzsche» (III, 229). *Demian*, with all its Christian terms, takes us into a secularized Christian universe.

There is only one principle that *Demian* teaches: that man has the duty to be himself. Those who live this way will be «new men» and lead humanity into the future. These «stigmatized» ones dare to break old rules and create new. Implied is the idea of an order of such men, a thought pointing to *The Steppenwolf*'s Immortals and the Wayfarers to the East. In *Demian* we find astrologers, cabbalists, yogi, buddhists, and Tolstoyites—men who have nothing in common except the wish to become, and be, themselves. Differences in religious and philosophical outlook are unimportant, because Hesse considers the whole world as « a manifestation of the One, the Divine» (VII, 497). Although he remained essentially a Christian all his life, his concept embraced all religions, never adhering to a particular dogma.

In *Demian*, Hesse brings us to the point where religion and depth psychology overlap, where no clear lines can be drawn to distinguish between «soul» and «unconscious,» religion and psychoanalysis. Christ is referred to both in Christian terms and also as Jung's suffering hero. The word «soul» is sometimes used in the Christian sense, but more often carries the meaning of «affective self,» referring to the Jungian collective unconscious. Mother Eva is the biblical mother of mankind as well as the Jungian *Magna Mater*. Both Eva and her son Demian are magical conjurations that lead Sinclair on his inward journey to self-fulfillment and the chiliastic vision.

Since the book describes an inward journey, there is—as in most of Hesse's works—very little «plot.» Recounting the life of the boy Emil Sinclair, the 40 year old Hesse retrospectively tells and comments on the story of his own adolescence, moving it into a different historical period, roughly the ten years preceding World War I. The boy grows up in a southern German town that looks like Calw. We follow his evolution from loss of childhood innocence, through puberty and a quest for identity, to the achievement of liberation.

Brought up as a Christian by loving but stern parents, the boy enjoys at first a happy childhood in a safe, undivided world, where all seems to be eternal-present. When he enters puberty, however, this safe totality collapses, and divides into two opposing worlds. One is «the light World of the Father,» where spirit, order, reason, stern moral laws, and purity reign (a world akin to André Gide's white world in *Les Cahiers d'André Walter*). The other world (corresponding to Gide's black world) is called «the dark World of the Mother,» representing soul, chaos, feeling, amoral and unconscious drives and sin.

As Sinclair struggles to maturity, we see him fluctuating between the two «Worlds». His goal is to reconcile them into a harmonious, undivided totality which, in *Demian*, he calls an «undivided god» (named Abraxas) that dwells in man as well as throughout the whole of nature.

The name Abraxas refers to a gnostic deity that is God and the devil at the same time. Another unifying symbol is a picture drawn by Sinclair—a picture that is «man, woman, girl, child, animal» (III, 211). Too, in a vision Sinclair recalls memories that go back to and beyond his childhood into former existences. Hesse wished not only to see the totality of one man's life and the unity of all human beings, but also to include pre-human existence in his vision. To this end he drew on his psychoanalytic experience, making much use of Jung's «collective unconscious» concept.

Although it is the story of Emil's liberation, achieved with the aid of his *Schicksalsbild,* Demian (III, 222), the novel is not limited to the fate of one man. It points beyond this, to the decline of an old world that was ready to die. Out of the cataclysm of death, a New World was to be born. Thus the symbol of the bird that breaks out of the egg (the world) also symbolizes the new man.

Hesse elaborates this idea of the decline of an old order in the essay, «The Brothers Karamazov or the End of Europe,» written in 1920. He points to the breakdown in Europe of ethical and moral order, whose bases were reason and consciousness. The breakdown manifests itself in a loosening of the instincts.[1] Hesse feels that «amoral» Eastern man (whom he calls Russian man and «soul man») invades Europe, bringing chaos and unconscious drives (the World of the Mother) into the well-ordered World of the Father. This is the conflict in *Demian,* but it is elevated in the essay to the level of cultural history, similar to the concept of «psychic evolution» popular at the end of the nineteenth century.

In another essay, «Thoughts on Dostoevski's *Idiot*» (1919), Hesse finds hope in the acceptance of the «two worlds» in the vision of unity of all life. Prince Myshkin suffers epileptic seizures, during which he experiences such visions. Hesse calls them «magical thinking,» illuminations of such great intensity that they are difficult to express in words. At the magic level, we are told, division of the world disappears. No longer are time and eternity,

[1] This thought corresponds to Bergson's *élan vital,* the unconscious flux of life in nature, as opposed to the order-imposing intellect.

inside and outside, reality and dream, good and evil, spirit and soul, life and death, opposites. All is One.

As Hesse confesses in «My Faith,» the idea of the fundamental oneness of all being is his deepest belief. Again and again he tries to communicate his noumenous experience, although he knows (and tells us in *Siddharta*) that no one can describe what happens to him in the hour of illumination. In *Aion*, Jung tells us that «one understands nothing psychological unless one has experienced it oneself.»[1] It is not surprising, then, that Hesse and his students are faced often with a non-tellable tale–the personal noumenous experience.

Hesse has outlined in «A Bit of Theology» the way the great religions conceive of the psychic evolution of the individual in three stages. The first is childhood, in which one indulges in a paradise of irresponsibility. The second takes place in the context of culture, religion, and morality. Here, upon reaching the knowledge of good and evil, one suffers the feeling of guilt because one realizes that absolute justice and virtue are unattainable. Sometimes the conflicts of this stage destroy the individual. Or he can move beyond them to the third stage, beyond morality and law, into a state of grace and redemption, into a new kind of «irresponsibility, or, in short, to faith.» And whatever form this faith assumes, its content is always the same: that a higher power, whose servant man is, and in whom he can confide, rules over him, and that man's duty is to strive to be virtuous. This, Hesse contends, is how the «awakened man» is expressed in a «European and almost Christian» way (III, 389).

Similar stages can be seen in non-Christian religions. First, there is naive man, living in fear and desire. Then there is the second step toward redemption by means of exercises such as yoga, which master the drives and teach

[1] C. G. Jung, *Aion, Researches Into the Phenomenology of the Self.* Collected Works, IX; Bollingen Series XX. New York, 1959, p. 200.

one to recognize the world of phenomena as a world of illusion. Yogic meditation concentrates on the individual soul, Atman, that is part of the world soul, Brahman. The third stage is reached when yoga is recognized as a kind of desire which is overcome by the awakened, who experiences that he, as Atman and part of Brahman, is eternal and indestructable; and that it doesn't matter whether he strives or does not strive, because this does not affect his Atman. (This third step of enlightenment corresponds also to Christian grace.) Hesse finds the same progress from striving to no-longer-striving in Taoism. To him, this confirms that there is a «central problem expressed everywhere in analogous symbols» (VII, 390), and that the world's great religions are all trying to cope with this problem.

Hesse believes, then, that there is only one unified pattern for the evolution of the soul to redemption. Similarly, he concludes (as have others–Goethe, for example, in *Dichtung und Wahrheit, 2. Teil, 9. Buch*) that there is «no diversity of men and spirits but only one humanity and only one spirit» (VII, 391). This humanity has as its highest aim the provision of «soul» (VII, 69) for the universe. It is born in the hearts of poets and artists who give it form. Hesse himself wished to write the history of his own soul, but felt that all his books were only «attempts» (III, 393). Such a viewpoint represents an apotheosis of art.[1] For Hesse, art is soul become form, «the highest form of all organic life» (VII, 70).

Hesse's faith transcends all dogma. He contends that «the true seeker could not accept any doctrine . . . But the man who had found himself could approve each and every doctrine, each Way, each goal; nothing separated him any longer from the thousands of others who lived

[1] In this Hesse agrees with Malraux who claims that modern art has, at least in the artist's eyes, stepped into the absolute's place. (See *Voices of Silence*, 1951, transl. by Stuart Gilbert, New York, Doubleday & Co., 1953, pp. 600–602.).

in the eternal, who breathed the divine» (III, 701).[1] Hesse's only «doctrine,» then, was to have no doctrine, since the belief in an all-embracing unity of life underlies most religions and cannot meaningfully be called a doctrine.[2] Clearly, theories and reasoning do not explain Hesse's visions which cannot be grasped in philosophical, theological, or psychological terms (helpful though these may be), but which must be «understood» solely as poetry.

Poetic inspiration came to Hesse as a process that was active and non-active at the same time. He was always «waiting for my fate to come to me with a new image» (III, 230), which would then dominate his imagination, and a new story would take form. Given this «technique,» it is understandable that poetic visions of unity and of mystical harmony with the universe provide the climactic moments in Hesse's works. In *Demian* there is the gigantic vision of the heavenly city, out of which millions of people flow into the Great Mother as into a great gorge. *Siddharta* envisions a stream of life's forms. In the *Märchen* «Iris,» Anselm finds the world of unity in the calyx of a flower.

In two other of Hesse's works–*Klingsor's Last Summer* and *Klein and Wagner*–the visions are particularly vivid. In the former, a frenzied painter burns himself out «like a flame» (III, 557) in Nietzschean fervor. Drinking to both life and death, he lives in exuberance that borders on blasphemy as he directs «the dance of the world» (III, 575). He knows that he is insane, «as every creative mind is insane» (III, 613).[3] The whole stream of life is cap-

1 Significantly, Hesse mentions Gandhi as one of those «awakened men,» along with Jesus, Buddha, and Socrates (letter of Aug. 10, 1950, to Fräulein Vogel, Hesse-Collection, Stadtbibliothek, St. Gallen).
2 At the end of *The Spa Visitor*, Hesse gives an even closer definition, saying that the unity he worships behind multiplicity is life itself.
3 In *The Steppenwolf*, also, we find the idea that schizophrenia is the root of art.

tured in his self-portrait, «an enormous, ruthless, shouting, moving, frightening confession» (III, 609), open to many interpretations. He is Faust, Karamazov, animal, and sage. Behind his face are «many, many faces» (III, 610). And behind all these faces are still others, «prehuman, animal, vegetable, stone» (III, 611). Drunk, candle in hand, Klingsor studies his face in the mirror. It is as if the last man remembered, just before his death, all forms, even those of his «prehuman existence» (III, 611).

Visions of the unity of all life are central also to *Klein and Wagner*. Klein has led the life of a good clerk and father, while harboring an alter ego resembling the musician Richard Wagner–the seductive, genial artist full of the lust of living. Guilt-ridden because he is not entirely bourgeois and does not lead a completely useful life in line with middle class mores, his guilt reminds him of the criminal schoolteacher Ernst Wagner who murdered his wife and children. One day Klein actually changes his name to Wagner, embezzles money, and escapes his dull existence–leaves because he fears that he might, like Ernst Wagner, kill his family. After a brief, sensuous freedom, he almost kills a pretty dancer in her sleep because he cannot reconcile the bourgeois and the artist-criminal-seducer poles of his existence. Again he flees, rows out into the lake, meditates, and–letting-himself-go, as taught by Master Eckehart–drowns in the water, a symbol of the World of the Mother. At the last moment, by «magical thinking,» he sees the gigantic «stream of forms» (III, 552), full of faces he knew; he sees also thousands of images–strangers, children, flowers–in two streams; one flows toward God, is breathed in; the other is exhaled. God, in the middle, is a blazing light in a transparent «dome of music» (III, 554)–music that comes from the eternal streams. Klein sees himself as a young man of twenty, with face «glowing in sacred ecstasy» (III, 553).

Now he has become a prophet and revealer, drifting in blissful consent, joining the music of the world-streams in the praise of God. His vision of the stream of life reminds us of the mysticism of the Upanishads and anticipates that of Siddharta who, too, flows into unity (III, 721).

Such magnificent visions had come also to Hesse, whose former life had been shattered and who, like Klein, had made a clean break with the past. In 1919, he left his family. His wife was in an asylum and the children were staying with friends. Preferring the south of Switzerland to Bern, Hesse moved into the Ticino. *Klein and Wagner* and *Klingsor's Last Summer* contain the barely disguised autobiography of this period. Later, Hesse was to call this time the fullest of his life. A prisoner broken loose, he enjoyed a new freedom. Yet his exuberance was close to despair, and nights with friends at an inn were followed by lonely days in the casa Camuzzi, a picturesque small baroque building at Montagnola. Yet Hesse was intensely alive and productive, writing and painting. In 1916 he had done some charcoal sketches; in the summer of 1919 he discovered the joy of aquarell painting. With his palette he would sit and paint the beautiful landscape, ablaze with colors. They found their way into Hesse's writings, though there, too, as in his life, blazing color and ecstatic mood alternated with dark feelings of doom and despair.

In the winter of 1919, at the casa Camuzzi, Hesse began the novel that was to become his most harmonious work—*Siddharta*. He completed it in 1920, and it was published in 1922. Though there were other of his works that he liked more than *Siddharta* (he mentioned *Klingsor's Last Summer* and *Knulp* as his favorites), in 1923, he thought it the work that had «the greatest merit» (Card to Joh. Kleinpaul, Montagnola, 4. Juli 1923).

As a child, Hesse had known about «Indian and Chinese sages» (IV, 449). Later he travelled to the Orient and consecrated years of his life to the study of oriental religions and philosophies, which led him to a synthesis of Christian and oriental thought. He would speak of «Buddha, Jesus and Socrates» (IV, 423) as of human gods–as men who had achieved self-realization according to their inner law, the «Godhead within» (VI, 156). Their doctrines were of secondary interest to him (though there, too, he found that they had much in common), for he studied religions not for their sake but for his own: in them he sought, and had confirmed, his «own» faith. We find professions of it scattered throughout Hesse's works, but particularly in an essay, «My Faith,» and in *Siddharta,* the «book where I tried to express my faith» (VII, 370).

His pious Protestant parents and their life of «service and sacrifice» before God (VII, 372) were the strongest formative influences on young Hesse. But the boy complained about the religious practices early. He disliked the gloomy little churches, boring ministers, and endless sermons.[1] At fifteen he wrote his parents that though they foresaw a better life after the one on earth, he thought differently, and therefore would either do away with this life or enjoy it. Yet, Hesse does not admit a break with Christianity–only «additions and evolutions.» He wrote, for example, that for him, «Christian mysticism . . . although not without conflicts . . . exists along with an Indian-Asiatic faith of which the sole dogma is the belief in unity» (VII, 373). This placed him in the stream of thought that leads from the mystical teachings of the Upanishads to Persian sufism through the neo-platonists

[1] That young Hesse also did not like his parents' sermonizing letters can be seen in the following quotation: «If you want to write me, please, not again about your Christ.» *Kindheit und Jugend vor Neunzehnhundert: Hermann Hesse in Briefen und Lebenszeugnissen 1877–1895,* edited by Ninon Hesse. Frankfurt: Suhrkamp Verlag, 1967, p. 265.

to the Christian mystics Eckehart and Tauler, and finally
to the philosophy of the great German mystic of the nineteenth century, Schopenhauer. He was able to synthesize
the Christian and oriental branches of mysticism because
he saw the common goal: the inward way to suprapersonal unity.[1]

Enlightened men, Hesse believed, are «stripped of the
temporary and personal» (VII, 383). Such men have been
teaching the same thing for thousands of years, and

> any theologian or any educated man trained in the
> humanities could say it, no matter whether he is in-
> clined to follow Socrates or Lao Tse ... or the Buddha
> ... or Jesus. All of them ... each awakened and en-
> lightened man, each true teacher of humanity, has been
> teaching the same, namely that man should not desire
> greatness or happiness, neither heroism nor sweet peace,
> that he should not desire anything at all, except a pure
> spirit, an alert mind, a brave heart and the ... wisdom
> ... to bear happiness as well as suffering, clamour as
> well as silence» (VII, 428).

Enlightened men are beyond personal egotism and bear
reverence and charitable love for their fellow men. They
also have a will to serve—«each true poet has a spark of it,
neither art nor religion are possible without it» (VII,
382). In short, for Hesse awakening and service are
linked, as are art and religion. Thus, his immortal teachers of humanity belong to different walks of life: they
are not only founders of religions like Jesus and Buddha,
but also philosophers like Socrates and Nietzsche, artists
like Mozart and Bach, and writers like Jean Paul and
Goethe. He perceives in all of these men a suprapersonal
wisdom, «because all wisdom transcends the individual»

---

1 In the *Chandogya-Upanishad*, the idea of unity is conceived as
residing within a small lotus blossom in the body, «the Self.» A. Hil-
lebrandt, ed., *Upanishaden*. Düsseldorf: E. Diederichs Verlag, 1921,
p. 122.

(VII, 381). It is in such men that Hesse sees hope for a future Kingdom of the Spirit.

Though the novel's sub-title is *Eine indische Dichtung,* in *Siddharta* Hesse expresses his own faith and thus—in addition to Hinduism and Buddhism—it includes elements of Christianity, Taoism, and Confucianism. Since the setting is India, there are numerous references to the Buddha's life and to the Indian pantheon. As with the *Pâli-Kanon,* which begins with the Buddha's life at a time when he dwelt on the shores of the river at the roots of the tree of enlightenment, the novel begins with Siddharta's youth on the shores of the river, in the shadow of the sacred Sal woods. He is a Brahman's son who converses with learned men, practices meditation, and utters the sacred syllable «Om,» mentioned in most Upanishads.[1] Siddharta has been taught that Atman, the individual Self, is identical with Brahman, the universe; but he is beset by doubts. Teaching, books—even the *Samaveda Upanishads*—no longer satisfy him. He seeks his own way «to the I, to the Self, to Atman» (III, 619).

Like the Buddha, Siddharta leaves with his friend Govinda, against his father's will, to join ascetics (the Samanas), to «become empty» (III, 628), free of desire, free of the empirical «I.» When this empirical «I»[2] has become numbed, he hopes to find the last, «the innermost» Self (III, 626) that is no longer «I,» but the Atman that serves man «as a light.»[3] Siddharta sleeps deeply and experiences a rebirth.[4] He has—also like the Buddha—visions

1 In the *Mundaka-Upanishad,* e. g., it is explained that «The ‹Om› is the secret religion that is the bow. The Self is the arrow, sharpened by meditation. The target is Brahman.» (*Upanishaden, op. cit.,* p. 183).
2 The *Brihad-Aranyaka Upanishad* calls it the physical, mortal form.
3 *Upanishaden, op. cit.,* p. 77.
4 In the *Chandogya Upanishad,* the Atman is defined as breath. In dreamless sleep, the Atman is breathed back into the Brahman, to be breathed out after sleep. Since all is one in Brahman, deep sleep and subsequent awakening are the same, like death and rebirth.

39

of other existences. He «killed his senses, his memory; he slipped out of his ‹I› into a thousand different forms, was animal, was carcass, was stone, was water» (III, 627).[1]

Siddharta's migration through various existences is also in keeping with the Buddhist scriptures, and is epitomized by references to the shedding of a snake's skin, symbolizing rebirth and movement toward final liberation.[2] Though Siddharta does not find «the Way of Ways» with the forest-dwelling ascetics, he does come to know that «nothing can be learned» (III, 630).[3] When he hears the great Gautama himself lecture, he finds an error in his doctrine of the unbroken chain of cause and effect; namely, the doctrine of redemption–Nirvana. The Buddha, Siddharta finds, presents a divided world. His friend Govinda, however, is impressed by the Illustrious One and joins him as a disciple. Unperturbed, Siddharta–who feels that teachers and doctrines have prevented him from knowing himself–decides that he must reach «his own goal alone, or die» (III, 643). The moment he reaches this firm resolution, the world becomes transfigured and suddenly beautiful in ways that it had never seemed before. It is no longer the world of illusion that it had been to the Brahman, who only sought the unity behind appearances. Siddharta suddenly feels deeply that «the One

1 The *Jâtaka-Book* of the *Pâli-Kanon* contains several hundred legends where the future Buddha is born as fish, frog, parrot, peacock, monkey, hare, snake, robber, barber, son of a king, priest, ascetic, tree-good–to name but a few.

2 In the scriptures it is said that «the monk whose thoughts are gathered in meditation succeeds in bringing forth an immaterial body, like someone who pulls a snake out of its skin.» (*Upanishaden, op. cit.*, p. 34.) The snake plays an important part in *Siddharta*.

3 This is confirmed by the Mahayana scriptures, where the transcendental absolute is said to be uncommunicable by words, but can only be experienced »by the devout in his innermost Self.» (*Upanishaden, op. cit.*, p. 150.) The *Mundaka-Upanishad* confirms that speech: The Gods, asceticism or works do not enable man to perceive Atman; only the awakened, whose «innermost Self has been cleansed by enlightenment» (III, 1) can experience him.

and the Divine» (III, 647) are everywhere: in the sky, in the woods, and in himself. He experiences the god of the Upanishads (particularly the *Brahma Upanishad*), »the only God that is hidden in all beings, pervading everything and living as soul in all creatures.»[1] He feels that he is no longer an ascetic or a Brahman. These existences he has shed and left behind. He was reborn at this magical moment, when the world melted away from him and «he stood alone like a star in the sky» (III, 649). «Shedding skins, eternal surrender of the ego to metamorphosis,» he knows, «leads to immortality» (IV, 248).

Siddharta is now on his Way, a saint's way, which for Hesse often leads through «sin» (IV, 346). Transgressing values shared by Brahmanism and Buddhism, Siddharta goes to experience the world. In the city, like Demian and unlike Klein, he lets himself fall into life. At first he listens to his inner voice, considering his introduction to love (by the courtesan Kamala) and into the world of business as a «game» (III, 666). However, as the years go by, the inner voice grows silent and he is caught and immersed in the game, the Sansara, as an end in itself. Although he is not like the child-men defined in «A Bit of Theology,» he has acquired a sickness of the soul, attachment to property, fear of old age and death, and a feeling of satiety. It is time for him to go back to the river that separates the world of the child-men from the world of the Samanas.

At the river, the symbol of changeless present and ever-present change, Siddharta looks at the reflection of his face and spits at it. Like Klein, he wants to let himself fall. Then, without thinking (and that is important), he utters the sacred word «Om.» In a flash of magical vision he overcomes the wish for suicide and falls into deep sleep, to awaken reborn, overjoyed to be free and to hear the inner voice again. He joins the ferryman, Vesudeva,

[1] *Upanishaden, op. cit.,* p. 217.

who «listens with a quiet heart, with ... open soul» (III, 698) and lives spontaneously, as the *Vedanta* and the *Tao-Teking* teach. They both learn from the river the eternal change and eternal sameness of the flow of life's forms. They echo Confucius, who said that «All flows like the river, without stop, day and night.»[1]

Siddharta is drawn into the world of the child-people only once more–when he tries to teach his son wisdom and realizes again that nothing can be taught. Again, he looks into the river and sees images flow by: his father and his son and many others all «become flow and rush along to find the sea and rise again in clouds to return to earth.» He hears thousands of voices–the «music of life» (III, 721)–and lets himself go, all desires extinct, to become part of unity. He has become a saint. Vesudeva, his former master, now radiant, leaves him. Now it is Siddharta's task to help Govinda and depart in turn.

Siddharta tells Govinda–a Buddhist monk still adhering to one doctrine–about his experience of Unity and of his conviction that the world is complete at each moment. Like St. Francis or Confucius, he preaches universal love, believing that the Buddha, too, had led a life of charitable love. Although Govinda is convinced that Siddharta is a saint, he is still reasoning, not yet «free, open, without goal» (III, 723). Only when he has kissed Siddharta's forehead does his will rest at peace and contemplation begins.

For Hesse, contemplation «is not search or criticism; it is nothing but love. It is the highest, the most desirable state of our soul: selfless love» (VII, 69). It is a state when time ceases to exist. If this state would exist forever, it would mean eternal bliss, for at such magical moments, devoid of a fixed perspective, nothing is seen «darkly and distorted» (VII, 68) by our selfish will. Nothing is subject to our willfulness; all becomes again part of na-

1 R. Wilhelm, trans., *Kung Futse. Gespräche (Lun Jü)*. Düsseldorf: E. Diederichs, 1955, p. 15.

ture, beyond polarities like old and young, beautiful and ugly, hard and soft. All forms become again expressions of «forever creative, immortal life» (VII, 69).

Siddharta has helped Govinda to «shed the skin,» has awakened in him selfless love. Now Govinda has a vision of the flow of forms. Like Klingsor, Klein, and Siddharta, he sees many, many forms—human faces, crocodiles, bulls, birds, gods—in eternal metamorphosis. Above this stream he sees Siddharta's masklike face, diaphanous and smiling, the smile of «unity above the flowing forms» (III, 732). Finally, Govinda, too, has experienced Unity by direct apprehension.

Hesse suggests that the experience of Unity and the professing of selfless love are Protestant traits (VII, 372). They may equally well be seen as Buddhist traits. In his youth Hesse had believed in Buddha and had thought of Nirvana as the return of the individual soul to the universal soul.[1]

Hesse called the *Bhagavat-Gita* a revelation and the best concept of the Self. In addition, he called Chinese wisdom «a second home . . . without whose ideal of wisdom and goodness I would not know how to live» (VII, 419). The idea of unity that underlies Confucianism and Taoism is one of cosmic complements. Confucius preaches «love for your fellowmen.»[2] Hesse found «mystic dynamism» in Lao Tse (VII, 373) and said of Goethe's supra-personal wisdom—which is akin to the wisdom of India, China, and Greece—that it is no longer subject to will or intellect, but only to «devotion, reverence and the will to serve Tao» (VII, 382). This idea of service points to *The Journey to the East* and *The Glass Bead Game*.

[1] The union with God in Christian mysticism corresponds to the union with Nirvana of the Buddhist mystic; both stress love for fellow man, but Buddhism places more emphasis than does Christianity on love of all creatures. Like Brahmanism, Buddhism emphasizes selflessness, freedom from desire, and good deeds and thoughts.
[2] *Kung Futse Lun Yü, op. cit.*, p. 159.

*Siddharta* is the profession of faith of a seeker who couldn't accept any doctrine, but who, when he found his Way, «was able to approve each doctrine» and was no longer separated from «the thousands of others who lived in the eternal and breathed the divine» (III, 701).

In *Siddharta,* with its magic synthesis, we have the most harmonious of Hesse's soul-biographies–in oriental apparel. Between it and the next major work to show dissonance juxtaposed to harmony, Hesse wrote *The Spa Visitor,* an essay of self-examination, «half-way from *Siddharta* to *Steppenwolf*» (IV, 914). When it appeared in 1924, *The Spa Visitor* came as a surprise to readers who had basked in the rhythmical, liturgical language and the legendary magical world of *Siddharta.* There is a different style, mood, and message: the suffering individual–in painful individuation within a world that demands conformity and worships technical progress–is juxtaposed to the poet, who «imposes his way of thinking on the whole world» (IV, 10). Though the bourgeois give preference to machines, the poet reveres great poetry, prefers the brightness of the stars and their «music of the worlds» (IV, 11). Such thoughts are *prologomena* to *The Steppenwolf.*

In 1923, when *The Spa Visitor* was being written, several events occurred in Hesse's life which were to have significant impact on his writing. Growing dissatisfaction with his German countrymen, whom the war had taught nothing and whose undemocratic behavior saddened Hesse deeply, made him abandon his German citizenship to become a Swiss citizen. His three sons were inducted into the Swiss army. In the same year he was divorced from his first wife.

Since his retreat to Montagnola in 1919, he had been working feverishly and had produced novellas, essays, articles, book reviews; he had edited the journal *Vivos Voco* and books of a number of his favorite writers. He was lonely, though, and soon began to leave his retreat (which he called his «home in the steppe») to visit friends, go on lecture tours, and make trips to a health spa near Zurich, Baden.

*The Spa Visitor* was mostly written there, while Hesse undertook a cure for his rheumatic ailments. The leisurely pace at the spa and the many kinds of visitors he met lent themselves to intense self-examination and brought about an appraisal, playful in tone, of the artist's isolation within the bourgeois world of «very intelligent anti-intellectualism» (IV, 19).

In the preface, Hesse points to the stars and to «the music of the worlds,» prefiguring the world of *The Steppenwolf*'s Immortals. Yet at times, he looks at himself in sorrow, believing that he has «a personal biology and mythology» where the psychic dominates to such an extent that he sees every sickness and even death as psychogenic (IV, 24). Days of depression alternate with days when he sees life as a game. One day he looks at »the stars mirrored in the rain puddles . . . in a moment of magical . . . beauty, that comes out of your own soul» (IV, 27). It is the transient beauty of a world that must die that mirrors the stars, just as it is «the spirit that must become flesh» in order to become part of the living world of forms (IV, 31).

In the next work, *The Nuremberg Journey*, we have again two perspectives: the timeless and the temporary, or «the eternal Self that watches the mortal ego» (IV, 159). This higher Self perceives that the poet is living «outside of bourgeois society» (IV, 160) and is only at home with his favorite writers: Goethe, Hölderlin, Kleist, and the Romantics–Jean Paul, Brentano, Hoffmann, Stifter, Eichendorff (IV, 156). From the temporary perspective, it would seem that the poet lives in the past, since all of these writers (as well as his favorite musicians, Händel and Mozart) lived before 1850. But to the eternal eye that is part of the other perspective, namely that which the pious call the Third Kingdom of God and what *The Steppenwolf* will designate as the realm of the Immortals, the world cannot be seen in fragments of time. It must be seen as a whole, as eternal; and the artist must be a messenger of the eternal. In this timeless perspective, names are irrelevant. It is immaterial whether we call the Immortal an artist, a prophet, a philosopher, or a saint. And posterity no longer exists. In eternity, Hesse contends in *The Steppenwolf*, «there are no epigones, only contemporaries» (IV, 345).

Only the simultaneous double perspective of the temporal and the divine enables the Immortals to laugh. It is only with this humor that the artist-saint can affirm at the same time that «the saint and the sinner ... bend the poles [of the two-voiced melody of life] together ... and even include the bourgeois in the affirmation» (IV, 239). In *The Nuremberg Journey*, the poet feels that all one can do about «the whole game of life» (IV, 179) is laugh, an art the Steppenwolf will have to learn before he can join the Immortals.

Because of their saving humor, *The Spa Visitor* and *The Nuremberg Journey* can be considered optimistic renderings of his mood toward the middle of the nineteen-twenties. This cannot be said of most of the poems he wrote at that time and published in *Crisis*. There, even the liberating flow into unity is followed by the bitter remark that these are only «beloved dreams» (V, 694). The poet also confides that he listens fearfully to his inner voice, «which he no longer believes» (V, 694). It is this mood of despair that dominates Hesse's next (considered by some his most daring) novel, *The Steppenwolf*, published in 1927.

*The Steppenwolf* is constructed around «The Tractate» «as strictly and rigidly as a sonata» (VII, 495).[1] The in-

1 See Theodore Ziolkowski, *The Novels of Hermann Hesse*, Princeton: Princeton University Press, 1965.

troduction–with its exposition, development, and re-capitulation–corresponds to the first movement of the sonata. Subsequent variations on the basic theme follow, and these can be likened to the second movement. As the third movement we can consider the tentative denouement that refers back to «The Tractate of the Steppenwolf.» In this work, the author's dream of putting into words the melody of the «two-voicedness of life ... two series of notes and notes that correspond with and complement each other, but that are at the same time antagonistic» (IV, 113) has probably come as close to realization as is possible for a writer to achieve.

Hesse's «sonata» has the ambition not only to portray one human life, «consisting of many ‹I's›» (V, 244), but beyond this to portray the genius's condition, by means of both reality and fantasy. When we remember that his own life seemed to Hesse to be «like a *Märchen*,» outer and inner worlds in a relationship that «I have to call magic» (IV, 484), we can see why *The Steppenwolf* seems to be a *Märchen*–the work of a magician who slips with ease from reality to surreality, blurring the dividing line, so that he achieves, paradoxically, magic reality.

*The Steppenwolf* is, like all of Hesse's work, the biography of a soul; the characters are «fragments of the poet's soul» (IV, 245). Like *Demian* and *Spa Visitor* it has an introduction which achieves a distancing effect from the main narrative. The writer of this introduction, an intelligent young bourgeois, is the publisher of Harry Haller's notes, which form the major part of the novel. He sees in the Steppenwolf a sad outsider, a man whose sickness seems to be the sickness of the age itself (IV, 205). In addition there is an insert, «The Tractate of the Steppenwolf,» containing analysis and advice given from the perspective of the Immortals, who represent Hesse's chiliastic vision. In addition to these three distinct perspectives there are numerous insertions of reflections and

47

commentary, forming an intricate web of thoughts and perceptions.

There is a good deal of autobiographical detail in Harry's life. Like his creator, he is separated from his wife, has lost most of his friends, hates himself, is lonely and in deep despair because he doubts his ideals and his vocation. He is also obsessed by guilt, believing that «all created things are guilty» (IV, 249). Like Hesse, he harbors «guilt feelings of individuation» (IV, 232), because, as a Nietzschean, he is different from the herd. Typically «Hesse-ian» that he is, he listens to an «invisible magician» (IV, 258), or a «bird» (IV, 367) inside, and is unwilling to accept a world of conformity and order, feeling only disgust «about the way people think, read, build, make music, celebrate, and run the business of education» (IV, 343). Life has become senseless; he longs for new values. Yet, paradoxically, Haller-Hesse learns from the «Tractate» that he has also been a bourgeois, all along: he has been a «specialist for poetry, music and philosophy ... The rest of his personality, the whole remaining chaos ... he has considered undesirable and called Steppenwolf» (IV, 319). With his fear of disorder and sensuality, he still lives in neat bourgeois houses and shuns prostitutes. He also has secret longings (like Thomas Mann's Tonio Kröger) to belong to the bourgeoisie. To liberate himself from bourgeois inhibitions and see the world from the perspective of the Immortals, Harry has to learn first to accept himself wholly, then to perceive life as a game, and finally to expand his soul to include the world in its totality. Only then may he partake of the Immortals' wisdom and share with them «the cool, bright, hard smile» (IV, 256) and see «God at his work» (IV, 212).

Years later, Hesse will write of his «catharsis by *The Steppenwolf*» (VII, 932). Similarly, his hero moves toward catharsis by going through the hell of his «own

soul» (IV, 368). Haller-Hesse takes leave of the bourgeoisie when he befriends the callgirl Hermine and is
initiated into the pleasures of the dancing halls and bars,
and meets the beautiful Maria, who in turn helps him
indulge in the pleasures of the senses. Finally sated by the
sensual life (as was Siddharta), Harry is driven on in
«eternal surrender to metamorphosis» (IV, 248).

Some of the fifteen sideshows of the Magic Theater
that Harry chooses not to enter were explored by Siddharta. One is the «Mutabor»–metamorphosis into animals
and plants; another, «Kamasutram» education in the
Indian art of love and the Wisdom of the East. Significantly, after the orgy of destruction of the automobile
hunt, Harry finds on one of the dead a card with the
phrase, «Tat twam asi,» a Sanskrit expression meaning
«this is you.»

Beside the destructive urge, evidenced in the automobile
hunt, there is the creative function of man as artist. The
artist, a schizophrene, can reconstruct his fragmented personality as he wishes, in all variations of the game of life.
The musician, the master artist of them all, is able to
transform «time into space by music.» To Haller-Hesse,
music «was without form ... it was only light, only
brightness ... what remains when a true human being,
having passed through suffering and sin, bursts into
eternity» (IV, 347). This realm beyond time and illusion
has been called elsewhere in Hesse's work the Third Kingdom of God, the Communion of Saints, or Brahman. It
is always the same and always fulfills the same function:
to replace the idols of the time with faith. «In *The Steppenwolf* it is Mozart and the Immortals and the Magic
Theater, in *Demian* and *Siddharta* the same values have
another name» (VII, 501).

The faith expressed in *The Steppenwolf* is in the timeless realm of the Immortals or the Communion of Saints,
represented in a golden sky. The Steppenwolf perceived

a «golden trace» several times and even felt that he had «partaken of the cool, bright, hard smiling wisdom of the Immortals» (IV, 256) at magic moments of his life. At such moments he «had affirmed all things, given my heart to all things» (IV, 212). Is not this «to become God, which means ‹to expand one's soul so much that it can encompass the whole Universe›?» (IV, 250). This bliss, however, lasts only moments. At the end of the book, Harry is unable to join the Immortals because he has not yet learned to perceive the eternal behind the temporary and to laugh at the game of life. But this does not justify considering *The Steppenwolf* a novel of despair, for it concludes on a note of hope for Harry.

As Hesse repeatedly stated, we have to see both time perspectives. Despair there certainly is, but at the same time there is bliss. But if we take the «Tractate» as the novel's center, we have to give greater significance to the timeless perspective than to the temporal. Faith in eternity was absolutely essential to Hesse: «I could not live or die without it» (IV, 347). This is demonstrated in all of Hesse's works, where the eternal has different names but is essentially the same. To become God–to enter eternity–means to leave personality behind, to go beyond the *principium individuationis*. This process the German mystics called «depersonalization.»[1] When Hesse speaks of the affirmers of life and nature–among them Goethe or (significantly enough) the Buddha–this affirmation is accompanied by a negation of the ego and «the desire to dissolve» (VII, 290). Harry, for example, says that «My personality had dissolved... like salt in water» (IV, 362); he had fallen out of time, «and was drifting along, near death, willing to die» (IV, 352).

Belief in the eternal, accompanied by the abolishment of time and personality, a key concept in Hesse's work,

[1] As Hesse knew, psychologically this term is called complete introversion (VII, 122).

is of great significance in *The Steppenwolf*. It is this that gives the work its affirmative quality.

Siddharta, Harry, and Goldmund–each one a brother of the others (VII, 493)– are all saints (to be sure, they are also sinners; but we have learned that sin is no barrier to sainthood, is possibly even a way to it) (IV, 346). Each lives according to his inner law; each believes in the suprapersonal and the supratemporal eternity. All three are at times tempted to commit suicide, as a means of flowing back to God. Their Way to Immortality is «surrender of the ego to metamorphosis» (IV, 248). At the same time, their lot is painful: «shedding of the skin» and rebirth (IV, 248). They move between the poles of existence with only moments of grace, when they are enlightened by a vision of the eternal. Each such truly exceptional individual is «driven by his inner destiny toward the Spirit, toward God–but drawn back to Nature, to the Mother, by his innermost longing: between both poles his life oscillates in fear» (IV, 247).

In Hesse's work, the central figure (occasionally two figures), «each a variation of my theme» (VII, 493), and identical with the author at a given time in his life, has to yield to metamorphosis. True to his belief in eternal metamorphosis, Hesse has to move on, both forced and willing to follow the inner law. Clearly, Hesse-Haller had not wished another «incarnation» (IV, 255) and another journey through hell. «Is it necessary,» Hesse asks himself, «that Camenzind, Knulp, Veraguth, Klingsor, Steppenwolf should be followed by a new incarnation?» (*A Night of Work*, written in December 1928, during his work on *Narcissus and Goldmund*, VII, 305). The answer is yes. Nothing can stop the author from creating and suffering. He will go on writing late hours, trying to cast imagination into form in a desperate but exhilarating effort. Speaking of Goldmund, «a figure that appeared to me in a vision almost two years ago» (VII, 304), he confides that such a figure becomes «for a while the symbol and bearer of my experience, my thoughts, my problems» (VII, 303). He adds that although his prose works are called novels, they are basically monologues in which «that mythical figure,» an incarnation of the author's mind, is examined in its relationship to the world and to its own Self. All of the figures together are «brothers, close relatives, and yet no repetitions» (VII, 306). Together they constitute the biography of Hesse's soul.

In *Narcissus and Goldmund,* as in *Siddharta,* the two worlds are separated by water, this time a brook that divides the outside world (the World of the Mother) from the Catholic monastery, Mariabronn (the World of the Father). Goldmund crosses the brook twice: first, when he illicitly visits the village; and later (as with Siddharta and the river), when he finally departs to enter the world and sin.

The structure of *Narcissus and Goldmund* is contrapuntal. Throughout, we have the «two-voicedness of the melody of life» in permanent oscillation between the two poles: Spirit and Nature. Narcissus, analytical thinker and theologian, represents Spirit. Goldmund, the dreamy artist who lives in the World of the Mother, embodies the world of nature and the senses, but has a longing for the mystical union of both poles. Although Narcissus and Goldmund are opposites, they are friends: each tries to comprehend the other and honor what the other is; namely, «contrast and complement» (V, 49).[1] Both live in danger, since Narcissus, who lives in the world of ideas, «may suffocate in airless space,» and Goldmund, the man of the senses, «may drown in sensuality» (V, 51). In Platonic terms, Narcissus sees in Goldmund «the other

[1] Hesse found that Chinese wisdom permits the wide swing between the world of Spirit and the realm of Sense. For the Chinese, «Nature and Spirit ... were not hostile, but friendly opposites» (V, 340). Narcissus and Goldmund complement each other like Yang and Yin.

lost half of his own nature» (V, 36). They share the will each to be himself (V, 287) and to reach eternal bliss and «return to God» (V, 48). This return is a matter of intellect for Narcissus, a disciple of Aristotle and Saint Thomas. He knows that God is eternal pure Being and that man, transitory and impure, can only strive to approach the Divine. His belief is that when man overcomes the accidental ego and recognizes the divine Soul as part of God (in Siddharta's terms, the Atman as part of the Brahman), he enters the Kingdom of God. It is his conviction that the same idea applies to the artist. For Goldmund, on the other hand, the religious quest is aesthetic: he believes that if he «frees the image of a person from accidental elements and reduces it to pure form,» he will have realized this image as an artist (V, 288). Since the pure image has to be present in the artist's soul first, before he can shape it into his work of art (e. g., Goldmund's statue), illumination has to precede artistic creation.

Narcissus can reason about «pure Being» but cannot experience unity because it cannot be reached by intellect alone. Goldmund, on the other hand, cannot reason. He lives only in images and knows that he has to follow «the call of the Mother» (V, 192), a very ambiguous call to which he listens all his life. First, he seeks and rediscovers the image of his own mother. Later, this image becomes part of the Great Mother, the Mother of Life. To Goldmund, the Great Mother is «love and desire, but one could also call her grave and decay» (V, 176). To seek her, he leaves the monastery. He experiences her first as love, being seduced by and seducing many women, but he soon realizes how transient this is. The transitoriness and death that he finds everywhere on his way make him yearn to find something that will last longer than the brief moment. He wants to «eternalize» it in art. He feels that the true work of art can be achieved only at a moment of awakening when all opposites are reconciled, time is abolished, and the world once more is made whole.

Like Siddharta, Goldmund sits at a river, gazing into the water. But instead of the «flowing stream of forms,» he perceives in the depths «formless radiance» (V, 189). The water keeps its secret: like «all real genuine images of the soul, they had no form ... they were ambiguous» (V, 189). Soul and dreams are made of such stuff, he thinks; they are immaterial, yet contain the possibilities of all forms.

At the end of his life, Goldmund still believes in the Great Mother, whose image he wishes to preserve in a statue in which he anticipates the union of the mind and the senses, the World of the Father and the World of the Mother. For Goldmund, a true work of art had to be both «male and female ... sensual and spiritual» (V, 177). Thus, this union «could begin in the most sensual experience and lead into the most abstract, or have its beginning in a pure world of ideas and end in bloodiest flesh» (V, 177). Art is the embodiment of the artist-saint's vision of the One. It is, therefore, both aesthetic and religious self-fulfillment. In other words, Hesse's (and Goldmund's) art is religion become form. The true artist is also a saint, a member of the communion of saints or of *The Steppenwolf's* Immortals—those who will be called in the next novel the travellers to the East (two of whom are named Goldmund and Hesse). And this is supported by the fact that the author speaks (in *Eine Arbeitsnacht* and in his correspondence) primarily about Goldmund and seldom about Narcissus, though he states in a letter that Narcissus «must be taken as seriously as Goldmund; he is the counterpole» (VII, 584).

Goldmund, although he has the soul image, does not have the strength to give it artistic form, his explanation being that the Eve-Mother «doesn't want me to make her secret visible» (V, 321). Nonetheless, his assertion that he has the soul image, even though he cannot give it form, makes it seem that he has fulfilled himself. For by his definition of the true work of art, this image would have to be a union of the Worlds of the Father and of the Mother, a vision of the One, although the vision still bears maternal features.

Beyond doubt, the mother image is of primary importance in the novel. It changes along Goldmund's way. First, it represents his own personal mother, an image that later becomes encapsulated, «like a kernel in a cherry,» within the image of the Great Mother (V, 191). Toward the end of his life, Goldmund perceives the image of the Great Mother «in the sky» (V, 320), a vision akin to the chiliastic vision of *Demian*. It is to this Mother that he longs to return. Before his death, his face expresses equanimity, and a smile full of «kindness and wisdom» (V, 321) reminds us of Siddharta and prefigures the Old Music Master of *The Glass Bead Game*.

It is no coincidence that Hesse's next prose work was called *The Journey to the East*. Eastern thought (both Indian and Chinese) had a great impact on his life and work: Old China's influence is seen in *Siddharta*, grows in importance in *Narcissus and Goldmund*, will be heavy in the last two mature works. The Chinese concept of totality as the unity of friendly opposites and the Old Chinese acceptance of both the world of the Spirit and the world of the senses were akin to Hesse's own convictions. He felt very close to his image of the Chinese sage, whom he saw as «an experienced man who had become wise and to whom humor was not unknown» (V, 340).

The Hesse who had turned fifty in 1927 could not have lived to write *Narcissus and Goldmund* had he followed the Steppenwolf's plan and killed himself on his fiftieth birthday. But he had developed wisdom and humor, and this enabled him to make writing the task of his life; so much so that he considered an evening spent away from it—listening to music or visiting with friends—as «lost» (VII, 302). Ironically, in this he believed he had failed, that he had set out «longing for life . . . for a real, personal, intensive life,» and had become «a writer, but not a human being . . .» (VII, 487). In a letter he confesses that he does not want «to live for life alone, not to love for woman alone» and that he needs «the detour via art, the lonely and secluded pleasure of the artist, in order to be satisfied with life, indeed, in order to bear it.»[1]

Nevertheless, he settled down for a life of creative activity and considerable personal contentment. He had met the Austrian art historian Ninon Dolbin (née Ausländer), twenty years his junior, who (in 1931) was to become his third wife (in 1924, he had been married, briefly, to Ruth Wenger). She was to be his devoted companion to the end of his life, three decades later. In 1931, one of his friends offered to build for him his dream house, and to lease it to him for life. The project materialized, the house is set high above the village of Montagnola, overlooking beautiful Lake Lugano and the surrounding mountain ranges. Once again Hesse has a real home and a garden where he can plant bushes and trees. He grows very attached to his little world. The house is comfortable. His library contains a rich selection of the treasures of Western and Eastern thought, from the *Upanishads* to the moderns of his day.

In his last two prose works the individual quest is no longer the center of the novel. In his next book, *The Journey to the East,* Hesse sees himself as part of «the procession of the creative and the suffering which passes through world history» (VII, 565). The focus has shifted to the assemblage of «awakened» individuals, which in *The Journey to the East* is called the League.

1 Letter to Christoph Schrempf, April 1931, Schiller National Museum, Marbach.

*The Journey to the East*, which can be seen as a preface to *The Glass Bead Game*, was begun in the summer of 1930 and finished the following April. Its action takes place several years after the First World War. Looking back, the author comments on these years, when the country was caught up by many beliefs, among them the faith in a Third Kingdom, adherence to bacchantic dancing communities or groups of ablutionists, and a turn to eastern mysteries and cults. (Hesse reflects these beliefs and activities in several works: in *Demian,* faith in the Third Kingdom; in *Steppenwolf*, a bacchantic dancing group; eastern mysteries in *Siddharta*; and the rite of ablution in *Narcissus and Goldmund*.) We are given the retrospective reflections of the author who–true to his existential nature–has continued his Way.

The voyage Hesse describes does not take place in geography. It is again an inward journey, outside time and space. Each wayfarer has his own personal «secret game in the heart» (VI, 21), but at the same time each shares with the others «the same faith» (VI, 21), and all have sworn the secret oath of allegiance. Together, they are on their way to the East, «the home and youth of the soul, the everywhere and nowhere, the unification of all times» (VI, 24). The East, then, is a metaphor in this work for the Kingdom of the Spirit, and the whole book is an «appeal» to a way of life that runs against the currents of the time.[1] When Hesse speaks of the «order» of the wayfarers, he perceives them as «a wave in the eternal stream ... of the human spirit toward the East, toward Home» (VI, 15). Since «nach Morgen» means not only «toward the East» but also «toward the morrow,» the travellers are on their way toward a future Kingdom of the Spirit that they themselves, artists and thinkers, create.

1 Card to Karl Isenberg, 2/5/1931, Schiller National Museum, Marbach.

*The Journey to the East* is, among other things, an apotheosis of art. Its heroes are the artist-saints. The narrator, HH, is a musician. Other travellers are painters, writers, or literary figures–among them Heinrich von Ofterdingen and Don Quixote, as well as figures from Hesse's own works, like Pablo and Goldmund. In addition, several personal friends appear in poetical disguise (this aspect is amusing, although the tenor of the work is deeply serious).

A mystery shrouds the purpose and structure of the Order, which must not be revealed by the travellers. Hesse comments that this commitment to secrecy can be interpreted in several ways. It can, for instance, be understood as a taboo against mentioning the name of God–that is, against defining and writing about the Divine. By Divine Hesse means the magic level that is the third and highest level of perfection (see «A Bit of Theology»).

The terrible difficulties of the narrator stem from the fact that he wishes to write about a journey which took place at the magic level, when he is no longer on that level. At the time of writing, he has regressed to the second level. From that inferior position, «the reality I once experienced along with my comrades is no longer present» (VI, 39). Memory has faded, focus is lost, reality and fancy intermingle. The narrative is very muddled. Instead of a narration of the journey, we are given a narrative that describes the vain attempts to formulate an «untellable story» (VI, 37). Everything dissolves when the narrator tries to convey it. He blames it all on the fact that he cannot reveal the secret of the League.[1] If he could do that, he reasons, then there would be a center around which he could construct the story. He does not see that one who is at the second level cannot convey

1 This is similar to Goldmund's defense of his inability to give artistic form to his image of the Eve-Mother–that she did not want him «to make her secret visible.»

what happened at the third. So the journey to the East remains, in the final analysis, untold.

In the depth of despair, HH realizes that he not only has no center, but has not even a coherent view of the journey. All he has are fragments of images «which have been reflected in something, and this something is myself, and this self, this mirror, proves to be nothing . . . but the uppermost layer of a surface of glass» (VI, 35). HH, we see, takes the existential viewpoint. He, the mirror which should give meaning to the world, is unable to reflect the third level of reality–the only one that matters to him. He is a useless mirror, a mere nothing. Facing this failure, HH contemplates letting-himself-fall (like Klein) «from the edge of the world into the void» (VI, 52). But at this point, as elsewhere in Hesse's work, a friend intervenes.

The friend's name is Leo. We first meet him as HH's servant. One day he disappears and (HH assumes) takes the League charter along. Disputes and apparent dissolution of the League ensue. Having lost his faith, HH slips back to the second level of despair. Found again, Leo guides HH. At that point Leo's identity and function become clear: he is HH's transcendental Self. Wholly leader and, at the same time, wholly servant, he is said to live in harmony with all creatures and with the Spirit. Life is for him a «game» (VI, 49). HH, selfish and tormented, is unable to accept Leo's message that, «Whoever wants to live long, must serve. He who wants to rule does not live long» (VI, 28). HH must learn that personalism has to be overcome before he can reach again the magic suprapersonal level of the League, where service becomes the foremost concern.

At the trial which he must undergo before he can be readmitted, HH accuses himself before an illustrious assembly. He is chastised with a smile and forgiven under the condition that he look at his file at the archives. It is now, when the enormous archives of the League are open to him, that he realizes how foolish he was to attempt writing a history of the League. He sees the fragment of his history—a meaningless, illegible piece of writing—and finally knows that the magic level cannot be communicated. In the file there is also a strange figurine consisting of two figures joined by a common back. One is HH himself, the other Leo. True to the principle of romantic irony—where life is viewed in double perspective from within and beyond the finite, thus giving the writer the double role of actor and spectator and the perception that life is a game—HH sees himself as weak, «dying or willing to die» (VI, 75) and melting over into Leo, the image of health and strength. He decreases; Leo increases. It can be anticipated that HH (who bears the author's own features) will be absorbed by Leo. This means that the literary figure (Leo) is more alive than its creator (HH, the narrator). It also implies that HH has returned to the magic level, the unification of polarities. He is ready to see the personal self die and the transcendental self (Leo) grow, because he has reached the distanced viewpoint where personalism no longer exists. One of the messages of *The Journey to the East* is, therefore, that the willful, personal self must die, and the suprapersonal self must increase. This means the liberation of the true self and, from a higher synthesis, the view of life as a game, an idea that prefigures *The Glass Bead Game*.

Actually, *The Journey to the East* refers to two journeys. One takes place within the divided self—HH and Leo. Its symbol is the figurine, which represents Hesse's Way, which can be called a Taoist's journey or the journey of an existential saint.[1] But in a broader sense, the individual Way must be seen in the context of the proces-

[1] At this point it does not matter to which religion we refer, although in this book Hesse borrows most of his symbolism from the Catholic church. In essence, *The Journey to the East* does not refer to any particular doctrine, although we can find traces of several.

sion of wayfarers, for Hesse's goal is no longer individuation, but service to humanity. He is part of the procession of the great artists who represent the eternal world of spiritual values, as they move forever through world history toward a Kingdom of the Spirit.

In *Demian* we were told that it is through those that «bear the mark» that humanity progresses toward new horizons. Now, years later, this belief is reaffirmed. In *The Journey to the East*, we are told that «it is good for those who bear the mark to know that they have comrades and to know that they are part of the journey ... This is our communion of saints; poor Villon and poor Verlaine belong to it as much as Mozart, Pascal, and Nietzsche» (VII, 565). It is to these stigmatized, the Eastern wayfarers, that the next book will be dedicated.

The narrator of *The Glass Bead Game* (1943), Hesse's next major work, shares the predicament that beset his colleague of *The Journey to the East*. An anonymous Castalian historian, living in about 2400 A.D., he faces an even more arduous task—or, rather, a series of tasks. He wishes to write the history of the Castalian order, a monkish institution in which the Glass Bead Game is played; he attempts to narrate the biography of one of the order's celebrated masters, Joseph Knecht, who died years before the narrator's time; and he has to collect and publish Knecht's literary remains. He is not completely successful in any of these endeavors, and he knows it very well. With irony he speaks of his «attempt» at a biography of the Magister Ludi, Joseph Knecht. Pretending objectivity and using a highly cerebral and overly-reflective style, he sets out to write what seems to be an account of Knecht's professional training and life. This is, of course, what we would expect of a Castalian, since the very heart of the Castalian order is service to the community and subordination of the personal to the suprapersonal. Fortunately, the historian is often carried away by artistic impulse and we have not only Knecht's functional, but also his personal *vita*. Of Knecht's literary remains, only thirteen poems and three fictitious autobiographies are appended (missing also is an unfinished fourth, very revealing, *vita*). Similarly, we expect more than we receive if we seek a clear elucidation of the Glass Bead Game. For, although the Castalian narrator speaks a great deal about the Game and attempts to give «a generally comprehensible introduction to its history,» he never fully explains–nor does he really ever intend to– the Game. This is reminiscent of *The Journey to the East*, in which the narrator is incapable of describing the journey.[1]

The books are similar in several other respects also, and it is no coincidence that *The Glass Bead Game* is dedicated to «the Travellers to the East.» In both books the narrators strive to be objective historians when they are essentially artist-mystics. Each tries to tell an «untellable» story, namely his own deepest psychic experience. Like some other of Hesse's works, these two define as a principle man's search for the Kingdom of the Spirit; and they share the belief that there is a community of geniuses or saints that serves and represents the Spirit at all times. When the Castalian narrator explains that the Glass Bead Game is «a symbolic form of the search for perfection ... an approach to God» (VI, 112), he could be speaking of *The Journey to the East*. Like the Journey, the Game has no beginning, having always existed «as an idea» (VI, 85). It is also shrouded in secrecy, being a «secret language ... a game with all the contents and

1 While Hesse was working at *The Glass Bead Game*, he wrote (about The Journey to the East) that the reader is not supposed to comprehend or explain the symbols but that he is to «let images enter his mind» and unconsciously «to absorb what they contain» as metaphors of life. (Letter to Alice Leuthold, 1931, Schiller National Museum, Marbach.)

values of our culture» (VI, 84). Similarly, in *The Glass Bead Game*, there is again a «religious» order which possesses an enormous archive, open only to the initiate. And again we are introduced to a utopian ideal as though it existed, the underlying reason being that it «be brought one step closer to existence and the possibility of being born» (VI, 79). It is clear that the same principal ideas underlie Hesse's two last major works, and there is good reason to believe that these ideas are at least latent in some of his other writings.

*The Glass Bead Game* differs from earlier works (wherein artistic vision prevails) in being highly formalized and didactic. Hesse's need to believe in the eternal Kingdom of the Spirit asserted itself more forcefully in this last great work because, in the Nazi regime and in the horrors of World War II, he was confronted with man's utter brutality. *The Glass Bead Game* is, among other things, an urgent plea for an all-embracing humanitarianism. The urgency produces a more didactic tone and a more explicit linkage with spiritual ideas of the past, like the philosophies of the ancient Chinese, Pythagoras, Leibniz, and Hegel.

For the same reason, Hesse's original plan was to write about an individual who lived through several incarnations at different historical periods and about a spiritual game that would show the mutual interdependence of spiritual achievements of the human mind. He wanted the Game to be «the *Unio Mystica* of all the separate elements of the *Universitas Litterarum*» (VI, 109). The link with the past—implicit from the beginning in his writings—is made conspicuous, so as to emphasize the timelessness and unconquerability of the human spirit. As Hesse explicitly states, the Glass Bead Game, «like every great idea ... has always existed» (VI, 85). And by dating his novel in the future, he implies that it always will exist.

When he tells us that the Glass Bead players dream

about extending the Game until it «encompasses the whole world» (VI, 220), we realize that Hesse is still speaking of the Kingdom of the Spirit that he visualized in *Demian*, but that he has undertaken now to formulate it in terms of Chinese universalism. Since the basis of his writing is the religious impulse, this Kingdom is viewed in religious terms. A *Ludus Solemnis* is, in fact, «almost synonymous with divine worship» (VI, 113). The Magister Ludi who performs it is «a prince or high priest, almost a divinity» (VI, 115). But despite this, and despite the apparent formality of the annual Game (carried out like a ritual dance around a holy center), we realize that it is still not conducted according to a particular doctrine, and that Hesse's Kingdom of the Spirit exists outside the established religions.

To the aesthete, the Game offers beauty; to the religious man, it gives in each ideogram the basis for meditation. Thus artist and saint are reconciled and formally acknowledged.

For many readers, the significance of *The Glass Bead Game* lies in the synthesis that it represents in Hesse's art and, perhaps, since he can only write what he has experienced, in his life. It is the work in which he reaffirms most strongly his belief in the Kingdom of the Spirit, seeing in the Game an eternal approach to this Kingdom or, to use religious terminology, an approach to God. Here an idea that we have seen in earlier works has been formalized in terms of the exact sciences. We are given a history of the Game, from the time (many years earlier) when it was played with glass beads to a later period when manipulating it meant dealing with symbols, the Game having become a symbol of the mystical union of all the separate elements of the *Universitas Litterarum*. Mathematics and, particularly, music—which have the capacity to express the interconnections and syntheses of relationships—thus play important parts in the Game.

The central figure is named «Knecht» («servant»), indicating that in one sense his main function is to serve the hierarchy. And, since Castalia demands an almost complete «absorption of the individual into the hierarchy» (VI, 80), the Castalian narrator knows almost nothing of «the servant's» personal life before Knecht joined one of the Castalian preparatory schools at the age of twelve.

The language and setting are often lyrical and romantic; at the same time, Knecht's friends represent ideas that influence and form him, ideas often couched in didactic prose. Plinio Designori stands for «the world outside Castalia» and its problems, Fritz Tegularius for «the esoteric, intellectual Castalian.» Pater Jacobus, whom Knecht meets as an adult, represents the view of the historian Jakob Burckhardt—that the history of civilization is the product of three forces: state, religion, and culture. The beatific Magister Musicae stands for the «perfect man» and is said to be like «an archangel from highest heaven» (VI, 129), a condition that is made even more evident when at death he undergoes a process of depersonalization and his face is transformed into a magic figure. The Older Brother, a legendary figure in his bamboo grove, represents Taoist mysticism. As teachers, he and the Old Music Master have the greatest impact on Knecht. Others, like Master Alexander, stand for Castalia, the rational spiritual order which follows Confucian principles.

Knecht, believing that he is Castalian, fulfills his duty as supreme Magister Ludi for eight years. But doubts assail him, even from the beginning. Slowly he realizes that he is (as Sinclair had been) aware of the polarities of the light World of the Father (Castalia) and the dark World of the Mother (the outside world). When he writes poetry, he breaks rules of the hierarchy that forbid artistic creation. When he experiences «awakening,» he is un-Castalian. Even the academic Castalian narrator notes that Knecht harbors two opposing feelings within his breast–one toward service to the Order, the other toward «awakening.» The irrational strain grows. Even while he defends Castalia to Plinio he feels a longing for the world outside. This sentiment increases in the presence of the overly-intellectual Tegularius and finds support in the teachings of the Old Music Master and the Older Brother. It finally leads Knecht to leave Castalia and go into the world as tutor to Plinio's son Tito. When he walks through the countryside in euphoria (like Goldmund), «without any obligation to think» (VI, 522), he sings songs and plays his flute. As with Goldmund, it is the artist in him that wishes liberation. To be sure, this is not what he gives as the official reason for his resignation. (He claims that exclusive devotion to the spiritual life in seclusion from the world leads to degeneration and esoteric play as pastime, and that his decision is to counter this by becoming a Castalian teacher in the outside world.) The decision to leave is not surprising, for several reasons. Perhaps the «official reason» has some truth to it. Much more important is the repressed artistic impulse.[1] Also, we have to remember the existential problem, best expressed in the poem «Steps,» written by the student Knecht (VI, 555). There the message is that man has to move on from step to step, in endless transition. His lot is never to remain on any one step. Castalia, too, has to be transcended.

When Knecht left, the Castalian narrator could have ended his biography, since departure meant the end of «the master and servant's» functional life as a Castalian. But the narrator follows Knecht's quest for self-fulfillment, as he obeys something from within–follows him until he drowns in the icy lake as the sun rises over the mountains of Belpunt.

Much has been said about the death of Knecht. Hesse

1 See Mark Boulby's «Der vierte Lebenslauf as a key to Das Glasperlenspiel,» Modern Language Review, LXI (1966), 635–646.

concurred that many interpretations were possible. For him, Knecht's death had the meaning of sacrifice; he felt that, far from «breaking off educating the young man» (VII, 640), Knecht had fulfilled his task as Tito's teacher. He has, indeed, caused a great change in Tito's thinking. The youth feels responsible for Knecht's death, and as he picks up the master's bathrobe and puts it on, he knows that his life has been changed and that he has now a commitment to achieve greater things than he had anticipated.

Like Knecht's death, *The Glass Bead Game* invites many interpretations. On one level, it restates Hesse's belief in man's ability to become himself and, once «perfected,» to help others by serving as an example, creating an eternal circle of master and disciple. As Knecht himself had been aided by the Old Music Master and the Older Brother (and Siddharta by Vesudeva, Sinclair by Demian), so Knecht leads Tito toward self-realization and service. From the perspective of the Spirit, teacher and disciple are interchangeable, it being «no longer possible to tell who was coming and who going, who was leading and who following» (VI, 310). Both are part of the game of life that flows on eternally, «divided into old and young . . . Yang and Yin» (VI, 311).

The hero's exemplary life has universal meaning. By affirming faith in the individual's perfectibility and will to serve, Hesse implies his belief in the coming of a better humanity, which will conquer chaos and barbarity. Like *The Journey to the East, The Glass Bead Game* expresses faith in the indestructibility of man's spiritual culture. This spiritual heritage is the content of the formal game. As an organist plays on an organ, the Magister Ludi plays with all those components of culture which represent the best thought and spirit of all times. They are *«Geist,»* which Hesse also calls «divine substance» (VII, 572).

Another approach, the novel as psychological game,

focuses on the player's psyche. He is to be brought into meditation, where he can receive enlightenment, not by active logical thought, but from within, passively, with an open heart. The highest aim is to achieve a harmony between reason and intuition. The Old Music Master, by definition a master of this game, has achieved this harmony between *Geist und Seele* (VI, 180) and has become «a saint and a perfected man» (VI, 352).

In essence, the saint and the millennium are the principal themes of *The Glass Bead Game*, as they were in most of Hesse's other writings and, indeed, in his life. The figure of the saint is drawn most clearly in Hesse's essay on Goethe. Goethe is suprapersonal. He is at home «everywhere and nowhere ... He is timeless, because all wisdom transcends the person» (VII, 381). In fact, his kind of wisdom is no longer «Goetheian»: «It is the wisdom of India, China, Greece; it is no longer will or intellect, but ... reverence, willingness to serve: Tao. Each true poet has a spark of it; neither art nor religion are possible without it» (VII, 382).[1]

The saint–the self-fulfilled and at the same time, paradoxically, the impersonal individual–can be recognized clearly, whether he is St. Francis, Vesudeva, Siddharta, Mozart, an Immortal, a Wayfarer to the East, Goethe, or the Old Music Master. He has reached the end of his Inward Way, where all opposites are reconciled. This center, Hesse writes, cannot be described in terms of one religious doctrine:

> The doctrine of Jesus and the doctrine of Lao Tse, the doctrine of the Vedas and the doctrine of Goethe are, as far as the eternally human is concerned, the same. There is only *one* doctrine. There is only *one* religion. A thousand forms, a thousand prophets, but only *one* call, only *one* voice.

1 This image fits all the travellers to the East, including, of course, Hermann Hesse.

The voice of God . . . is in you and in me, in each one of us . . . there is only *one* eternally valid truth. It is the doctrine of the «Kingdom of Heaven» which we carry «within us» (VII, 94).

The suprapersonal spiritual world of the saint is present after *Demian*, bearing various names. As early as 1920, Hesse wrote that the sacrifice of the «empirical I» is the only way to the saint, «the strongest model» for him.[1] He adds that writing is for the confessional poet a long «way,» the goal of which is to express the «I» so completely that it dissolves, bringing into being something higher: the suprapersonal. Art would be transcended and «the artist would be ripe to become a saint . . . I do know that I do have to go that way.»[2] He knows that it is a difficult way and that confession is sacrifice. It is appropriate that in *The Glass Bead Game*, the book in which Hesse wished to «summarize and terminate» his whole work,[3] the artist-saint is formally installed in the eternal and invisible Kingdom of the Spirit, the end of his Inward Way.

As he had planned, *The Glass Bead Game* is Hesse's last major work. But he continued to be active, writing short prose, essays, poetry, and many letters. Indeed, it is impressive in how personal a manner Hesse answered letters that he received from thousands of persons whom he did not know, but whose personal misery moved him. For many he had become a sage, priest, or physician who could be approached for counsel. Although he would repeat over and over that he was not a leader, he did not withhold advice. He would address his correspondents as equals, encouraging them to persevere in «going their Way,» speaking about generally human concerns, voic-

1 «Aus einem Tagebuch des Jahres 1920,» *Schweizerische Landes-bibliothek*, Bern, p. 84.
2 *Ibid.*, p. 78.
3 Letter to Fredy Leuthold, 1932, *Eidgenössische Technische Hoch-schule*, Zurich.

ing his opinions on problems of the day. Seen as a whole, Hesse's correspondence gives a history of his time and complements his works. For his thousands of correspondents his letters meant very much, as we can see in those preserved in archives, nearly 16,000 of them at the Schweizerische Landesbibliothek Bern alone.

During the last years of his life, many honors were conferred on Hesse, among them, in 1946, the Nobel Prize. Although his health problems grew, his way of life did not change. He remained at Montagnola most of the time, but his mail and visitors kept him in close touch with the world around him. He died at the age of 85 on a summer morning in August, 1962.

But death may have had little significance for one who «has already died many deaths,» and who knows that his «own most personal life and thinking were involved in the eternal stream of great ideas» (III, 157); for one whose consciousness was freed from the world and whose art is a universe of its own; most of all, for one who had the courage to go his own Way and to enter the abyss of himself to find the Kingdom of the Spirit.

# 2

THEODORE ZIOLKOWSKI
SIDDHARTHA: THE LANDSCAPE OF THE SOUL

One of the most salient characteristics of the reaction against the nineteenth century was a reawakening of interest in the Orient. The East, with its aura of mystery, has been a symbol of revolt against rationalism in Germany at least since the twelfth century, when the authors of medieval romances such as *König Rother* and *Herzog Ernst* sent their heroes off to Constantinople and beyond in search of adventure and magical knowledge that were no longer in evidence in Europe. Not until Herder, however, was a mythical image of India created that inspired, on the one hand, the scholarly investigations of Friedrich Schlegel, Friedrich Majer, and Josef von Hammer-Purgstall, and, on the other hand, the poetic vision that permeates the writings of Novalis, the older Goethe, and Schopenhauer—to mention but a few characteristic examples.[1]

With the reaction against positivism and the advent of modern mysticism that is so conspicuous in the works of Maeterlinck, Yeats, Hofmannsthal, and others, the mystical image of the Orient received a new impulse. Alfred Döblin, with his *The Three Leaps of Wang-lun* (*Die drei Sprünge des Wang-lun*; 1913), was one in a line of expressionists that included poets such as Else Lasker-Schüler and Franz Werfel, who exploited Oriental materials in their effort to find a correlative substance for their new conceptions. This interest was disseminated in popularized form to thousands of readers in many languages by Hermann Count Keyserling, whose *Travel Diary of a Philosopher* (1919) gave an account of his trip around the

[1] See, in this connection, A. Leslie Willson, *A Mythical Image: The Ideal of India in German Romanticism* (Durham, N. C., 1964).

world in 1911 and 1912 as well as an introduction to the mystical thought of the East. The Orient became a popular province for all those—writers, theosophers, and readers alike—who sought a philosophy of unity and totality to offset the fragmentation of existence produced by the scientific and technological progress of the West, whose decline Spengler was gloomily prognosticating.

### Hesse and the East

While Keyserling was making his subsequently publicized tour of India, he might have encountered Hermann Hesse, who, with the painter Hans Sturzenegger, was taking a quiet trip through the East in the same year (1911). In his *Picture Book* (*Bilderbuch*; 1926) and in the journal *Out of India* (*Aus Indien;* 1913) Hesse published his own far less spectacular account of his impressions. India was a goal for Hesse, toward which he had long been striving, and at the same time a disappointment. In many of his stories and essays he has told of his childhood, surrounded by the objects that his grandfather Gundert had brought back from thirty years of missionary work in India. India, it can safely be maintained, was one of the most influential conditioning factors in Hesse's childhood. «From the time I was a child I breathed in and absorbed the spiritual side of India just as deeply as Christianity.»[2] As a boy he had before him the constant stimulus of that same grandfather, who continued in Germany his scholarly enterprises on Indic languages; and his father also published works dealing with his years in the Orient.[3] «For over half of my life I was concerned

[2] GS, VII, 371.
[3] For an account of these matters see Joseph Mileck, *Hermann Hesse and His Critics* (Chapel Hill, North Carolina, 1958), pp. 3–4, and E. A. F. Lützkendorf, *Hermann Hesse als religiöser Mensch in seinen Beziehungen zur Romantik und zum Osten* (Burgdorf, 1932).

with Indic and Chinese studies,» Hesse wrote in *Picture Book*, «—or, so as not to get the reputation of scholarly authority, I was accustomed to breathe the air of Indian and Chinese poetry and piety.»[4] Anyone who takes the trouble to glance at essays like *A Library of World Literature* (*Eine Bibliothek der Weltliteratur*; 1929) can easily obtain a quick synopsis of Hesse's impressive range of reading in Oriental literatures and philosophy.[5] It was only natural that he should desire to see with his own eyes the lands that had so long filled his imagination. And, indeed, he found there the India of which he had dreamed; his disappointment lay in the realization that he himself, as an Occidental, was unable to partake of this Oriental paradise.

«We come to the South and East full of longing, driven by a dark and grateful premonition of home, and we find here a paradise, the abundance and rich voluptuousness of all natural gifts. We find the pure, simple, childlike people of paradise. But we ourselves are different; we are alien here and without any rights of citizenship; we lost our paradise long ago, and the new one that we wish to build is not to be found along the equator and on the warm seas of the East. It lies within us and in our own northern future.»[6]

What he brought back from his trip was «a deep reverence for the spirit of the East,»[7] whether in its Indian or Chinese form. But Western Man can never hope to return to that state of primitive innocence; rather, he must seek his own paradise in the future. Not cyclical, but progressive regeneration is his destiny, and that fact separates him irrevocably from the primeval Golden Age of which he dreams.

4 «Besuch aus Indien»; GD, III, 856.
5 «Eine Bibliothek der Weltliteratur»; GS, VII, 307–343.
6 *Aus Indien*; reprinted extensively in *Bilderbuch* (GD, III, 786–862); here p. 845.
7 GD, III, 851.

Hesse's attitude toward the East is at this time not one of enthusiastic affirmation, but rather of critical assessment. The magic of the East, which he clearly regards as an image of a lost and irrecoverable paradise, exerts an ineluctable attraction upon his mind and imagination, and he returns to it again and again. Yet he pores over the lore and wisdom of the East with a skeptical eye, striving to single out those elements that are relevant to his own problems and, in turn, testing and sharpening his own thoughts on the systems that he discovers there. This is particularly evident in his journals from the year 1920, precisely during the composition of *Siddhartha*.

«My preoccupation with India, which has been going on for almost twenty years and has passed through many stages, now seems to me to have reached a new point of development. Previously my reading, searching and sympathies were restricted exclusively to the philosophical aspect of India–the purely intellectual, Vedantic and Buddhistic aspect. The Upanishads, the sayings of Buddha, and the Bhagavad Gita were the focal point of this world. Only recently have I been approaching the actual religious India of the gods, of Vishnu and Indra, Brahma and Krishna. And now Buddhism appears to me more and more as a kind of very pure, highly bred reformation–a purification and spiritualization that has no flaw but its great zealousness, with which it destroys image-worlds for which it can offer no replacement.»[8]

This evaluation is perfectly consistent with Hesse's thoughts as we know them already; it is the reproach that Sinclair, the poet, made to Pistorius, the analyst. A purely abstract vision of the world is insufficient for men who require substance and life. This brings us directly to the story of Siddhartha, the Brahman's son who rebels against the strictures of his caste and predestined office in life.

After all that has been said it is no surprise that Hesse

8 «Aus einem Tagebuch des Jahres 1920,» *Corona*, 3 (1932), 201–02.

undertook to write a novel about India; by the same token, it would be naïve to read the book as an embodiment or exegesis of Indian philosophy. Hesse found this book difficult to compose because he was engaged in coming to terms with India as he wrote. *Demian* was poured forth within the period of a few months in 1917; *Siddhartha: An Indic Poem* required almost four years of effort although it is shorter than *Demian* by one quarter. Hesse began the book in 1919 and quickly wrote the first four chapters, which were published separately in the *Neue Rundschau* (1920). Then there came a break during which he wrote the expressionistically flavored story «Klingsor's Last Summer»; later in the winter of 1919-1920 he went on to compose the next group of four chapters (the Kamala episode).[9] Then he suddenly found himself unable to go on.

«My Indic poem got along splendidly as long as I was writing what I had experienced: the feelings of Siddhartha, the young Brahman, who seeks the truth, who scourges and torments himself, who has learned reverence, and must now acknowledge this as an impediment to the Highest Goal. When I had finished with Siddhartha the Sufferer and Ascetic, with the struggling and suffering Siddhartha, and now wished to portray Siddhartha the victor, the affirmer, the subjugator—I couldn't go on.»[10]

It was not until 1922, after a complete revision of his views of India, that Hesse was finally able to finish the last third of his novel and publish it in full.

### The Elements of the Plot

Siddhartha, feeling that the teachings of Brahmanism do not lead to salvation, decides to try other paths. He

9 Hugo Ball, *Hermann Hesse . . .*, p. 162.
10 «Aus einem Tagebuch des Jahres 1920,» p. 193. A similar explanation can be found in Hesse's correspondence with Romain Rolland, to whom the first part was dedicated.

leaves home with his friend Govinda (chapter 1) to join
the ascetic Samanas, with whom he spends three years.
But gradually realizing that asceticism and yoga are only
leading him further away from himself, he goes with
Govinda to hear the teachings of Gautama the Buddha
(chapter 2). Govinda remains with the great teacher, but
Siddhartha perceives that everyone must seek out his own
path (chapter 3). Departing from Buddha, Govinda, and a
life of the spirit alone, Siddhartha determines to expose
himself to the world of the senses and experience (chapter
4).

Crossing a river on a ferry, he reaches a large city where
he quickly meets and desires the love of Kamala, a famous
courtesan (chapter 5). Aided by Kamala, who has taken
an interest in the poor stranger, Siddhartha soon becomes
wealthy and is able to afford all the pleasures of life that
he desires—including Kamala herself (chapter 6). After
many years, however, he realizes that this path was just
as foolish as that of asceticism; that his luxurious life has
lulled his true self to sleep just as perniciously as the
exercises of yoga had done before. He decides to break
his way out of the world of Sansara and illusion (chapter 7). Unaware that Kamala is now pregnant with his
child, Siddhartha steals secretly away from the city and
returns to the river where, at the heigth of his despair, he
almost commits suicide. But as he sinks toward the water,
he suddenly feels a stirring of his old self and realizes that
escape by suicide is impossible (chapter 8).

He decides to stay by the river and to try to learn to
understand himself again: he regards his years as ascetic
and then as profligate as two necessary evils that cancel
each other out, leaving him once again in his original state
of innocence—with the added dimension of knowledge of
good and evil. Living with the wise ferryman Vasudeva,
Siddhartha learns many secrets from the river: primarily
that there is no time and that all being is a unity (the

awareness of simultaneity and totality!) (chapter 9), but before this knowledge can be of real significance, it must be conditioned by love. After twelve years have passed, Kamala comes to the river with her son in search of Buddha. She dies from a snake bite, and Siddhartha begins to care for the boy. He loves his son desperately, but the spoiled young city boy yearns only to get away from the two senile old boatmen and to return to life in the city. Eventually he succeeds in escaping, and Siddhartha experiences for the first time the pangs of love and, then, pure unselfish devotion (chapter 10). When he has reached this stage, Vasudeva dies, for Siddhartha can now take over the tradition and his knowledge (chapter 11). Govinda passes by one day and, in a mystic relevation, realizes that Siddhartha in his own way, like Buddha, has achieved absolute peace and harmony (chapter 12).

It is immediately apparent that, though the scene has changed, many elements of the plot are similar to those of *Demian*. Like Demian (and later Sinclair) Siddhartha is characterized by an almost physical illumination that is a reflection of his inner control and mental powers. Here, too, we have a dichotomy between the world of the spirit and that of the senses. Accordingly, Siddhartha passes through the stages of saint and profligate, like Sinclair, on his road to fulfillment. His development also involves the seeking out and consequent transcending of a series of teachers. Vasudeva's death, with the symbolic embrace, has the same significance of mystical transference as the death of Demian. And, finally, Siddhartha's development follows the triadic rhythm that we have already noted as characteristic of Hesse's novels, indeed his whole conception of human growth. Here, to be sure, the initial stage of childlike innocence is not portrayed, for Siddhartha, when we meet him, already has the seeds of knowledge and doubt in his heart. Yet that stage is clearly implied, for instance, in Siddhartha's words after his awakening on the bank of the river: «Now I stand again beneath the sun as I once stood as a small child: nothing is mine. I have no powers, no accomplishments, I have learned nothing.»[11] And the harmony that he attains at the end of the book is, of course, the third stage of higher innocence.

Apart from those familiar to us from *Demian*, there are other elements of the plot that are clearly discernible: namely, elements borrowed from the life (or legend) of Gautama Buddha.[12] Siddhartha, in the first place, has the same name as the Buddha, who in addition to the proper name Gautama also bore the epithet Siddhartha («the one who has reached the goal»). Both are supposed to have been first among their fellows, as children, in all competition. Buddha left his wife and newly born son to become an ascetic; Siddhartha leaves his beloved Kamala and their still unborn son for the same purpose. Both spent time among the ascetics, learning the practice of yoga. Buddha spent six years meditating on the bank of a river; Siddhartha's last years are spent at the river, where his final relevations come to him. Buddha's relevations came to him under the Bo-tree, while Siddhartha makes his most important decision while sitting under a mango tree. During his three vigils under the Bo-tree Buddha experienced in a vision all of his previous existences, the condition of the present world, and a revelation of the relationship of all things to one another; this is precisely the essence of Siddhartha's final vision in the novel: a view of the world as simultaneity and totality.

These parallels do not mean that Hesse is writing a life of Buddha or using Buddha as a typological prefiguration. On the contrary, any attempt to analyze the novel according to Buddha's life or his teaching about the Four

11 GD, III, 688.
12 I refer especially to the biographical evidence for the life of Buddha in Maurice Percheron, *Buddha in Selbstzeugnissen und Bilddokumenten*, trans. Joachim Rassat (Rowohlt-Monographien, 1958), pp. 17–33.

Truths and the Eight-fold Noble Path does violence to the natural structure of the book.[13] The book includes, certainly, an implicit critical exegesis of Buddhism,[14] but Hesse's entire view of life and development is explicitly opposed to that of Gautama. In his diary of 1920 he states categorically that he opposes Buddha's conscious attempt to postulate an established pattern of development, maintaining instead (just as Siddhartha does) that he hopes «to fulfill the will of God precisely by letting myself drift (in one of my stories I called it ‹letting one-self fall›) . . .»[15] As a matter of fact, recent studies indicate that the *thought* of *Siddhartha* has more in common with Chinese than with Indian philosophical and religious systems.[16] However, questions of this nature are out of place here since, as in *Demian,* Hesse defines his symbols adequately within the framework of his fiction.

13 Here my interpretation differs from that of Leroy R. Shaw, «Time and the Structure of Hermann Hesse's *Siddhartha,*» *Symposium,* 11 (Fall 1957), 204–224. Shaw regards the novel as an expression of the Four Noble Truths (chapters 1–4) and the Eightfold Path (chapters 5–12) of Buddha. I believe that this view is structurally fallacious for the following reasons. In Buddhism the Eightfold Path is the way to the perception of the Four Noble Truths, which represent fulfillment. If Siddhartha achieves the Truths in the first part of the novel, then it is contextually pointless and structurally inconsistent for the novel to continue. But more important : the whole novel is Hesse's attempt, as we shall see, to reject the Buddhist way. If that is so, then it would be illogical for Siddhartha to follow the Eightfold Path in his own development. Finally, Shaw's interpretation is predicated upon an acceptance of the superficial disposition of the material: namely, two parts of, respectively, four and eight chapters. I believe, as the following analysis will show, that this approach ignores the essential triadic structure of the novel.

14 Particularly informative on this point is the dissertation by Johanna Maria Louisa Kunze, *Lebensgestaltung und Weltanschauung in Hermann Hesses Siddhartha* ('s-Hertogenbosch, 1946). Miss Kunze, however, seems, like Shaw, to be unaware of the very important journal of 1920 from which I quote.

15 «Aus einem Tagebuch des Jahres 1920,» p. 206. (The story to which Hesse refers is *Klein and Wagner*.)

16 See esp. Edmund Gnefkow, *Hermann Hesse: Biographie 1952* (Freiburg im Breisgau, 1952).

The parallels to Buddha's life are, rather, contributing factors to the *legendary* quality of the novel, for the legend is the genre that Hesse seems consciously to be imitating here. The legend, as one can easily verify by a cursory comparison of selections from the *Acta Sanctorum*, consists substantially of an ideal life whose episodes are filled by traditional «motifs» or, in the terminology of André Jolles,[17] by «linguistic gestures». These incidents or motifs are, as a rule, traditional and transferable; precisely in this way Hesse has transplanted various motifs from the life of Buddha to the life of Siddhartha–not as typological prefiguration, but in order to sustain the legendary quality of the narrative. Hesse, of course, is not attempting to write a model legend; he exploits the possibilities of the genre only insofar as he can do so without obstructing the development of the novel. Yet there are certain other features of the legend *per se* that appear as elements in his novel and contribute to its structure. In the first place, Siddhartha is clearly regarded as a «saintly» figure–he is, in Jolles' words again, an *imitabile*–not in the sense that his road can be emulated, but rather his goal of absolute peace. Then, his reunification with the All at the end of the book corresponds to the miraculous union with God in Christian legends. As in Christian canonization trials, his saintliness must be attested by witnesses: namely, Vasudeva, Kamala, and Govinda, all of whom recognize in his face the aspect of godliness and repose. These elements of the plot unquestionably heighten the legendary atmosphere of the story.

The quality is maintained above all, however, in the language. The style here is just as highly consistent with the theme as in *Demian* and hence, properly, is unique

---

17 *Einfache Formen* (2nd ed. Darmstadt, 1958), esp. pp. 23–61: «Legende.» Cf. also the article «Legende» by Hellmut Rosenfeld in *Reallexikon der deutschen Literaturgeschichte,* II (2nd ed. Berlin, 1959).

and different from the style of the earlier novel. As a matter of fact, in the latter part of the novel one can find passages in which Hesse did not quite succeed in sustaining the pure simplicity of the earlier pages. This is accounted for by the fact that the first part of the book, as we have seen, was written in a mood of reflection whereas the second part was a voyage of discovery for Hesse himself. Thus in the beginning the style is more controlled. It is characterized essentially by extreme parataxis of syntax (which corresponds to the parataxis of structure, as we shall see), consciously archaic phraseology, epic repetition and epic cataloguing of detail (joined by many passages of iterative-durative action to denote the passing of time), Homeric simile, and, in general, by a highly stylized presentation. This is the basic tone of the entire book although in the excitement of the second part Hesse occasionally lapses into discongruous passages of extended hypotaxis and less leisurely presentation.

### The River as Symbol

The central symbol around which the plot and substance of the novel are organized is the river. Unlike those in *Demian,* this symbol is not complicated or complemented by other symbols or motifs; it alone bears the full burden of communication. The river, as so often in literature from Heraclitus to Thomas Wolfe, is a symbol for timelessness, and with this symbol Hesse aligns himself with many other modern authors who are obsessed with the problem of the tyranny of time: Proust, T. S. Eliot, Hermann Broch, Thomas Mann, and Faulkner, to mention only a few.[18] In Hesse's case this symbol of simultaneity is expanded to include the realm, already anticipated in *Demian,* in which all polarity ceases: totality. It

18 For a stimulating and informative discussion of this topic, with explicit reference to the river as a symbol, see Hans Meyerhoff, *Time in Literature* (Univ. of California Press, 1955), pp. 14–18.

is a realm of pure existence in which all things coexist in harmony. Fluidity is a corollary of what, in *Demian,* we called magical thinking, or what Siddhartha expresses thus: «... of every truth it can be said that the opposite is just as true!»[19] For in any system that regards all polar extremes as invalid, as interchangeable, traditional values are indeed in a state of flux. Hence we find in *Siddhartha* many symbols of fluidity, and this extends even to the vocabulary, which returns to expressions of fluidity just as consistently as the language of *Demian* to the style of the Bible. Further: another corollary to the principle of magical thinking is metamorphosis. Just as fluidity might be regarded as the mode of totality in space, metamorphosis—in the Indian sense of transmigration of the souls—is its mode in time. Thus the concept of the «cycle of transformations» *(Kreislauf der Verwandlungen)* plays an important role in the argument of the book, for Siddhartha's ultimate goal, as exemplified in the final vision, is to escape the wheel of metempsychosis by realizing that all possible transformations or potentialities of the soul are possible not only consecutively, but simultaneously in the human soul. «In deep meditation there is the possibility of annulling time—to regard everything that has been, that is, and that will be, as simultaneous.»[20] Siddhartha explains this idea to Govinda by using the example of a stone: «... this stone is stone: it is also animal, it is also God, it is also Buddha. I love and venerate it not because it might someday become this or that—but because it has long been all these things and always will be ...»[21] Siddhartha's redemption lies in the fact that he has escaped the circle of metempsychosis: his Nirvana is no more than the recognition that all being exists simultaneously in unity and totality. As Hesse states it in his diary excerpts: «Nirvana, as I understand it, is the liberating step back

19 GD, III, 725.     20 GD, III, 726.
21 GD, III, 727.

82

behind the *principium individuationis*; that is, religiously expressed, the return of the individual soul to the All-soul.»[22]

All of this is nothing new: we met it in Demian's magical thinking and in many of Hesse's essayistic utterances. And in the story «Pictor's Metamorphoses,» which was written in the same year (1922), Hesse transports us to a fairy-tale realm where the hero actually does undergo the various transformations that Siddhartha experiences only psychologically. Through the powers of the magic carbuncle Pictor is physically transformed into a tree and other natural objects. But nowhere else has Hesse employed a more appropriate symbol for his ideas than here: for the river is in essence fluidity and simultaneity. This is made clear repeatedly:

«This is what you mean, isn't it: that the river is everywhere at the same time—at its source and at its mouth, at the waterfall, at the ferry, at the rapids, in the sea, in the mountains—everywhere, at the same time—and that for the river there is only the present, without the shadow of a future.»[23]

In the river Hesse found the perfect symbol for his views. Demian's Abraxas, Harry Haller's Magic Theater, and the Glass Bead Game itself are all symbols for precisely the same concept; but they are invented or esoteric symbols that have to be explained, whereas the aptness and significance of the river is instantly apparent to the reader. But Hesse did not stop at the symbolic function of the river. He uses it in addition as the central structural element. Substance, symbol, and structure are so closely welded that it is almost impossible to separate these functions, for the meaning is not put into words, as in the other works, but must be derived from the action of the book itself.

22 «Aus einem Tagebuch des Jahres 1920,» p. 206.
23 GD, III, 698; for similar passages see pages 699 and 720.

It is only on the river, this realm of totality and efface-ment of polarities, that Siddhartha could have ex-perienced the visionary dream that he has as he departs from Govinda to experience the life of the senses in the city.

«Sad was the appearance of Govinda, sadly he asked: Why did you leave me? Thereupon he embraced Go-vinda, wrapping his arms about him, and as he drew him to his breast and kissed him, it was no longer Go-vinda, but a woman, and from the woman's garments there burst a full breast; Siddhartha rested his head upon this breast and drank, sweet and strong tasted the milk of this breast. It tasted of woman and man, of sun and forest, of animal and flower, of every fruit, of every passion. It made him drunk and unconscious.»[24]

In this dream, which comes to Siddhartha as he spends the night in the ferryman's hut beside the river, we have a transition from Siddhartha's previous ascetic life, personified by Govinda, to his new life in the arms of Kamala. But here on the river itself the two realms—spir-it and senses—are united in the embrace of the strange hermaphroditic figure of his dream (a figure strongly re-miniscent of the male-female dream-ideals of Sinclair in *Demian*). This dream plays a key role in the structure of the novel, for it is at once a transition between two parts as well as an anticipation of yet a third part, in which the two worlds will be reconciled in Siddhartha's vision of totality and simultaneity on the river.

### The Structural Principle

Superficially the novel is divided into two parts with, respectively, four and eight chapters. Any attempt to analyze the book on this basis, however, is fallacious, for it is quite obvious that the book falls into three natural sections: Siddhartha's life at home, among the Samanas,

24 GD, III, 652.

and with Buddha (four chapters); his life with Kamala and among the «child people» of the city (four chapters); and his life with Vasudeva on the river (four chapters). We have three parts of roughly equal length, each devoted to a distinct period of Siddhartha's development.

Temporally and spatially the periods are delimited by Siddhartha's initial crossing of the river and by his subsequent return to it.[25] Only with reference to the river is it possible to determine the fact that the three periods are of equal duration. And the river, as the natural symbol of synthesis, is the natural border between the realms of spirit and sense in which Siddhartha attempts to live before he achieves the synthesis upon its very banks. What we have, in other words, is a projection of Siddhartha's inner development into the realm of space: the landscape of the soul.

It can be ascertained that each section encompasses roughly twenty years of Siddhartha's life.[26] There is very little to go on. When Siddhartha leaves Kamala to go and

[25] Shaw, p. 212, is mistaken when he writes that «Siddhartha will cross and recross the river many times during his errorladen search. . . .»

[26] See Marianne Wagner, «Zeitmorphologischer Vergleich von Hermann Hesses Demian, Siddharta [sic!], Der Steppenwolf und Narziss und Goldmund zur Aufweisung typischer Gestaltzüge» (Bonn, 1953). In this unpublished dissertation, written under the influence of Günther Müller and his seminar, the author attempts to establish a precise chronology of events by referring to such things as rain seasons and banana crops. She assumes a lapse of one year between parts I and II, states categorically that Siddhartha is 57 years old when Vasudeva dies, and figures Siddhartha's own age at the end as sixty-one. However, the argument is unconvincing despite its subtleties; there is simply not enough evidence for a detailed chronology of this sort. Far more persuasive is the approach of Marianne Overberg in her dissertation for Müller: «Die Bedeutung der Zeit in Hermann Hesses Demian» (Bonn, 1948), for the author assumes that Hesse is interested not in any specific chronological time, but rather in »biological-inner» («biologisch-innerseelisch») time. Even Miss Overberg is tempted at times to be unnecessarily specific, as when she establishes the first chapter of Demian in the month of September «soon after the apple harvest.»

live by the river he is «only in his forties.»[27] Yet when he
first meets Kamala he is still a «youth,»[28] and Vasudeva
recalls that he had ferried Siddhartha across the river
once before: «It must have been more than twenty years
ago.»[29] Roughly, then, Siddhartha is in his early twenties
when he first crosses the river, and approximately twenty
years elapse before he returns to it. When Siddhartha sees
Kamala again, the son conceived on the night of his departure is eleven years old.[30] After this reference there is
no other specific statement: we read only that «long
months» passed before the son fled back to the city. And
the opening pages of the following chapter are filled with
expressions indicating the passage of time. So we should
be justified in assuming, for reasons of parallelism if for
none other, that at least twenty more years elapse before
Siddhartha's final interview with Govinda. Thus, the narrated time in each major section or life-epoch[31] is roughly equivalent.

Within the sections the time scheme is different. It is
obvious from the total time structure of the novel that
Hesse must operate, in this book more than in any other
he has written, with compression of narrated time within
the epochs. This is achieved, in the first place, by the frequent occurrence of passages indicating iterative-durative action. A good example is the opening paragraph.

«In the shade of the house, in the sun of the river bank
by the boats, in the shade of the Sal forest, in the shade

27 GD, III, 677.
28 GD, III, 657.
29 GD, III, 695.
30 GD, III, 706.
31 I use here the terms suggested by Eberhard Lämmert in his excellent study, *Bauformen des Erzählens* (Stuttgart, 1955). Lämmert uses
the term «epoch» *(Lebensepoche)* to designate the large units of time
into which a story naturally falls and the word «phase» *(Lebensphase)*
for specific periods of action within the larger epochs. The terms *Zeit-
raffung* (compression of time by various techniques) as well as iterative-durative compression stem from Günther Müller and are
employed by Lämmert and others in a restricted technical sense.

of the fig tree Siddhartha grew up, the handsome son of the Brahman, the young falcon, along with Govinda, his friend, the son of the Brahman. Sun browned his fair shoulders on the river bank, during the bath, during the sacred ablutions, during the holy sacrifices. Shadow flowed into his dark eyes in the mango grove, during the children's games, during the songs of his mother, during the sacred offerings, during the teaching of his father, the scholar, during the conversations of the sages.»

Although the novel begins when Siddhartha is about eighteen years old (he spends three years with the Samanas before he crosses the river for the first time), we receive, in passages of this sort, a clear impression of Siddhartha's childhood and an almost tactile sense of time passing.

From this general continuum of time that lasts for some sixty years, certain phases are isolated as characteristic examples for each of the three epochs. In general Hesse is operating here with two-day phases in all three sections, and these phases fall, in general, at the beginning and end of each epoch. The intervening time is filled—never simply omitted or ignored!—with iterative-durative action of the type just mentioned. In the first epoch we find a two-day phase beginning with Siddhartha's decision to leave home and continuing to the next day when he and Govinda join the Samanas. The second phase takes place three years later, when Siddhartha accompanies Govinda to the grove of Jetavana, where they meet Buddha; forty-eight hours after their departure from the Samanaś, Siddhartha also takes leave of Buddha and sets out on his new adventure.

The first phase of the second epoch relates the crossing of the river and his first full day in the city. The following twenty years, however, are expressed by time compression:

«Siddhartha thanked him and accepted, and now lived in the merchant's house. Clothes were brought to him, and shoes, and a servant prepared his bath daily. Twice a day a plentiful meal was laid out, but Siddhartha ate only once a day, and neither ate meat nor did he drink wine.»[32]

This passage is a particularly good example because it shows a transition from phase style to iterative-durative style. The first sentence is actually the last sentence of the preceding phase and is a specific answer to a specific proposal by Kamaswami. In the next sentence, however, the change takes place. The fact that clothing and shoes were brought to him is still specific, referring to the first day in Kamaswami's house; but the last part of the sentence is already iterative-durative: his bath was prepared not only on this one occasion, but every day for the next few years. From this point on, the epoch is not interrupted by another specific phase until the end of the twenty-year period when Siddhartha, who is now a wealthy merchant with his own house, possessions, servants, suddenly tires of his life and decides to leave it behind in order to start out all over again. This decision is again related in a two-day phase, which begins with Siddhartha's terrifying vision of his degeneracy and lasts until he finds himself on the river bank two days later, after his near-attempt at suicide by drowning, whereupon he decides to remain with Vasudeva, the ferryman.

The last epoch is richer in phases. The first, which takes place when Siddhartha has been with Vasudeva for twelve years, describes Kamala's arrival with her child and her subsequent death. The next phase relates the son's flight, many months later, and Siddhartha's realization that he cannot keep the boy with him or determine his way in life. The third phase depicts Vasudeva's death some years later; and the final phase is Siddhartha's

32 GD, III, 665.

mystical transfiguration before the eyes of Govinda. Yet between these eight specific phases, which form the slight action of the novel, the sense of time is never suspended, but is kept flowing by a variety of iterative-durative devices that leave us with a full impression of Siddhartha's life over a period of some sixty years.

The flow of time has two important functions in the novel. In the first place, the flow of time in Siddhartha's life must be depicted in order to make the symbol of the river plausible as an analogy for human life; the *tertium comparationis* is flux. In the second place, time is necessary to allow Siddhartha's own development. He must have time to exhaust fully the possibilities of two aspects of life and, in his third epoch, to adjust to the totally new synthesis of which he becomes aware on the banks of the river. In its own way, the novel *Siddhartha* is a *Zeitroman* in Thomas Mann's definition of his *The Magic Mountain*—a novel *about* time.[33] And the time in *Siddhartha* is as carefully structured as that in Mann's novel although the structure is a totally different one.

The temporal structure of the novel, which can be determined only by reference to the river, is paralleled by the spatial structure and what might be called the symbolic geography of the book. We have seen that the river symbolizes the goal of simultaneity and totality that Siddhartha aspires to achieve. Simultaneity and totality, however, imply the resolution of polar opposites. In *Siddhartha* the polar opposites to be reconciled—the spirit and the senses—are restricted geographically to realms divided by the river. The river by its very nature has part in both realms: it is not an obstacle to be crossed (as in Buddhistic symbolism) but rather constitutes in itself the natural synthesis of extremes. Siddhartha's wanderings in geographical space thus parallel his inner development.

33 Thomas Mann, «Vorwort,» *Der Zauberberg* (S. Fischer, 1950), p. XXIII.

Siddhartha leaves home in the first chapter in search of «Atman, It, the Only One, the All-One,»[34] which he had not discovered in Brahmanism. «And where was Atman to be found, where did It reside, where did Its eternal heart beat, where else but in the own Self, in the innermost being, in the indestructible part that everyone bears within himself?»[35] These are all periphrases for the word «soul» as we have seen it in *Demian* and Hesse's various essays. Accordingly, Siddhartha sets out to find Atman in asceticism and yoga, for he is still persuaded that the answer lies in exercises of the mind and denial of the world of senses. Yet, in the crucial phase at the end of his first epoch he is forced to conclude: «I sought Atman, I sought Brahma, I wished to dismember and unpeel my Self in order to find in its unknown interior the kernel of all shells, Atman, Life, the Divine, the Ultimate. But in doing so I lost myself.»[36] As he wanders on he meditates:

«He now had to experience himself. . . . The body was surely not the Self, nor more was the play of the senses; yet thinking was not it either, nor reason, nor acquired wisdom. . . . No, this world of thoughts also was not part of the beyond, and it led to no goal if one killed the random I of the senses in order to fatten the random I of the mind and of erudition. Both of them, thoughts as well as the senses, were nice things. But the ultimate meaning lay hidden behind both of them; it was important to listen to both of them, to play with both, neither to despise nor to overestimate either—and to perceive in both the secret voices of one's innermost being.»[37]

With this perception in mind he crosses the river and proceeds to the city, where he devotes himself to the sense

34  GD, III, 619.
35  GD, III, 619.
36  GD, III, 646.
37  GD, III, 651–52.

pleasures of the second section. We have here the familiar polarity of spirit and nature, but in *Siddhartha* the two realms are not mingled as was the case in *Demian,* where Sinclair pendulated constantly between the light and dark worlds. Instead, one section (twenty years) is devoted to the cultivation of intellect and another section (twenty more years) to the cultivation of the senses. Geographically, however, these are also different realms, and they are separated by the symbolic river which Siddhartha crosses. Twenty years later, when he returns to the river, he realizes that his life among the «child people» had merely cancelled out his preceding experiences in the realm of spirit and asceticism: «That was why he had had to go into the world, to lose himself in desire and power, in women and money; that is why he had had to become a merchant, a gambler, drunk and avaricious–until the priest and the Samana within him were dead.... He had died, and a new Siddhartha had awakened from the sleep.»[38] The return to the river is, of course, not accidental; if Hesse had not intended it as a structural element, he would not have described Siddhartha's first crossing and meeting with Vasudeva, which include certain elements anticipatory of the final resolution.

What we have is a geographical parallel to the temporal structure: in the first section Siddhartha spends twenty years in the realm of the spirit on one side of the river; in the second section, twenty more years in the realm of nature and the senses on the other side of the river; and the last (twenty) years of his life are spent *on* the river, which represents the synthesis of nature and spirit, the unity, totality, and simultaneity of all being. It is of interest to note that Siddhartha also begins his life on the banks of a river. (In the paragraph quoted above, the river is mentioned several times as an important feature of his childhood.) We have no indication that it is

[38] GD, III, 692.

the same river. Yet it is significant that his period of childlike innocence (the first of his three stages) was spent on a river; he leaves the river when the seeds of doubt have sprung in his heart and returns to it only when the poles of spirit and senses have cancelled each other, leaving him again as a child. For although rivers occur elsewhere in the book (there is, of course, a river in Kamala's city), they are mentioned only in passing and play no structural role.

It might be added that the parallelism between the first two epochs extends further to include the characters who play an important role. The significant dream that invades Siddhartha's mind before he first crosses the river calls our attention to the parallel function of Govinda and Kamala:[39] both stand for the essence, or the ideal, of the realm that they respectively represent. Buddha himself, who has achieved fulfillment, does not fit into the realm of the spirit any more than does Vasudeva: both show by anticipation the state upon which Siddhartha will enter when he has advanced far enough. But the Samanas, as representatives of the extremes of asceticism repel Siddhartha just as instinctively as does the village maiden who, at the beginning of his second epoch, invites him to engage in a little amatory sport from the *Kama Sutra:* she is not the essence of sensuality, but its gross extreme.

Through the projection of inner feeling into the realm of geography we have followed Siddhartha's development from the pole of spirit to the pole of nature and back to the synthesis of totality and simultaneity in the symbol of the river. In the final vision of the book Hesse renders Siddhartha's fulfillment visually by reversing the process. For as Govinda looks into Siddhartha's face at the end, what he perceives is no longer the landscape of

39 Kamala's name, like that of Kamaswami, is based on the Sanskrit root *kama*, meaning «love,» or Kama, the god of desire.

the soul, but rather: the soul as landscape. Siddhartha has learned the lesson of the river so well that his entire being now reflects the totality and simultaneity that the river symbolizes. As in a painting by Marc Chagall or in Rilke's poem «The Death of the Poet,» the landscape is actually reflected in Siddhartha's face. He has reached fulfillment by affirming the totality of the world and by accepting it as part of himself and himself as part of the development of the world.

«He no longer saw his friend Siddhartha's face, he saw instead other faces, many, a long row, a streaming river of faces, hundreds, thousands, all of which came and went, and yet all seemed to be present at the same time, all of them seemed to be changing and renewing themselves constantly, and yet all were Siddhartha. He saw the face of a fish, a carp with its mouth opened wide in infinite pain, a dying fish with breaking eyes—he saw the face of a new born child, red and full of wrinkles, drawn up to cry—he saw the face of a murderer, saw him plunge a knife into the body of a man—he saw, in the same instant, this same criminal kneeling in chains and his head being cut off by an executioner with a blow of the sword— he saw the bodies of men and women naked in the positions and battles of furious love—he saw corpses stretched out, still, cold, empty—he saw heads of animals, of boars, crocodiles, elephants, bulls, birds—he saw gods, saw Krishna, saw Agni—he saw all of these forms and faces in a thousand relationships to one another. . . . and all these forms and shapes rested, flowed, reproduced, swam along and streamed one into the other, and over all of them there was constantly something thin, insubstantial and yet existing, drawn like a thin glass or piece of ice, like a transparent skin, a shell or mold or mask of water, and this mask smiled, and this mask was Siddhartha's smiling face. . . .»[40]

40 GD, III, 731–32.

## The Beatific Smile

Siddhartha's smile in the preceding passage is the best example of the new dimension that we find in this novel. Here, in brief, we have the same story that we encountered in *Demian*: a man's search for himself through the stages of guilt, alienation, despair, to the experience of unity. The new element here is the insistence upon love as the synthesizing agent. Hesse regards this element as «natural growth and development»[41] from his earlier belief, and certainly as no reversal or change of opinion. In the essay «My Faith» (1931) he admitted «that my *Siddhartha* puts not cognition, but love in first place: that it disdains dogma and makes the experience of unity the central point. . . .»[42] Cognition of unity as in *Demian* is not the ultimate goal, but rather the loving affirmation of the essential unity behind the apparent polarity of being. This is the meaning of Siddhartha's transfiguration at the end of the book. The passage goes on at length, developing all the images of horizontal breadth in space and vertical depth in time that we have indicated. But the whole vision is encompassed and united by «this smile of unity over the streaming shapes, this smile of simultaneity over the thousands of births and deaths.»[43]

The beatific smile is the symbol of fulfillment: the visual manifestation of the inner achievement. As a symbol, it too is developed and anticipated before the final scene in which Govinda sees it in Siddhartha's face. It is the outstanding characteristic of the two other figures in the book who have attained peace: Buddha and Vasudeva. When Siddhartha first sees Gautama he notices immediately that his face reveals neither happiness nor sadness, but seems rather «to smile gently inward.» Everything about him, «his face and his step, his quietly

41 «Mein Glaube» (1931); GS, VII, 372.
42 GS, VII, 372.
43 GD, III, 732.

lowered gaze, his quietly hanging hand, and even every finger on this quiet hand spoke of peace, spoke of perfection.»[44] When Siddhartha departs from the Buddha he thinks to himself:

«I have never seen a man gaze and smile, sit and walk like that. ... truly, I wish that I too might be able to gaze and smile, sit and walk like him. ... Only a man who has penetrated into his innermost Self gazes and walks in that way. Very well—I too shall seek to penetrate into my innermost Self.»[45]

Siddhartha acknowledges in the Buddha a conscious ideal, but it is Buddha's goal and not his path to which the younger man aspires. The symbol of this goal is the beatific smile behind which, almost like the smile of the Cheshire Cat, the individual disappears. The same smile appears again when Vasudeva is portrayed, and we see it grow on Siddhartha's own face.

«And gradually his smile became more and more like that of the ferryman; it became almost as radiant, almost as illumined with happiness, similarly glowing from a thousand little wrinkles, just as childlike, just as aged. Many travelers, when they saw the two ferrymen, took them to be brothers.»[46]

At the moment of Vasudeva's death the unity of this smile is clearly expressed: «His smile shone radiantly as he looked at his friend, and radiantly shone on Siddhartha's face, too, the same smile.»[47] The words here are not used in a figurative sense, for it literally is the same smile. The smile is the symbol of inner perfection, but inner perfection for Hesse means the awareness of the unity, totality, and simultaneity of all being. It is thus appropriate that the three men who share this perception

44 GD, III, 637.
45 GD, III, 644.
46 GD, III, 699.
47 GD, III, 721.

should also share the same beatific smile, even though each reached his goal by following a completely different path.

## The Epiphany

The beatific smile as the symbol of fulfillment recurs in many of Hesse's novels: we shall find it again in *The Steppenwolf*, *The Journey to the East*, and *The Glass Bead Game*. But before we leave *Siddhartha* we must discuss one major point: the achievement of Siddhartha's affirmation of existence.

Siddhartha's development to the point of loving affirmation is marked by a technique of modern fiction that James Joyce defined as the epiphany, but which occurs regularly in much prose, German and French as well as English, of the early twentieth century.[48] In the epiphany the protagonist perceives the essence of things that lies hidden behind their empirical reality, and as such the epiphany is another symptom of the modern turn away from realism toward a new mysticism. The epiphany reveals the essential integral unity of a given object in a burst of radiance (what Joyce, in the words of Aquinas, calls the *integritas, consonantia,* and *claritas* of the object), and the observer is able to enter into a direct relationship of love with the object thus newly perceived. It is this element of loving perception, missing in the cooler cognition of *Demian*, that we find here in passage after passage. The most striking example occurs in the «awakening» scene of Chapter 4 after Siddhartha has made up his mind not to follow Buddha, but to seek his own way in the world of the senses:

«He looked around as though he were seeing the world for the first time. Lovely was the world, colorful was

48 For a full discussion of this term, its use in literature, and relevant bibliography, see my article «James Joyces Epiphanie und die Überwindung der empirischen Welt in der modernen deutschenProsa,» *Deutsche Vierteljahrsschrift,* 35 (1961), 596–616.

the world, strange and mysterious was the world! Here was blue, here was yellow, here was green. The sky flowed and the river, the forest towered up and the mountains, everything lovely, everything mysterious, and magical, and in the midst of it all–he, Siddhartha, the Awakening One, on the way to himself. All this, all this yellow and blue, river and forest, entered Siddhartha for the first time through his eyes, was no longer the magic of Mara, no longer the veil of Maja, no longer the senseless and accidental multiplicity of the world of appearances, contemptible for the deepthinking Brahman who disparages multiplicity and seeks unity. Blue was blue, the river was river, and even if the One and the Divine lay hidden in the blue and river within Siddhartha, it was still simply the manner of the Divine to be yellow here, blue here, sky there, forest there, and Siddhartha here. Sense and Essence were not somewhere behind the things. They were in them–in everything.»49

The points to be noticed in this and other epiphanies (including, of course, those written by the young Joyce) are, first, the impression of radiance aroused by the entire description, which here is created largely by words such as «blue,» «yellow,» and «sky.» Then: these are all objects encountered constantly in daily life, but here *perceived* for the first time. And finally: what Siddhartha realizes is that the meaning of these things is inherent within them and not some abstract ideal that lies behind their reality. They are radiant and meaningful as manifestations of the One and the Divine, hence as symbols of unity and totality.

A further characteristic of the epiphany–one that is inherent in its very nature but not usually present in the actual epiphany scene–is the subject's feeling that words, phrases, and concepts detract from our ultimate percep-

49 GD, III, 647.

tion of the object, that they lie as a veil between the viewer and true reality. (This is a syndrome that we discussed earlier as the language crisis.) In *Siddhartha*, as well as Hesse's works in general, we find this attitude, which provides the background for the experience of the epiphany. Siddhartha's final interview with Govinda makes it clear that he has been able to attain his affirmation and union with the All only because he eschews the easy way of convenient words and phrases as explanations of reality. «Words are not good for the secret meaning. Everything is always slightly distorted when one utters it in words—a little falsified, a little silly.»[50] He goes on to confide that he does not make distinctions between thoughts and words. «To be perfectly frank, I don't have a very high opinion of thoughts. I like *things* better.»[51] And he concludes by asserting that any ostensible difference between his views and those of Buddha is only illusory, the product of word-confusions. In essence, despite all superficial differences, they agree. The final vision, in which Govinda sees totality and simultaneity revealed in his friend's face, is also an epiphany: a direct revelation to Govinda of the essential unity of being that Siddhartha was unable to convey through the medium of words.

It is through epiphanies that Siddhartha breaks out of the rigid schematism of Buddhism and Brahminism (their «highly bred reformation» quality of which Hesse speaks in the diary of 1920) and begins to enter into an immediate contact with the world, though it first leads him to the false extreme of sensualism. Since love is the new dimension of Siddhartha's world, he must, as his final trial, learn to affirm even the rejection of his love by his own son. Only after he has suffered the torment of rejection can he perceive the final truth, which had hitherto been

50 GD, III, 727.
51 GD, III, 728. (My italics.)

purely intellectual: no two men have the same way to the final goal: not even the father can spare his son the agonies of self-discovery. When Siddhartha accepts this truth, he perceives with visionary clarity that in the realm of simultaneity and totality even he and his own father are one. Just as he had once deserted his father, so had his son left him.

«Siddhartha gazed into the water, and in the flowing water pictures appeared to him: his father appeared, lonely, grieving about his son; he himself appeared, lonely, he too bound by the bonds of longing to his distant son; his son appeared, he too lonely, the boy, storming covetously along the burning course of his young desires; each directed toward his goal, each possessed by his goal, each suffering. . . . The image of the father, his own image, that of the son flowed together; also Kamala's image appeared and merged with the stream, and the image of Govinda, and other images, and flowed one into the other, becoming one with the river. . . .»[52]

Not until he has recognized and then affirmed the loss of his son is Siddhartha ready to enter the state of fulfillment. Only at this point does he affirm with love the insight which had been purely intellectual cognition when he departed from Buddha. For even in the case of his own son he is forced to concede that each man must find his own way in life, that no man's path can be prescribed. Thus the highest lesson of the novel is a direct contradiction of Buddha's theory of the Eightfold Path, to which, as we saw at the beginning of this chapter, Hesse objected in his diary of 1920; it is the whole meaning of the book that Siddhartha can attain Buddha's goal without following his path. If rejection of that doctrine is the essence of the novel, then it is futile to look to Buddhism for clues to the structural organization of the book.

52 GD, III, 719.

Rather, the structural principle is to be found precisely where the meaning of the book lies. Just as Siddhartha learns of the totality and simultaneity of all being—man and nature alike—so too the development of the soul is expressed in geographical terms and, in turn, the landscape is reflected in the human face. The book achieves a unity of style, structure and meaning that Hesse never again attained with such perfection after *Siddhartha*.

It would be futile to deny, on the other hand, that this unity has been achieved at the expense of the narrative realism we customarily expect from fiction. Just as the characters and landscape have been stylized into abstractions by Hesse's poetic vision, likewise the dialogue and action have been reduced—or escalated—to symbolic essentials. As in *Demian* the action is almost wholly internalized: the excitement of this externally serene work is entirely within Siddhartha's mind. It is ultimately beside the point to judge this work by the criteria of the traditional realistic novel. Like Hermann Broch, who insisted that his *The Death of Vergil* was «lyrical work» and that it be read and criticized as such, Hesse had good reasons for calling *Siddhartha* «an Indic poem.» In both works there is a stratum of realistic narrative, but each as a whole represents the symbolic projection of an inner vision and not an attempt to capture external reality mimetically. Like his heroes, who vacillate between nature und spirit, Hesse as a narrator feels conflicting impulses toward realism and lyricism. In *Siddhartha* he reached an extreme of symbolic lyricism; his next major work, *The Steppenwolf*, comes closer to realism in its characterization, dialogue, and plot than anything else Hesse has written.

# 3

MARK BOULBY
THE STEPPENWOLF

One of the doors of the Magic Theater, one which Harry does not choose to enter, carries the inscription: «The essence of art. The transformation of time into space through music» (IV, 386). For the solution of this particular enigma one might well turn first to «Old Music» (1913):

There, a high strong note from the organ. Growing, it fills the immense space, it itself becomes space, envelops us totally. It grows and lingers, and other notes accompany it, and suddenly they all rush in hasty flight down into the depths, bow down, worship, also defy and tarry subdued in the harmonic bass. And now they are silent, a pause like the breath before a storm moves through the halls. And now once more: powerful notes arise in deep, magnificent passion, swell tempestuously on, cry out in lofty devotion their lament to God, cry again and more urgently, more loudly and fall still. And once again they go forth, once again this daring and self-absorbed master sends forth his powerful voice to God, laments and invokes, weeps out his song mightily in charging files of notes, and rests, spun in his mesh, and praises God in a chorale of reverence and majesty, spans golden arches through the high twilight, raises pillars up and ringing groups of columns and builds the vault of his adoration until standing it rests in itself, and it still stands and rests and encloses all of us after the notes have died [VII, 41–42].

This was an evening in the cathedral at Basel, quite possibly the very place where later Harry Haller (IV, 325) was to hear a similar music. The imagery prefigures the vision of the drowning Friedrich Klein–«a transparent sphere or dome of notes, a vault of music, in the middle of which sat God.» Music–that is, time–is transformed into architecture, into space–«it itself becomes space.» A dome of worship is built, and golden arches are raised in the high twilight. Then follows a melody rich in arabesques, which seeks only to express the harmony of this earthly world, and «the beauty of a contented, happy soul.» Finally Bach transcends all these limits, builds at a much higher dome, «lifts up and rounds out his edifice of notes far above the church into a starry space full of noble, perfect systems, as though God had gone to rest and had handed over his staff and his cloak» (VII, 43). The vision opens out onto the starry vault of the universe, perhaps the most persistent and potent figure in the whole complexity of *The Steppenwolf* (1927). Time and space as alternative manifestations of music, the moment of transcendent freedom which music may bestow and which is colored gold, music as form for the passionate impulse of worship–in this short passage from «Old Music,» indeed, much of the essence of the later novel is already incapsulated in a quite extraordinary way. And there are yet other associations: what the drunken Klingsor, in the grotto, had achieved in the imagination only, the domination of the heavens, this composer has actually attained in the work: «He thunders in massed clouds and then opens up free and clear spaces of light, triumphantly he brings forth planets and suns. ... And he ends splendidly and mightily like the setting sun and subsiding leaves the world behind him full of brightness and soul» (VII, 43).

Upon the dualism of «brightness and soul» *(Glanz und Seele)*, surface brilliance of form and fathomless depths of being, turns Hesse's view of music. «I was in music,» he tells us, «inclined to be conservative, like most writers,»[1] with a long-lasting attachment to the great Roman-

1 «Recollections of Othmar Schoeck» (IV, 652).

tic composers. Never an *avant-gardiste*, the course of his relationship with musical tradition was sharply different from that of Thomas Mann, had indeed a different starting point, Chopin rather than Wagner. In *Peter Camenzind*, Wagner's *Meistersinger* is a symbol of health, but tensions did later arise not unlike those in Mann, as the dubious light in which the composer appears in «Klein and Wagner» shows. Already in *Rosshalde*, in the argument between Albert Veraguth and Otto Burckhardt, we may note the beginning abandonment of the Romantic position, although there was never a clean break. The significance of music as a vehicle of austere religious experience is already pre-eminent in the virtuoso performances of Pistorius, and yet Emil Sinclair's reaction to these pre-Classical offerings has much about it that is both Romantic and sensual, as the language at this point betrays.

One suspects that it may well have been the religious feeling of the Bach chorales which first drew Hesse toward the music of the eighteenth century, to the music, it is worth recalling, of the great age of Protestant Pietism. And as his interests move in this direction, music becomes for him less a prop of poetry and the poetic temperament, and more an objective entity, a paradigm of transcendent harmony. The contemplation of such paradigms sometimes seemed to Hesse the true object of the aesthetic impulse; they might be discovered in a statue by Michelangelo, a Tuscan cathedral, or a Greek temple, or else a composition by Mozart. Moreover, the «Northern European» could experience, for instance in the music of Bach, something of what the Moslem and the Buddhist, secure in their religious traditions, were vouchsafed every day: the feeling «of belonging to a transcendental community and of drawing strength from an inexhaustible magical source.»[2] Music became for Hesse a symbol of

2 «India» (IV, 850).

spiritual community as well as a source of magical insight; its paradigmatic aspect turned it into a sort of hieroglyphic of the soul, a hieroglyphic giving only «the approximation of what we have heard,» as Hoffmann had said,[3] its highest content an austere fervor, «the genuine serenity *(Heiterkeit)* of the soul.»[4] For the Schlegels, architecture had been conceived of as frozen music, in Hesse's later work the characteristic design of music in space is the gothic arch, but it also may be said to form patterns in ice, diagrams of feeling coolly drawn by mind, or as *The Steppenwolf* has it, it becomes «time frozen into space» (IV, 347).

*Spa Visitor* (1924), a work originally more informatively entitled *Psychologia Balnearia* and which is close to *The Steppenwolf* in both date and mood, tells of the author's exacting struggle to achieve a musical form in his writing, an invertible counterpoint, «this two-voicedness and eternally progressive antithesis,» a form «where constantly melody and counter-melody should be simultaneously visible,» a form which would give expression to his own experience of duality: «For life consists for me exclusively in the fluctuation between two poles, the back and forth between the two fundamental pillars of the world» (IV, 114), the duality, moreover, of phenomena and noumenon, multiplicity and the One.

Hesse several times compared the structure of *The Steppenwolf* to a musical prototype; he said that the novel was constructed around the «Tractate of the Steppenwolf,» the intermezzo, «as strictly and tautly ... as a sonata,»[5] and also that «the *Steppenwolf* is as strictly con-

3 «Johannes Kreislers Lehrbrief,» in E. T. A. Hoffmann, *Das Kreislerbuch* (Leipzig, 1903), p. 365.
4 To quote from one of the prime sources of this view of music, Wilhelm Heinrich Wackenroder. See Wackenroder and Tieck, *Herzensergiessungen,* ed. A. Gillies (Oxford, 1948), p. 134. Music, for Wackenroder, is «the land of Faith» (p. 131).
5 *Letters* (VII, 495). The «musical» form of *The Steppenwolf* has been analyzed in detail by T. J. Ziolkowski, «Hermann Hesse's

structed as a canon or a fugue and has been given form to the utter extent of my capacity. It even plays and dances.»[6] Sonata form, indeed, would appear well adapted to display the fundamental dualism on which the novel is founded, as to a lesser extent might the canon and the fugue or double fugue with its contrapuntal structure. The introduction, the first section of Harry's journal and the tractate may be regarded as the first movement, having a tonic and a dominant, a development and a recapitulation;[7] perhaps the «wolf» is the tonic, the «bourgeois» the dominant. Certainly in his musical analogies the author seeks to stress that the texture of the novel must be regarded as woven of two principal subjects set forth, restated, developed, and contrasted, and eventually resolved.

A curious remark of Hesse's, however, leads to a deeper level of interpretation than this; the novel dances: «But the serenity out of which it does this has its energy sources in a degree of coldness and despair of which you know nothing.[8] There is no form without faith, and there is no faith without previous despair, without previous (and also subsequent) acquaintance with chaos.» Faith, earlier novels teach, is the acceptance of fate, the sometimes side-long recognition of a secret order in chaos; this order, when imposed upon the material of the imagination, is the form of the work of art (itself therefore an act of faith). The form of *The Steppenwolf*, then, is in some way intimately related to the spiritual agony from which the novel springs. Certainly it discloses the genetic pattern discernible in all the author's works, to which he inevitably submits despite the yearning to resolve this

*Steppenwolf:* A Sonata in Prose,» *Modern Language Quarterly,* XIX (1958), 115–133.
6 *Letters* (VII, 525).
7 Ziolkowski, *op. cit.,* p. 120.
8 I quote from a somewhat ironical letter in reply to a lady inquirer (Oct., 1932) (*Letters;* VII, 525).

dualism in a new stylistic synthesis. The strictly devised, musically conditioned form of the novel itself introduces an austere, an ascetic element which leads away from *Märchen* and legend, away from synthesis and magic realism as attained in *Siddhartha,* toward the intensest possible expression in novel form of the irresolvable counterpoint of the self. (The resolution we are offered is, not to put too fine a point on it, spurious.)

The difference from *Siddhartha* is apparent from the very outset, for *The Steppenwolf* has a preface or introduction. It is a revealing fact that those three novels of Hesse's in which the reflective aspect predominates, namely, *Demian, The Steppenwolf,* and *The Glass Bead Game,* are all framework novels and all have such a preface; there is a note in the introduction to *The Steppenwolf* which reminds us at once of the preface to *Demian*: «I do not want to recount my confessions or *to tell stories*» (IV, 192; my italics); within a framework of common sense we have a set of memoirs which may or may not be «fiction» (IV, 203), may or may not be «pathological fantasies» (IV, 205). Both *Demian* and *The Steppenwolf* are, within the framework, first-person narratives; *The Glass Bead Game* is not, but here the renewed importance of the element of legend makes a great difference. Whether the existence of the introduction in *The Steppenwolf* actually results in an intensification of the novel's realism is open to doubt, as it is in the case of *Demian;* the introduction equally (or correspondingly) has a distancing, depersonalizing effect. The tractate, the novel's most curious formal feature, goes much further than the introduction in objectifying and universalizing the problems of Harry Haller; like the introduction it is remarkable for the sobriety and matter-of-factness (which to Harry merely seems crudity) of its presentation. Except here and there, where for instance the bourgeois narrator talks in the introduction about a «sickness of the age,» the portentous note of the preface of *Demian* is missing; the use of imagery is restrained in both introduction and tractate. The bourgeois narrator, an elder cousin of Mann's Serenus Zeitblom, is duly reticent about himself; the author of the tractate is both reticent and mysterious, although a little familiarity with Hesse's earlier novels serves quickly to identify him. The problem of the novel's form, and hence the understanding of the work as a whole, turns really upon the nature and function of the tractate.[9]

What has happened here is that the element of tract discernible in the style of earlier novels has been hypostasized as a specific entity; Schiefer points out acutely the analogy between the tractate and the Christian tracts of the Protestant missionary societies.[10] The Calw printing house where Hesse's father worked published such things; their style was a matter of poignant familiarity to the novelist, as was their purpose–to preach the truth and the gospel, to awaken and convert. Thus we have the valuable insight that the tractate derives from the Pietistic tradition; we may even note in Harry's own journal reminiscences of the Pietistic tradition of the examination of conscience; the dissociation of the personality which occurs in Hesse's works has its roots here too. None of Hesse's novels is so clearly indebted to his Pietistic heritage[11] as is *The Steppenwolf*; the form is the imposition by faith of order upon chaos, the theme is the reflections

9 In all editions of the novel the tractate is printed differently from the remainder of the book, and in some early ones had its own colored binding.

10 P. Schiefer, «Grundstrukturen des Erzählens bei Hermann Hesse,» p. 73 a. There are other significant features; for instance, the opening of the tractate is a parody of *Märchen* style: «Once upon a time there was a man called Harry . . .»; and the ironic question is posed whether Harry was «sometime, maybe before his birth, changed by magic from a man into a wolf» (IV, 225).

11 Which he had earlier contrasted negatively with the «healthy» Roman Catholic religion. «Aus einem Tagebuch des Jahres 1920,» *Corona*, III (1932–1933), 200.

of a Pietist upon the way of life of a profligate with aspirations to sainthood. The saint, in any case, Hesse defines as one «in whose soul-state the chaos of the world is turned into meaning and music.»[12] The choice of music as the paradigm could be, but of course is not, wholly adventitious, for such music not only offers discipline, austerity, ascetic control, but is also itself connected with the appropriate religious sources[13] (the question of jazz, naturally, is a somewhat separate one). The book is saturated with allusions and symbols drawn from the Pietistic sphere, the tractate itself makes use of significant parallels–for example, «as no rule is without its exception and as a single sinner may be dearer to God than ninety-nine of the just» (IV, 227)–and reveals from time to time a faint but detectable puritanism. Not only the tractate but also the novel which contains it preaches a gospel, teaches a lesson; interpretative and reflective like *Demian*, and equally aspiring to normative definitions, the formally more consummate *Steppenwolf* is at heart a didactic novel.

The roots of its form, therefore, lie in the Pietistic view of the world, so it is not surprising that its theme should be that of the outsider. The English term first occurs in *Spa Visitor*,[14] then again in *The Nuremberg Journey* (1927)–and here a second time in the outlandish compound «*Outsiderwurstigkeit*»[15]–twice in *The Steppenwolf* and later on also in *The Glass Bead Game*.[16] *Spa Visitor* and

12 *Ibid.*, p. 197.
13 Music, however, is the direct analogue of the *moral* condition–and therefore the developing destiny–of a civilization, a point Hesse makes strongly by allusion to the appropriate Chinese sources (*Letters* VII, 571). Both Novalis and Fichte had identified the supremacy of inner over the outer with the triumph of the *moral* principle.
14 IV, 58.
15 IV, 161 (for both instances).
16 Cf. also «poor outsiders and steppenwolfs,» in *Letters* (VII, 730). How this word found its way initially into Hesse's vocabulary has not been cleared up.

*The Nuremberg Journey* may both be regarded as prolegomena to the major novel. The former deals with Hesse's first stay as a sciatica patient, taking the waters, at the Swiss spa of Baden, the second with a reading tour he undertook in Bavaria.

*Spa Visitor* is a work of some importance; Hesse later characterized it as «a mood of contemplation and self-examination, halfway from *Siddhartha* to *The Steppenwolf*.»[17] An ironic stocktaking and mannered self-persiflage, *Spa Visitor* owes something to Jean Paul, to whose humorous vision—as well as to his eccentric narrative techniques—Hesse turned for inspiration in these years. It states and restates theoretically a number of propositions central to the author's outlook, for instance the notion of fate—cited in those very words of Novalis already once used in *Demian*[18]—and the concept of unity. The gambling motif (gambling may be spiritually reinvigorating, it may restore the lost delight of childhood) links with *Siddhartha,* more specifically with «Klein and Wagner,» where the description of high life has a similar luster; one passage at least points directly forward: «And now at isolated moments my soul trembles alarmed and recalcitrant, like an animal of the steppes which suddenly awakens prisoner in a stall» (IV, 79). Return home to Montagnola from Baden is «return to my steppe» (IV, 79). In its depersonalization and its hostility to the self, *Spa Visitor* is positively Strindbergian. There are, indeed, direct analogies to be made with *Inferno* (which certainly influenced Hesse), for instance the neurosis of hotel living, but of course the persecution mania is less frenzied in Hesse than in Strindberg and the scatological obsessions are absent;

17 «Notes While on a Cure in Baden» (1949–1950; IV, 914).
18 «Yes, just as fate and the feeling self were names for one and the same concept» (IV, 17). Recent major studies of Hesse (Ziolkowski and Rose) have indicated the important debt to Romantic writers—Novalis, Jean Paul, and also Hoffmann—discernible in both themes and forms of *The Steppenwolf.*

*Spa Visitor,* though it is by no means gentle, lacks the matchless misanthropy of *Inferno.*[19] Humor is the solvent for the agony of outsiderdom here, as it is in the major novel, and the rituals of spa life are viewed comically as a banalization of religious exercises: «I had wanted to achieve by the way of penance, punishment, and good works, bathing and washing, doctors and Brahman magic, what can only be achieved by the way of grace» (IV, 103–104). Burlesqued though it is in this case, the association of bathing and washing with spiritual exercises points to a significant symbolic motif in Hesse's later novels. *Spa Visitor,* to sum up, may be regarded as a rather wry discourse upon the futility of good works as well as an aggressive attack, in the footsteps, though scarcely the mood, of *Siddhartha,* upon the curse of the intellect.

The rather slighter *Nuremberg Journey* takes up once more the question of the nature of humor, debates the justification of literature in this modern age, expresses horror of technology, and may be summed up as a commentary, both overt and oblique, upon the incapacity for naïve experience, the chronic condition of self-observation which the author constates in himself, whether this be incipient «contemplation,» the *sine quâ non* of self-development, or merely sickness, schizophrenia. Of the *Nuremberg Journey,* Hesse wrote later that it had been composed «in a critical and often virulent period of my life, when catharsis by means of *The Steppenwolf* had not yet been achieved.»[20]

The pessimism, aggression, and self-denigration of this period are most acutely caught in the remarkable collection of poems entitled *Crisis,* original confessional literature which, though crude at times, is astonishingly

19 Hesse reviewed the German translation of *Inferno* (Berlin, 1919) in *Vivos Voco,* I (1919–1920), 720.
20 *Letters* (VII, 932).

strong.[21] The *Crisis* poems certainly provide a rich fund of material for the psychoanalyst's casebook; when the work appeared, as Hesse wrote to his future wife, the despair which had given rise to it was already past[22]– *The Steppenwolf* was already finished. The link between the poems and the novel is extremely intimate.[23] The poems, Hesse said, dealt with «the misery and despair of physical life»[24]–itself a very Halleresque theme. *Crisis* reflects a desperate and vain effort to drown the corrosive, cauterizing intellect in sensual experience, the blur of wine and dancing, perhaps above all the former; Harry Haller stands «in the sign of Aquarius, a dark and damp sign» (IV, 202), and *Crisis* adds:

> Ich will zum Wassermann und zu den Fischen
> Und heim in das gewohnte Elend gehen.[25]

> (I go to Aquarius and to the fish
> And home as always to my misery.)

The poem «Missglückter Abend»[26] recounts almost exactly that same incident which is made a pivotal point

21 *Krisis: Ein Stück Tagebuch* (Berlin, 1928). There were 1,150 copies, of which 1,000 were put on the market. Hesse's uneasiness about the degreee of selfexposure in these quite untypical poems is evident in that the majority (and many of the best) were not reprinted. A number appeared in the *Neue Rundschau*, XXXVII (1926), 509–521, under the title «Der Steppenwolf: Ein Stück Tagebuch in Versen,» and also as «Aus einem lyrischen Tagebuch» in the *Neue Schweizer Rundschau*, XX (1927), 625–627. Some were even thought harmless enough to find their way into *Trost der Nacht* (Berlin, 1929) and the later *Gesammelte Gedichte*. See also *Gesammelte Schriften*, V, 688–702. The original volume is now rare.
22 Cf. *Letters* (VII, 478).
23 «A New dance, a foxtrot,» writes Harry Haller, «called ‹Yearning› conquered the world that winter» (IV, 363). The use of the word «that» *(jenem)* inadvertently destroys the immediacy of Harry's journal and reaches the true standpoint of retrospect and hindsight occupied by the author.
24 *Letters* (VII, 572).
25 «Nach dem Abend im Hirschen,» *Krisis*, p. 18 (also V, 689).
26 *Krisis*, p. 15.

of *The Steppenwolf*–the visit to the professor's house. Harry Haller's maddened hatred of the bourgeoisie and of their sham religiosity is reflected in the story of the master baker who runs the poet down in his car and is himself killed but of course goes to Heaven (as the poet does not), for he is a Catholic.[27] There is a sarcastic detachment from the new self-knowledge and the poet's erstwhile guru, Dr. Lang,[28] while the theme of the profligate sounds strongly:

> Rot blüht die Blume der Lust,
> Rosig lächelt die Knospe auf deiner Brust,
> Schaudert bebend unter meiner Zunge.
> Einst war ich ein kleiner Junge,
> Lernte Griechisch und ging zur Konfirmation,
> Eines frommen Vaters vielversprechender Sohn.[29]

> (Red blooms the flower of desire,
> Rosy is the smiling bud upon your breast,
> It shudders trembling beneath my tongue.
> Once I was a little boy,
> Learned Greek and went to confirmation,
> A devout father's promising son.)

But the Promising Son became the Prodigal Son, the criminal, the masochist, the potential sex-murderer:

> Ich bin heraus aus eurem Garten gebrochen,[30]
> Schweife flackernd umher in der Wildnis,
> Noch verfolgt und gequält von jenem Jugendbildnis,
> Das ich mich mühe zu tilgen und langsam zu morden.
> Vielleicht morde ich's Mädchen, in deiner Seele.

27 «Besoffener Dichter,» ibid., p. 73.
28 «Abend mit Dr. Ling,» *ibid.*, p. 51.
29 «Der Wüstling,» *ibid.*, p. 62 (also V, 695).
30 Cf. Gide in *Le Retour de l'enfant prodigue;* there is here a similar contrast between garden within and desert without.

Vielleicht, noch eh' diese Stunde der Lust verglüht,
Drück' ich die Hände um deine zuckende Kehle.

(I have broken out of your garden,
Errant I roam in the wilderness,
Still pursued and tormented by that picture of youth
Which I struggle to erase and slowly to murder.
Perhaps, my sweet, I will murder it in your soul,
Perhaps, before this hour of pleasure fades
My hands will press around your quivering throat.)

The Prodigal is constantly referred to in these poems:

Nun ziehe ich vor, gleich dem verlorenen Sohn
Brüderlich zwischen den Schweinen zu sitzen[31]

(Now I prefer, like the Prodigal Son,
To sit in brotherhood with the swine.)
He even appears in conspicuous association with another notable figure:

Legen Sie ab Ihre werte Persönlichkeit
Und wählen Sie sich als Abendkleid
Eine beliebige Inkarnation,
Den Don Juan oder den verlorenen Sohn[32]

(Discard your worthy personality
And for your evening suit select
Any old incarnation,
Don Juan perhaps or the Prodigal Son.)

The wall which separates the poet from the universe must be pierced, the open cosmos is the world of the Immortals, the great sinners:

31 *Krisis*, p. 61.
32 *Ibid.*, p. 49.

Und hinübertreten zu den großen
Sündern . . .[33]

(And to cross over to the great sinners . . .)

The way into «starry space» may be through cruci-
fixion, but then the note of scepticism typical of *Crisis*
intrudes:

Aber diese kühlen Sternenräume,
Diese Schauer der Unendlichkeit
Sind ja leider nur geliebte Träume.

(But these cool starry spaces,
These shivers of eternity,
I'm afraid they're just beloved dreams.)

«Am Ende» repeats the words of *Spa Visitor*, the
sounding of the retreat:

Packe meinen Koffer, fahr' zurück
In die Steppe, denn es gilt zu sterben.[34]

(Pack my case and travel back
To the steppe, for there's dying to be done.)

For *Crisis* has none of the optimism of the novel itself;
it mixes pessimistic longing for extinction with masochistic contempt, and all under the supreme sign of blasphemy. It reflects:

Wer des Lebens Wonnen kennt
Mag das Maul sich lecken.
Außerdem ist uns vergönnt
Morgen zu verrecken.[35]

33 «Ahnungen,» *ibid.*, p. 67 (also «Gewissen» [V, 694]).
34 *Krisis*, p. 79.
35 «Zu Johannes dem Täufer/Sprach Hermann der Säufer,» *ibid.*,
p. 25.

(He who knows life's pleasure
Can slobber at his leisure.
We've another grace as well:
Tomorrow we can go to hell.)

This sums up the mood. The depression is in truth partly anchored in physical despair, in the pains and frustrations of middle age.[36]

Harry Haller is Hermann Hesse's «fifty-year-old man»; Hesse made the association with Goethe's novella of that name quite consciously: «The ‹fifty-year-old man› has little reason to collect congratulations.»[37] Harry harps upon his age, his physical decline; his proposal to cut his throat is compared with Adalbert Stifter's act. This note is by no means new; in «Aus dem Tagebuch eines Wüstlings» (1922–1923) it is sounded strongly: «Aging as I am,» groans the diarist, «I dissipate my days like a student.»[38] Perhaps the most intensely personal of all Hesse's imaginative creations, there is in Harry something of almost all this author's previous protagonists, Peter Camenzind's Rousseauism, Hans Giebenrath's morbid regression, Knulp's introverted vagabondage, Klingsor's frenzy, and Klein's decadent self-crucifixion on the cross of introspection.

The Neo-Romantic issue of the justification of the artist has evolved into the question of the justification of the psychopath: «whether in certain historical and cultural circumstances it is not more important, nobler and more right to become a psychopath than to accommodate oneself to these circumstances by sacrificing all one's ideals.»[39] As the tractate points out, those who begin to perceive the true nature of their own ego are frequently locked up

36 Hesse suggests that this is a reason for the constant misinterpretation of *The Steppenwolf*, especially by young people. Cf. VII, 413.
37 «Nachwort an meine Freunde,» in *Krisis*, p. 81.
38 *Simplicissimus*, XXVII (1922–1923), 19.
39 *Spa Visitor* (IV, 58).

by the majority as schizophrenics. The characteristics of the outsider may often seem identical with those of the psychopath, or those of the artist, or those of the genius *per se*. The lone wolf artist is a well-known type with particular advantages over those of his colleagues who are *engagés*, but many lone wolves lack special artistic gifts, they have only «a plus in mind and imagination, a capacity for experience, for empathy, for resonance.» Such individuals are those in whom the highest possibilities of humanity are periodically realized, they justify the vanity and the waywardness of genius. One day, confronted by a call which they cannot respond to in any other manner, they immolate themselves and thus become saints: «These are they who truly love, the saints.»[40] The outsider is therefore justified in the last resort because he is a potential saint, and we see that his goal is decreed by his origins, is perhaps innate in the Pietism of Calw.

Hesse's fifty-year-old man bemoans the loss of his youth, his poetry, his ideals; now he is bitterly involved in «the crisis in a man's life around his fiftieth year.»[41] He has gout in his fingers, his walk is that of a sick man. The bourgeois narrator, proud of his own healthy instincts, is inclined at first to dislike Harry, suspicious of his manner, his style of life, his fear of the police; he concludes from the mobility and sensitivity of his features that he is «a genius of suffering» (IV, 193), as Nietzsche was. A gifted intellectual, disillusioned with men, sad at their insincerity, their pretention, and their histrionics, Harry has habits which are very much those of his type: he has no regular work, sleeps late, lives in a room stamped with eclecticism and chock full of symbolic miscellanea—photographs of home, a Siamese Buddha, a reproduction of Michelangelo's «La Notte,» a picture of Mahatma Gandhi, a whole library of eighteenth-century

40 *Letters* (VII, 719).
41 *Letters* (VII, 545).

literature including the memorable *Sophiens Reise von Memel nach Sachsen,* a well-thumbed Goethe, Novalis[42] and Jean Paul, volumes of Dostoevsky, of Baudelaire, the odor of cigars, empty Chianti bottles.

Not only are his eating habits irregular and his digestion bad–he is «an evening man» (*Abendmensch,* punning the prefix «Abend–» in its sense of «Western»)–but the drinking is evidently central, as one might expect of a budding saint, especially in the era of the author of *Crisis,* «Hermann the Tippler.» The «old-style tavern» (IV, 216) which he frequents is a hideaway for crusty, nostalgic, and would-be bachelors, «lonely lads like me who'd gone off the rails» (IV, 217). The word «lad» is quite enough here to summon up Peter Camenzind, and it is no surprise to find that Harry's taste is for «light, modest local wines without particular names» (IV, 217). Later on in the book we have it again: «Dear to me was my hard seat, my peasant glass» (IV, 353); there is a romantic atmosphere reminiscent of Harry's boyhood where inn, wine, and cigar were still forbidden delights. Those youths Peter and Emil, as may have been suspected, were bourgeois after all! They too suffered, it is true, from melancholia, and between their headaches and hangovers had but a few tolerable days; they too had talked themselves into their loneliness, as Harry into his; but still they were both *young* tipplers, both had their teachers and helpers, some sort of providential guidance or at any rate the remains of a poetic youthful faith in themselves. But this fifty-year-old man has used up all his placebos; demanding absolute freedom, he has all but obtained it. The iron

---

42 In 1925 there appeared *Novalis: Dokumente seines Lebens und Sterbens,* eds. Hermann Hesse and Karl Isenberg. In his postscript to the edition Hesse describes the work of this poet as «the strangest and most mysterious . . . in the history of the German mind» (VII, 282). *Spa Visitor* also discloses the revival of interest in Novalis at this period in Hesse's career–as also Jean Paul, to whose writings *The Steppenwolf* makes direct allusion (IV, 218). Cf. T. J. Ziolkowski, «Hermann Hesse and Novalis» (diss. Yale University, 1957).

justice of the *Märchen*, of which genre Harry's life is in some sense a parody, has him in its vice–what he longs for he gets, but «more than is good for human beings» (IV, 230); the «magic wish» (IV, 231), once wished, cannot be taken back; as Hesse's protagonists all learn: «There is no way back at all» (IV, 249). In the inn, under the wine, the rich memories flood in; memory alone–the aesthetic experience and its recall–seems to make the Steppenwolf's existence valid: «Who still thought»–in his treeless novel, at any rate– «of that tough little cypress high on the hill above Gubbio? . . . The Steppenwolf did» (IV, 219).

*The Steppenwolf* is a novel of the city (either Zurich or Basel)–although Harry does live in a garden suburb, this is scarcely evoked at all. His is the sharp and intolerable loneliness of the city streets; he has found that he cannot have community, not any more, however much he may desire it. People may not dislike him actively–indeed, he casts a certain spell to which the aunt and later her nephew, the bourgeois narrator, succumb–but they all avoid him. He knows full well, as a partly awakened man, that it is hopeless for one like him ever to try to fulfill the demands and obey the commands of society.[43] For him there is only the coldness–and the wondrous silence– of absolute loneliness, «wonderfully still and great like the cold, still space in which the stars revolve» (IV, 220).

With this there sets in the imagery of the cosmos, later to be developed so richly in what can be called the main section of the novel, that is, that part of «Harry Haller's Notes» which follows the tractate. These memoirs are «only for madmen»; nothing in them is quite on the level of reality of the prosaic introduction. But there are several levels of reality in *The Steppenwolf*. The tractate also, and the Magic Theater, are «only for madmen»–the latter, in the reflection of the illuminated sign on the asphalt, being «only–for–mad–men!» (IV, 215). *Ver-rückung* («de-

43 Cf. «In Memoriam Christoph Schrempf» (IV, 773).

rangement»)—this is the process by which the novel proceeds from the real to the superreal: to receive the message of the Magic Theater one must be «crazy . . . and far »removed from ‹everyman›» (IV, 258).

At the end of the first movement, if we follow the musical analogy, comes the tractate, a summing up constituting the chief attempt in Hesse's entire work at a theoretical statement of the nature of his protagonists' conflict with society and its conventions, with the bourgeois outlook. The bourgeois narrator, in the introduction, shows us Harry from the outside, recalls his ambivalent first impression of the Steppenwolf, the latter's tristful features at the celebrity lecture at the Aula, their encounter on the stairs where Harry sits entranced before the potted araucaria, the symphony concert at which the Steppenwolf seems transported by a work of Friedemann Bach. The bourgeois narrator is himself a type, portrayed with a certain dry objectivity, his satirical potential scarcely explored; in comparison with him, the author of the tractate is clearly of a totaly different origin. Harry compares his own poem

«I, the Steppenwolf, trot and trot . . .»[44]

with its significant mixture of aging weariness and blood lust, with the tractate, and finds the former a sad, subjective picture, whereas the latter is a cool analysis, «seen from without and above,» composed by «one who stands outside» (IV, 253), outside the charmed circle of introversion, an Immortal, as one presumes. Thus it seems to him, but in fact, of course, the author of the tractate sees Harry not from without but from within, the voice is the voice of his «friend,» the higher reflective self, the «invisible magician» (IV, 258). He speaks to Harry rather as the Armenian astrologer speaks to Klingsor,

44 Cf. also the same poem, entitled «Steppenwolf,» in *Krisis,* p. 34 (also V, 692–693).

though more sharply; what he relates is not the socially conditioned observation of the bourgeois but the truth of an esoteric gospel. Thus the tractate is on a different level from the introduction, and is written in a different style, self-assured in its diagnosis and coolly ironical.

The world of the bourgeoisie is etched in in its contrasts with Harry's world by the employment of symbols of cleanliness and order; when Harry first enters the aunt's house he sniffs appreciatively—«Oh, here it smells nice» (IV, 186). This nasal reference, like others—«I stood for a minute sniffing» (IV, 221),—points to that ubiquitous specter, the wolf; the various allusions to teeth throughout the novel are also signs of the omnipresence of the beast. The two cleaned and dusted plant pots on the landing which contain the araucaria (or *«Kinderbaum»!*) and the azalea are pillars of a bourgeois temple; in this house Harry finds «a superlative of bourgeois cleanliness, care, and precision, dutifulness and fidelity in small things» (IV, 197), all that he could possibly want, things he both loves and needs, for his mother was a bourgeoise. It seems that the Steppenwolf loves the bourgeois world as he says he does, without any irony; however, Harry, having neither family life nor social ambition, also regards this bourgeois sphere with a good deal of contempt, although he cannot do without it, has money in the bank and supports his relatives, dresses discreetly and respectably, tries to live at peace with the tax office. He is willy-nilly drawn by a «strong, secret longing for the small world of the bourgeoisie» (IV, 235), he lives in the province of the burghers, and all that he does stands in some relationship to them, be it only one of revolt. Dwelling in such clean middle class homes is, he thinks, simply «an old sentimentality of mine» (IV, 210).

The tractate censures him for this cowardice; for those with some understanding of the teaching of Gotama Buddha it is absurd and unforgivable to live in a world «in which common sense [Hesse uses the English expression], democracy, and bourgeois culture rule» (IV, 251). This is to serve false gods–an idea expressed vividly years before *The Steppenwolf* in «The Hiking Trip» (1920): «You cannot be a vagabond and an artist and at the same time a bourgeois and a respectable, healthy person. You want the ecstasy, so you have to take the hangover» (III, 409). The tractate points out, and the Steppenwolf later comes to understand, the concealed and shabby compromises and philosophical inanities on which the life of Harry Haller has so far been founded; educated in a *petit bourgeois* milieu, he has prejudices against prostitutes, thieves, and revolutionaries, as Friedrich Klein had.

The tractate proceeds to a normative definition of the term «bourgeois»: «The ‹bourgeois,› as a permanently existing condition of man, is nothing else but the attempt at an equilibrium, the striving for a balanced middle position between the countless extremes and antithetical poles of human conduct» (IV, 236). Characteristically, the author of the tractate selects saint and profligate as his exemplary pair, and sets up a typological model. A man can choose between devotion *(Hingabe)* to the aspirations of the saint or else to the drives of the senses, he may elect to martyr his instincts or his spirit; between both poles stands the bourgeois, characterized above all by the wish not to surrender his own ego to anything at all but to contain it, appalled by the postulates of any kind of ethical absolutism. Intense experience is only possible at some cost to his ego, rudimentary though this ego may be. Here and there the Nietzschean tone is unmistakable; Harry has to learn «that ‹man› is not something already completed, but a challenge of the spirit» (IV, 247): bourgeois are all weak and fearful creatures, a herd of lambs who survive solely because of the vitality of the Steppenwolfs amongst them.

These «wild ones» are the prisoners of the bourgeoisie,

held to it by «infantile feelings» (IV, 238); the reserve of the act of transcendence is, as we have seen before, infantile regression. The dominant cosmic imagery leads to an analogy between the bourgeoisie and Mother Earth, for the tractate speaks of «the heavy maternal planet of the bourgeoisie» (IV, 239), which is then contrasted with «soaring into free, wild cosmic space» (IV, 239). The author of «The Hiking Trip» remarks that he is partial to neurotic extremes and dislikes the golden mean, what Harry calls contemptuously «comfortable room temperature» (IV, 209). Unable quite to achieve sainthood, despite breathing exercises and the rest, Harry's ascetic impulse shows its fundamental masochism, turns him into a potential suicide, an assassin of his own ego. His aggression upon the outside world is in reality only self-destruction, encompassed by symbols of lupine savagery, blood, and murder. Even the act of eating has the bestial nuance (cf. IV, 217). Or of another act, as we have it in *Crisis*; «Blood blooms in bed.»[45] In fact, it is not to be denied that murder lies in the pun which stands at the very opening of Harry's journal *(herumgebracht/umgebracht)*. In Harry's polemics against the bourgeois world, the language is always harsh, ugly and shrill, full of ill-contained violence: «Those bad days of inner emptiness and despair, in which, in the middle of an earth destroyed and sucked dry by joint-stock companies, the world of men and so-called civilization grins at us at every step in its concealed and debased rubbishy fair-ground luster like an emetic, concentrated and intensified to the peak of intolerableness in our own sick ego» (IV, 208).

By and large Hesse attributes to two megalomanias, that of technological progress and that of nationalism, the present condition of man.[46] He regarded it as his life's

45 «Der Wüstling.»
46 Cf. «Expression of Thanks and Moralizing Reflections» (1946; VII, 457).

work to help defend the individual existence against the threat of mechanization. That new invention, the radio, of which the technologists are so proud, merely causes Harry to think of the ancient Indians, who knew all about ubiquity and uchronicity; the relativity of space and time is no new discovery. In any case, Hesse's community of Romantic castaways, infantilists all, are not really hostile to the railway and the automobile so much as to «the forgetting of God and the trivialization of the soul.» In that they have faith in something real, they have perhaps more genuine hope and longing for the future than do the «devout apostles of progress»[47]—and he thinks amicably of Knut Hamsun (though perhaps he should have thought rather of Naphta in *The Magic Mountain*). In *The Steppenwolf*, Romantic aggression is turned particularly against the automobile, a neurosis which was prefigured in *The Nuremberg Journey* (IV, 175).

Cars and the death-wish are closely associated. The Catholic master-baker in *Crisis*, transcendental in his smugness, reappears in just this context in «Dream Traces»[48] in the same year as *The Steppenwolf:* «It could happen that the automobile of one of the lords of this world, a newspaper publisher or a rich master baker, might run over him at a street corner» (IV, 423). In the novel itself we hear of these pseudo-Christians, «the taciturn business-faces of these merchants and master bakers« (IV, 260)—the subject was clearly much on Hesse's mind. Eventually, in the Magic Theater, Harry Haller dreams his automobile hunt, a war to the death between man and machine. In the company of his boyhood friend Gustav, who has subsequently become a professor of theology but is now glad to exchange this role for one

47 «Madonna d'Ongero» (III, 891).
48 «Dream Traces» itself appeared under the title of «Inner Experience» («Inneres Erlebnis») in *Die Horen,* III (1927), 11–20.

of actual violence, the pacifist Steppenwolf commits mayhem among carowners. Harry's meditation that such insane actions as theirs may help to re-ennoble a life reduced to cliché by the American and Bolshevik rationalizations is disposed of by the pragmatic Gustav as «a bit too dreamy» (IV, 383). The pretty prisoner, Dora the secretary, gets kissed on the knee, and this gesture leads on to a Freudian fall in which the dream concludes.

Satire of the bourgeoisie, of its twentieth-century hypostasis in technology, and of the outside world in general is but an inverted form of attack upon the self. All comes back to the critical contemplation of the ego, the tormenting of the libidinous will. Even the bourgeois narrator is under no illusions as to the origins of it all in Harry: «(he) was brought up by strict and very devout parents and teachers according to that approach which makes the ‹breaking of the will› the basis of education ... Instead of erasing his personality this had merely succeeded in teaching him to hate himself» (IV, 193); self-hatred, indeed is the Steppenwolf's form of piety, his Christianity. Harry's disgust when he witnesses the sanctimonious sham of a funeral ceremony send him on one of his meaningless peregrinations through the gray streets of the city. Meeting a youngish professor of his acquaintance, an orientalist, Harry accepts an invitation for that evening, a folly which, as he shaves himself morosely, leads him to meditate upon all the mechanical functions of life which protect men from self-insight und upon the social activities which cannot mean anything to him, «as if I still belonged to that delightful childlike world of eternal play« (IV, 265). The social life, the elegant life, the life of the theaters, bars, and cafés is a frivolous, childish game from which wolves are by definition excluded. As for the professor, he is satirized as an example of the devoted scholar half buried from reality, understanding nothing of the great changes, such as the war and the theory of relativity, which have recently overturned the whole world. Worse, he is a chauvinist. He abuses a publicist namesake (as he thinks) of Harry's, «that traitor Haller» (IV, 267), who had ridiculed Kaiser Wilhelm and blamed Germany for the war. His wife possesses an appalling portrait of the older Goethe, thoroughly *embourgeoisé*. All this arouses in Harry the «Steppenwolf with grinning fangs» (IV, 268); sick und feeling his age, Harry hits out, predicts with bitter anguish the approach of another war brought on by the chauvinists, and confesses that he himself is the aforesaid treacherous publicist–having first of all angrily deplored the disgraceful treatment that Goethe has received at the hands of the portraitist. It is of special note that he declares his interest in things oriental, in Krishna and such antiquarian rubbish, long since at an end.

His precipitate departure from his host's house is no triumph, however, but rather a retreat and a flight. The imagery now becomes characteristically physiological and violent: «I had taken my leave of my former world and home, of middle-class life, propriety and learning, just as a man with a stomach ulcer takes his leave of roast pork» (IV, 271). He apologizes for his behavior–after all, he is a schizophrenic.

The poem «Missglückter Abend» tells us of this dismal withdrawal:

Traurig bin ich davongezogen,
Um irgendwo ein kleines Mädchen zu kaufen,
Das nicht Klavier spielt und sich nicht für Kunst inter-
essiert.

(Sadly did I take my leave,
To go and buy a little girl somewhere,
One who doesn't play the piano and has no interest
in art.)

Harry's escape from the professor's house onto the dark streets of the city is a total victory for the wolf in him.

The typical act of flight, the rush to suicide, which, however, ends in the beginnings of enlightenment, the encounter with Hermine–these features may even recall Siddhartha's flight from Kamala. But in this case the flight is *to* woman. Encounter with the «shadow» (that is, the wolf) is but the first stage in a Jungian analysis, is the approach to something deeper, the anima. There is thus a sense in which the escape may be compared more closely with Siddhartha's flight from the Samanas and from his «shadow» Govinda. Harry finds his way to a dive, The Black Eagle, and there he discovers his *dame aux camélias*; she does indeed wear the appropriate flower and she has moreover certain appropriate additional qualities–«She was indeed like a mama with me» (IV, 279). The bourgeois Harry, the compromising Harry, appears finally to have been torn to pieces by the wolf; what Hermine, «the wonderful friend» (IV, 290), has to offer is of course neither the Way of the bourgeois nor the Way of the wolf, but some third Way, that which leads to the Third Kingdom of the Spirit. Of Hermine, Harry says: «She was the little window, the tiny light aperture in my dark cave of fear. She was redemption, the way outside» (IV, 294). The imagery is familiar; Harry the outsider is outside all walls except that which he has built around himself.

A situation of considerable complexity obtains here. The «wolf» is defined in the tractate as «a dark world of instincts, of savagery, cruelty, unsublimated, raw nature» (IV, 242). The tractate chides Harry for the crude mythology in which he divides himself into «man» and «wolf,» points out that the wolf, though healthy, is also no ideal savage, but has his longings and his sufferings just as the child has his: «There is no way back at all, neither to the wolf nor to the child» (IV, 249).[49] Clearly

49 Cf. again in «On the Soul»: «Not back to the child, the primitive . . .» (VII, 72).

the «wolf,» in one of his aspects, is the Jungian «shadow,» the «inferior self,» which «stands, so to speak, on the threshold of the way to the «Mothers», to the collective unconscious.»[50] Harry makes the mistake of idealizing those impulses he also consciously represses, this is the source of much of his sickness. But the meaning of the wolf is scarcely exhausted by these explanations; Harry Haller's is an inverted world, and the fearsome wolf with his teeth and his blood lust is not only Wagner, but in a sense is also his opposite, Klein. For the wolf is the instrument of masochism (it is the wolf who tears to pieces the «bourgeois man» in Harry); and the masochist is the frustrated saint. Thus the wolf may be seen in his inverted aspect as a terrible perversion of the Pietist's will-to-God, his rending of Harry Haller as a satanic variant of the struggle to destroy the Natural Man; he is, maybe, the repressed world of the mother, but he is also a bestialization of the demands of the father in Harry's heart. In his savaging of Harry, the bourgeois, he tends to present not one extreme, but *the* extreme.

Harry's error in dividing himself, in his own imagination, into only two is of course a baneful crudification of the richness and subtlety of human nature. It has been remarked before that this reveals a Lutheran heritage in the novel;[51] the tractate points emphatically to original sin—«all created things, even the apparently most simple, are already guilty» (IV, 249) Harry's meeting with Hermine might therefore for this reason also be called his escape from the Samanas, from the clutches of asceticism. Hesse's writings are full of commentaries upon that condition of consciousness in which there are two I's, an observing and an observed: «In each one of us there are

50 J. Jacobi, *The Psychology of C. G. Jung*, p. 146. Jacobi notes specifically (p. 144) that Hesse's *Steppenwolf* is an example of the artistic use of the shadow motif.
51 Anni Carlsson, «Vom Steppenwolf zur Morgenlandfahrt,» in Hugo Ball, *Hermann Hesse*, p. 252.

two I's, and whoever could know where the one begins and the other ends would be infinitely wise.» First of all there is «our subjective, empirical, individual I,» and then a second I not fully separated from the first: «This second, lofty, sacred I . . . is not personal, but is our part in God, in life, in the whole, in the unpersonal and the super-personal.»[52] In practice a distinction must be made, and indeed emerges quite clearly from Hesse's writings, between the genuine moment of enlightenment, self-centered detachment, and the obsessive self-oberservation of the decadent for whom naïve experience is but a dream. In the former case everything falls into place, for there are differences of level; in the latter everything jars, for all is on the same level. Harry's stupid error of dividing himself into ego and id–«the fairy tale of the wolf» (IV, 251)–the secondary delusion that the personality is dualistic whereas it is manifold, this derives from the primary delusion that the personality is a unity. All make this mistake, which is caused largely by the apparent one-ness and permanence of the body; here the classical drama with its unity of character contrasts with the ancient Indian epic, the heroes of which are «not characters but groups of characters, successive incarnations» (IV, 245). Modern authors frequently portray unconsciously the same disunity of the personality, their characters being fragments of a higher unity–«if you like, the writer's own soul» (IV, 245). Here the author of the tractate mentions *Faust* and may also have had *Peer Gynt* in mind, for he compares the personality to an onion. I's succeed each other in time, moments of transformation occur in which whole selves are sloughed off, each change triggered by a moment of self-confrontation. The Steppenwolf knows this as Siddhartha did, but he finds it an agonizing proc-ess, from which he would fain escape forever; he is afraid to look in a mirror, he maneuvres to avoid this very

52 *Letters* (VII, 635–636).

self-confrontation.[53] Only suicide offers him the hope of achieving his aim permanently.

Immortality, says the tractate, can be hoped for only through nonattachment and through «eternal surrender of the ego to metamorphosis» (IV, 248). It is just this sacrifice of the will of which the Steppenwolf is incapable. To go on living seems to him quixotic; suicide constantly hovers therefore before him, now nearer now farther, as the only way out. The bourgeois narrator, observing Harry's habits, remarks with unconscious irony that he is leading «the life of a suicide» (IV, 203). In fact for one of his type suicide is quite clearly the ultimate form of inverted aggression, and a total surrender to the delusions of Maya besides. Like Siddhartha and like Klein, Harry must know that suicide «is after all only a rather shabby and illegitimate emergency exit» (IV, 233), but nevertheless he sets his fiftieth birthday as the day on which to decide wheter to kill himself, and when he meets Hermine he had in mind to hasten the deed that selfsame night. Psychologically all this is acutely enough observed.[54]

---

53 The highly important mirror motif (and the related motif of reflection in water) occurs—as has been shown—in almost all Hesse's major works. It happens that it is also inseparable from the problematics of Goethe's novella *Der Mann von fünfzig Jahren*. Goethe's Major imagines he is experiencing «the return of spring,» and yet, when he stands before a mirror, he is most dissatisfied with his appearance and is persuaded to undertake a course of facial and general physical rejuvenation. Cf. here «Bei der Toilette»:

> «Einst war das Auge klar, die Stirne licht,
> Wange und Lippe lachender und weicher,
> Da braucht ich Puder und Pomade nicht»
> (*Krisis,* p. 40; also V, 700).

> (Once my eye was clear, my brow was light,
> Cheeks and lips more laughing and more soft,
> Then I needed neither powder nor pomade.)

54 «But anyone who refuses to experience life must stifle his desire to live—in other words he must commit partial suicide. This explains the death-fantasies that usually accompany the renunciation of desire» (Jung, *Symbols of Transformation,* p. 110).

The treatment of suicide throughout Hesse's work offers an intriguing pattern; a clue to it all may be found where it occurs in «Child's Soul.» In his bitter desperation the little fig thief wishes he were dead: «One ought to take poison, that would be best, or hang oneself» (III, 442); then this is transformed into the kindred impulse toward an act of externally orientated violence, «something horrible but liberating» (III, 443), revenge on the world, to set fire to the house, or–to kill his father. Suddenly Franz Kromer is conjured up before us, offering the knife to Emil Sinclair; worse the awful specter of schoolmaster Wagner butchering his whole family, and his pupil Klein about to stab the sleeping Teresina («Child's Soul» was written in January 1919, in Basel; «Klein and Wagner» in May-June of the same year, in Tessin; the two works certainly have much in common, especially the main theme–theft–and the bloodthirsty undertones). Govinda's vision included a murder and the execution of the criminal, and so also the boy in «Child's Soul» visualizes his own execution and his Cain-like glorying in his crime. «Der Wüstling,» in *Crisis*, takes up the theme again, as does «Sterbelied des Dichters»:[55]

> Liege bei den jungen Weibern,
> Reibe meinen Leib an ihren Leibern,
> Kriege sie satt und drücke ihnen die Gurgel zu,
> Dann kommt der Henker und bringt auch mich zur
> Ruh.
>
> (I lie with the young women,
> Rub my body on theirs,
> Tire of them and throttle them,
> Then the hangman comes and quiets me too.)

Thematically, these aggressive dreams are manifestly linked with childhood experience, and that such notions play so significant a part in Harry's imaginative life is

55 *Krisis*, p. 10.

striking confirmation of the sources of his neurosis. As late as the second «autobiography» in *The Glass Bead Game,* «The Father Confessor,» we find a condemnation of the idea of suicide as the work of the Devil (VI, 615).

In *The Steppenwolf* the firm resolution to cease being «the noble Don Quixote» (IV, 256) and to kill himself, sends the hero to bed in a calmed state of mind:

At the ultimate instant, however, at the final limit of consciousness, in the moment of going to sleep, that curious section of the Steppenwolf pamphlet flashed before me, where it speaks of the «Immortals,» and with this was linked with a sudden start the memory that I had often and indeed quite recently felt myself near enough to the Immortals to experience with them in a bar of old music the entire, cool, bright, hard smile of the Immortals' wisdom. This rose up, gleamed, died away, and sleep laid itself as heavy as a mountain on my brow (IV, 256).

The second-long lightning flash of memory, of recalled aesthetic experience, is a moment of awakening alongside the intention of suicide; it is a close parallel to Siddharta's recollection of *«Om,»* as he bends suicidally over the water, and like that it is at once followed by sleep «heavy as a mountain»—*Tiefschlaf.* In Harry's case this does not rescue him at once from the threat of self-murder, but it points to the source from which salvation is to come. In the tractate there is a discourse on that whole class of people[56] who are designated «suicides,» whether or not they ever lay hands upon themselves; they are those who live constantly exposed at the edge of existence in a sense of imminent danger, «on the narrowest of rock pinnacles» (IV, 232), Romantic at root, «inflicted with the guilt feelings of individuation» (IV, 232), long-

---

56 In «Aus einem Tagebuch des Jahres 1920,» Hesse talks of the various journals he is writing or should write. One should be «a suicide's journal» (*op. cit.,* p. 195).

ing for the mother, yearning to be reabsorbed into the universal flow. When Pablo enjoins Harry to commit «a little sham suicide» (IV, 371) as a necessary preface to entering the Magic Theater, suicide has become a figure for the sacrifice of self-delusion prior to descent into the soul. The death-wish, indeed, is intimately connected with something else, with «*Om*,» with enlightenment.

Such moments are defined by the author of the tractate, in a central passage, as containing the real meaning of the Steppenwolf's life: «Even in this man's life it seemed at times as if all the ordinary everyday, well-known, and regular things merely had the function of undergoing a second-long pause, of being interrupted and giving way to the extraordinary, to miracles, to grace» (IV, 228). This is «the froth of the happiness of the moment,» «precious fleeting froth of happiness,» it elevates a man for an instant so high above his fate, «that his happiness shines like a star» (IV, 228). Harry Haller remembers that moment of bliss which the bourgeois narrator, at the concert, had observed from without:

> I had flown through Heaven and seen God at his work, had suffered blissful agonies and no longer struggled against anything in the world, no longer feared anything in the world, had affirmed all things, surrendered my heart to all things. It hadn't lasted long, perhaps a quarter of an hour, but that night it had returned in my dreams and since then, through all the barren days, it had occasionally secretly flashed out again, sometimes I saw it clearly for minutes pass like a golden, divine trace through my life [IV, 212].

There are the expected figures here from religious poetry—flying through the heavens, for instance. The color gold, in association here—as in 1913—with music, is evidently an epithet for the experience of the awakened soul. For the religious source of the epithet we must turn to the scene in which Harry takes Hermine's head in his hands and kisses her on the brow; as he does this the sunlight plays on the golden inscriptions on the spines of his books[57] and recalls what she has just said about the communion of saints: «this was formerly portrayed by the painters in a golden sky» (IV, 346). And we may note yet another account: «By happiness I understand something quite objective, that is: the totality itself, timeless being, the eternal music of the world, what others have called the harmony of the spheres or the smile of God. This essence, this endless music, this full-ringing and gold-gleaming eternity is pure and perfect presence.»[58] From the delighted moment of 1913, through the dry prose of the tractate and the passionate memory of Harry Haller, to one of Hesse's last essays, the pattern is the same, the object of description the same, an experience of totality both aesthetic and religious, a condition of pure and perfect presence. From one such experience to another, by way of Maya and Sansara, stumbles the *vita* of the profligate-saint.

The motif of the «golden trace» occurs several times in the first section of Harry's memoirs; aggressive hatred of society gives way over wine to a moment of glorious memory: «The golden trace had flashed, I was reminded of the eternal, of Mozart, of the stars» (IV, 219).[59] Equally significant is the longing which possesses Harry for a friend, in some attic somewhere, complete with violin, with whom he might while away the nighttime hours; but Pistorius was rejected in an earlier novel, and *Crisis*

57 Cf. in «Old Music» (VII, 39) «the golden letters.» The adjective is, of course, extremely common as a cliché of Romantic language and occurs frequently in *An Hour beyond Midnight* and in *Hermann Lauscher*. It is, in general, a secularized religious epithet, but the point is that in Hesse the religious nuance is still quite detectable: Hermann Lauscher's mother used to tell «stories of Jesus with a golden background» (I, 101).
58 «Happiness» (1949–1950) (IV, 891).
59 Mozart's name is associated with such an experience at least as early as 1920; cf. «Aus einem Tagebuch des Jahres 1920,» *op. cit.*, p. 192.

is very skeptical about «Dr. Ling.»[60] To see through his «crude simplification» of himself, to penetrate the nature of his own ego, it is necessary for Harry to observe himself from another level, to break the vicious circle of one-level thinking in which it is so easy to drown.[61]

The tractate points out the possibility of self-knowledge for the Steppenwolf, «be it, that he lays hands on one of our little mirrors, or be it that he encounters the Immortals or perhaps discovers in one of our magic theaters what he needs for the liberation of his derelict soul» (IV, 241). *The Steppenwolf* is a novel full of mirrors, from the wet asphalt, when Harry first paces the streets, onward. The whole world in which Harry Haller moves may be interpreted as merely the reflection of his own mind. It is no surprise that Harry's friend, when he finds one, is really but a piece of himself, though it is new that this «friend» turns out to be a woman.

Hermine's first words to him, it has been well observed, are no more than «precisely what one would expect from a prostitute with long experience in handling drunks and mothering would-be suicides.»[62] It is perhaps worth adding that Harry talks to her with some touches of condescension, which she resents. In the episodes with Hermine and Pablo the novel is indeed moving on two, if not more, levels of reality and gives in some degree «the effect of a sustained pun.»[63] Just how far one should go, however, in assigning the prostitute Hermine to the

60 Cf. «Abend mit Dr. Ling» *(op. cit.).*
61 Cf. Novalis, «Die meisten Menschen wollen nicht eher schwimmen, (als) bis sie es können» (Most people aren't willing to swim until they can swim) *(Schriften,* III, 217). Harry quotes this aphorism to the bourgeois narrator with approval. The idea actually comes from Fichte, whose Idealism was indirectly a significant source of Hesse's thought. Harry compares learning to swim to learning to think: to think means to leave solid ground behind for the water, and eventually to drown (IV, 199).
62 Ziolkowski, «Hermann Hesse's *Steppenwolf,*» *op. cit.,* p. 125.
63 *Ibid.,* p. 124.

«real» world and the ideal Hermine (and all her mantic utterances) to Harry's projective imagination is an uncertain matter. She has, of course, her unmistakable forbears: «I saw her clearly, the pale, firm face with the blood-red painted mouth, the bright gray eyes, the smooth cool brow, the short stiff lock of hair before the ear» (IV, 274). The identity of this description with that of Klein's Teresina is extraordinary: the pale face, the blazing lips, the gray eyes, the allusion to the ear. The fascinating, complex conversation between them when Harry takes her out to dinner slips from one level to another, at first almost imperceptibly but then with a quite conspicuous change of style: «Slowly, as though producing each word unwillingly, she said . . .» (IV, 298). Hermine herself is described as extremely changeable and «always only moment» (IV, 302); even when she is but her frivolous self she can be extraordinarily perceptive, as for instance when she designates Harry «you Prodigal Son» (IV, 301). We may recall that Kamala turned into a Buddhist, that the religious vein in the life of the prostitute is a cliché since Dostoevsky, and we may therefore find Hermine's confession about her former piety and her enduring preoccupation with the saints entirely in character: «The saints, they are the genuine human beings, the younger brethren of the Saviour» (IV, 345). Nonetheless, there is without doubt a great deal in the view, which Harry himself asserts, that many of the utterances of Hermine and Pablo are but projections of his own higher self; the constant emphasis upon the change of level–«All the same I could not leap back into the probable and the real with the same tightrope walker's facility as Hermine could» (IV, 301)–must charitably be interpreted as a deliberate pointer to the «double perception»[64] on which the novel is based and not as the uneasy effort to remedy a sensed weakness of composition.

64 *Ibid.*, p. 123.

Hermine puts out a hand and rescues Harry; Hermine is the first human being «who shattered the opaque glass globe[65] of my deadness and stretched in her hand, a kind, beautiful, warm hand» (IV, 290). She is a «child,» she understands how to play the moment. She introduces the Steppenwolf to jazz, which used to appear to his raw lupine imagination «like the steam from raw meat» (IV, 220), as «American» (symbol for Harry of all that is streamlined and intolerable), and as a music of doom. She introduces him to dancing, with a strong emphasis upon the sexual pleasure thereof, the world of *boîtes* and cafés, night life in the superlative; one of the *Crisis* poems remarks that this is no place for one who used to be «brother of the trees, friend of the lakes and the rivers»:

> Nun, altes Männlein, kämme hübsch den Scheitel,
> Rasier dich gut und schlüpf' ins Abendhemd!
> All dein Bemühn ist doch vermutlich eitel,
> Du bleibst in dieser Welt doch immer fremd.[66]

> (Now, old fellow, comb a nice parting,
> Have a good shave and slip into your dress shirt!
> But all your efforts are doubtless useless,
> In this world you'll always be strange.)

He is too old:
> Traurig seh' ich ein, ich alter Knabe:
> Dieses Tun ist lächerlich und nichtig,
> Das ich viel zu spät begonnen habe,
> Nicht einmal den Onestep kann ich richtig![67]

65 Mauerhofer points out the frequent occurrence of glass imagery in the thoughts of introverted and schizoid personalities (*op. cit.*, p. 29).
66 «Bei der Toilette,» *Krisis*, p. 40.
67 «Kopfschütteln,» *Krisis*, p. 13. Hermine's Horror at his ignorance: «Not even the one-step?» (IV, 275) may be compared. The dance is, as it was for Nietzsche's Zarathustra, the supremely unreflective form

(Sadly I perceive, boy that I am grown old,
These doings are absurd and vain,
Which I've started much too late,
I can't even do the one-step properly.)

Hermine tells him that he has always occupied himself
with the most complex and difficult matters, and hence
cannot cope with the simple ones such as dancing—and unless he has first tried these simple things he has no right
to say he has found nothing worth having in life. Harry
the «hermit» (IV, 320) puts up some resistance to the
suggestion of importing a gramophone into his «cell,»
but eventually gives way. Then on a night after he has
been listening to music in the cathedral his initiation is
continued by an emissary from Hermine, Maria, a sensuous little creature whom he finds in bed in his lodgings,
and gradually, instead of the church music «which once
had been my home» (IV, 326), he becomes at home in
«the world of dance and entertainment halls, cinemas,
bars, and hotel lounges» (IV, 330). Maria's naïve enthusiasm for an American hit song tears great holes in Harry's aesthetics; from all sides fresh and jolting experience
forces its way in—«New things, feared things, solvents
into my life which up till now had been so sharply cir-
cumscribed and so strictly shut off» (IV, 319). He feels,
indeed, that what he needs is «experience, decision, a
push and a leap *(Sprung)*» (IV, 294); his escape over the
wall of his enclosed self is facilitated in that the Without
comes a great way to meet him, forces its way into his
hermitage and begins to dissolve it from within. Like
Siddhartha, he has to learn to play; this Hermine can

of self-expression. In «Nachwort an meine Freunde,» Hesse asserted
that *Crisis* was to be understood as a reassertion of the sensual element in his nature, «this half of me up till now repressed» (p. 82).
He then adds, recalling for us the confessional doctrine of *Demian:*
«One cannot have the ideal of honesty and always desplay only the
attractive and significant side of one's nature» (p. 82).

teach him; he has to learn how much of him is still bourgeois, for instance his fear of death; once again he must
needs slough off a skin. He has to rediscover the delights
of concrete things, of luxury articles and toiletries, all of
which help one to live in the present. In Maria's arms,
«out of the well of this night of love» (IV, 333), rises a
whole host of memories of things past, mother and childhood, «stars and constellations,» «experiences turned into
stars» (IV, 332), all the women he has ever loved, and his
own wife who fell victim to mental illness. Above all he
recalls a legendary figure, the «legendary Hermann» (IV,
332), the friend of his youth with whom he committed
his first «spiritual excesses and dissipations» (IV, 315) and
of whom Hermine at once reminded him. In rousing these
memories, Maria also shows that she is able to give him
naïve experience, it is the lesson «to entrust myself like
a child to the game of the surface, to seek the most fleeting pleasures. To be child and beast in the innocence of
sex« (IV, 350), «playful sensuality» (IV, 299)–for the
first time in his life Haller-Klein has sexual experience
which is free of a feeling of guilt; with Maria he finds
himself in a warm garden, a pleasure garden like that
of his Indian precursors, a state of bliss which he realizes,
however, is but a transitory stage: «Once more I ran
flickering and full of desire through all the paths and
thickets of her garden, sank my teeth once more into the
sweet fruit of the tree of paradise» (IV, 351).

As for the saxophonist Pablo,[68] «this handsome *cabal-
lero*» (IV, 314) for whom music is not to be talked about
but only to be played, he is the representative, in a

68 He appears in the poem «Neid» as an ideal:

> «Wenn ich doch Banjo könnte spielen
> Und Saxophon in einer Jazzband blasen»
> (*Krisis,* p. 28).
>
> (If only I could play the banjo
> And blow the saxophone in a jazz band.)

curious sense, of the outlook of *l'art pour l'art*, an expert in the most licentious refinements of the «game.» It appears to Harry that Pablo's creole eyes hide «no romanticism, no problems, no thoughts» (IV, 314); he is surprised to learn that Pablo has remarked of him: «Poor, poor fellow. Look at his eyes! Can't laugh» (IV, 315). Pablo is a «metaphysician of the body»; he uses narcotics (as indeed Harry himself is not averse to doing), he plays with the senses, he offers homosexual as well as heterosexual delights; he organizes orgies—for example, «a love orgy for three» (IV, 336)—and Harry peremptorily declines participation, as he also affrontedly refuses the offer to sell one night's rights to the circulating Maria in return for twenty francs. Hermine asks if Maria has as yet shown the Steppenwolf «a particular game of the tongue while kissing» (IV, 338), and admits to a Lesbian connection with the other girl.

These manifold new relationships and possibilities recall to Harry the thousand I's of which the tractate spoke. Hermine's «boy-face» (IV, 296), her boyish lock of hair, remind him constantly of Hermann, of which name, of course, hers is the feminine form. It is indeed a hermaphroditic spell which she casts, she is Harry's anima—hence the authority which she can exercise over him—«all too near to me ... my comrade, my sister» (IV, 315). The legendary Hermann takes physical shape at the masked ball, when Hermine is dressed as a youth. What they all of them, Hermine, Maria, and Pablo, teach Harry might be regarded as merely what the young Siddhartha contemptuously dismissed as «ways away from the ego,» obtainable in every tavern and brothel; they introduce him to the experience of orgiasm, «the ecstasy of festival, the secret of the submersion of the individual in the crowd, of the *unio mystica* of joy» (IV, 362). Pablo—his teacher—duly kisses him; and Harry also impresses a sacramental kiss on Hermine's brow. The deep anoetic state which Harry reaches—«in this deep, childlike, fairy-tale happiness» (IV, 362)—has evidently connections with the world of the child and the *Märchen*, both of which are the sphere of the hermaphrodite: «For she often talked to me about Hermann and about childhood, mine and hers, about those years of puberty in which the youthful erotic capacity embraces not only both sexes, but everything, the sensual and the spiritual, and endows everything with the love-spell and the fairytale power of metamorphosis which returns occasionally in later times of life solely to the elect and to poets» (IV, 360). Transvestism is the Steppenwolfian form of metamorphosis; Pictor's paradise reappears in this novel in the guise of orgy; and all is under the sign of increasing age and of—to use Goethe's phrase—«recurrent puberty.»

No wonder, therefore, that Goethe has his part to play in all this. If *The Glass Bead Game* is Hesse's *Wilhelm Meister*, *The Steppenwolf* is perhaps his *West-Östlicher Divan*.[69] Both Hesse's novel and Goethe's book of poems parody another style (in Hesse's case a musical form), both glorify the temporary resurgence of potency, both unite the mystical and the sensual in a peculiar blend and above all both are hermaphroditic in their innermost sense and structure. The history of Hesse's changing attitude to Goethe is interesting. «Gratitude to Goethe» (1932)

69 A comparison with *Faust* has also been made by E. Schwarz: «Zur Erklärung von Hesses *Steppenwolf*,» in *Monatshefte für deutschen Unterricht*, LIII (1961), 191–198: Harry and Faust are both «elderly» men rejuvenated by magic and led into the world of sense experience; Harry and Maria is a relationship reminiscent of Faust and Gretchen (?), and the artists' ball is seen as a kind of Walpurgisnacht. This scholar also notes analogies with *Wilhelm Meister:* Hermine resembles Mignon, while the Magic Theater has something in common with the Society of the Tower in Goethe's novel. However, the much more striking relevance of «Der Mann von fünfzig Jahren» has been overlooked. What is really of dominant interest throughout these analogies—and what might make further comparison with the *Divan* particularly apt—is the emphasis on the recovery of potency in the fifty-year-old man and the problems raised by this event.

tells us that Goethe, though not his favorite author, was the one who—with the possible exception of Nietzsche—had stimulated and provoked him most. As a youth in Tübingen, Hesse had been much preoccupied with that poet he later called «the star of my youth,»[70] and there are important references in *Hermann Lauscher* and *Peter Camenzind*. A recurrent discrepancy between Goethe the poet on the one hand and Goethe the humanist, teacher, and man of letters on the other plagued Hesse's judgment until the First World War; Goethe, it seemed, had never quite succeeded in blending Tasso with Antonio, «and at times this made him really disagreeable and embarrassing for me».[71] Then during the war Goethe became a symbol for international truth, for the European spirit above all partisanship and contemptuous of all chauvinisms—Hesse's position and that of Romain Rolland.[72]

But the real secret of Goethe revealed itself only later, as an esoteric mystery, disclosed to the perceiving eye here and there in the works of the older Goethe, in his letters, in sections of *Faust* Part Two, above all, and the *Novelle:* this is that wisdom of Goethe's which is impersonal or superpersonal: «no longer will and no longer intellect, but piety, reverence, readiness to serve, Tao.»[73] The analogy between Goethe's wisdom and Chinese thought was drawn already in «Goethe and Bettina» (1924): the older Goethe «produces all around him like a Chinese magician that double atmosphere, that air of Lao-tzû, in which doing and nondoing, creating and enduring are no longer separable.»[74] Geniuses of the Goethe type are precisely those who do not burn up young, they are positive and affirmative; but at the same time Goethe, Leo-

70 «Gratitude to Goethe» (VII, 380).
71 VII, 377.
72 Cf. «O Friends, Not These Sounds!» (VII, 44 f.).
73 VII, 382.
74 VII, 289.

nardo, Rembrandt, Frederick the Great, they all in old age become «depersonalized»: «Affirmers of life, affirmers of nature, they are however all of them deniers of themselves, of man. The more they ‹perfect› themselves, the more their life and work takes on the tendency to dissolve in the direction of an apprehended distant possibility which is not called man anymore, at the most superman.»[75]

Depersonalization in this sense of the word becomes an essential element in the solution which is eventually proposed for Harry Haller. At the professor's house the Steppenwolf reacts antagonistically to the bourgeois characterization of Goethe–there was enough of the bourgeois in Goethe, as there is enough of the bourgeois in Harry, to bring about this painful crisis of conscience. Humored by Hermine into a drunken sleep, he comes to dream of Goethe: received by the Olympian, Harry–embarrassed by the attempts of a dream scorpion to run up his leg–speaks to this stiff little man with the *star* on his «classic's breast» (IV, 283), rebukes him for his dishonesty, for his sins of suppression and aversion: «You have rejected and suppressed the voices of the depths . . . in yourself just as in Kleist and Beethoven» (IV, 284). Goethe defends himself; the discussion begins to turn upon time and death, Goethe's fear of death, the Faustian issue of transience–a theme Hermine then goes on with when Harry wakes up. Goethe talks of his own innate childlikeness, his «play impulse,» says slyly that such games are now at an end, then, however, warns Harry not to take the pompous older Goethe too seriously, for the Immortals like fun above everything: «Seriousness, my boy, is an affair of time; it arises . . . from an overvaluation of

75 VII, 290. Cf. «Aus einem Tagebuch des Jahres 1920»: «Then what is higher could also follow, what is superpersonal and supertemporal, art would be transcended, the artist would be ripe to become a saint, or at any rate a priest» (*op. cit.*, p. 197).

time» (IV, 286). To show what he means he discloses a lady's leg of diminutive proportions contained in a leather and velvet case, which then transforms itself into the somewhat too symbolic scorpion.

On the way to the masked ball, the local annual artists' jamboree, Harry calls in at a cinema and watches an Old Testament epic. His contained outrage at this degradation of the holy tales of his childhood puts in a nutshell the essence of his outsiderdom. We now enter the concluding movement of the novel, the «theme with variations,»[76] as the Magic Theater has been called. Don Juan now descends into hell. The Strindbergian motif of hell, essential to the novel, is first concretized by the bourgeois narrator, who defines the Steppenwolf's memoirs as «quite literally a passage through hell, a sometimes nervous sometimes bold passage through the chaos of a darkened soul-world, undertaken with the will to traverse hell, to face up to chaos, to endure the evil to its end» (IV, 205). This attitude of truculent, persecuted resolve is exactly that of the author of *Inferno*. Hermine tells Harry that she has snatched him up and saved him even before the very gate of hell. After an exhausting and fruitless evening at the ball, Harry—the observing «I» who sees behind «falsifying masks of feeling» (IV, 241) as the tractate calls them, and who therefore alone is both unmasked and uncostumed—receives a message: «Hermine is in hell» (IV, 357). Waylaid for a time by a Spanish dancing girl (Maria), Don Juan presses on as fast as he can toward his goal: «Never has a sinner been in such a haste to get to hell» (IV, 358). «Hell» is in fact a basement room of the hotel, appropriately decorated: «on pitch-black walls sinister glaring lamps, and the devils' band playing feverishly» (IV, 359). Here Harry meets the transvestite Hermann, recognizes and for the first time definitely falls in love with Hermine. «Masque...

76 Ziolkowski, «Hermann Hesse's *Steppenwolf*,» *op. cit.*, p. 132.

*Märchen* . . . game and symbol . . . dream paradise . . . ecstasy . . . *unio mystica* of joy»–in such terms as these Harry now describes the experience of the ball.

Meanwhile the prospect of the Magic Theater looms–«Entrance costs your sanity» (IV, 357). On the first night of his narrative Harry recounted how, tramping along the rainy streets, he had noticed the gothic portal for the first time, cut unexpectedly in the familiar old monastery wall (certainly not an accidental association), constrasting so sharply with the doors leading down into the ubiquitous *boîtes de nuit,* and then the flickering lettering like an illuminated advertisement: «Magic Theater: Entrance not for everybody» and «only for madmen» (IV, 215). The light on the glistening black asphalt had momentarily brought the «golden trace» to mind and filled the Steppenwolf with a longing, «for the door to a magic theater, only for madmen» (IV, 216).

Now as the ball shrinks to its conclusion, as room after room empties, Hermine reappears disguised as a pierrette; with her as she is now dressed, that is, with his feminine self, Harry can dance a wedding dance, the preamble to the preordained hermetic union. At the end of this: «Entranced we gazed at one another, my poor little soul gazed at me» (IV, 366), the personification of the self in Hermine has now become transparent; even Pablo's eyes are those of Harry's soul, now characterized by that old epithet «the lost frightened bird» (IV, 367). Pablo takes them both into a strange circular room, where they sit «in a layer of very thinned-out reality» (IV, 368); the opium cigarettes, now handed round, have–we are hardly surprised to learn–a smoke which is «thick as incense» (IV, 368)–even in these circumstances, or perhaps especially now, the dominant orientation of the novel is retained in this simile. Drugs will take Harry into the

77 «Normal,» Hesse says in effect, is merely a term for the conservative function: cf. «Fantasies» (1918; VII, 153).

world of his own soul; reality is within. Pablo says: «I can give you nothing which does not already exist within you. I can open for you no other hall of pictures but that of your soul» (IV, 368–369). Mirrors–Pablo's «tiny mirror in the hand» (IV, 371) (for *The Steppenwolf* constantly parodies the *Märchen*)–and then an enormous mirror in the Theater itself, now dominate the action; in them Harry sees the reflection of the shy wolf within him. Pablo laughs; the purpose of the whole performance is said to be to teach Harry to laugh, to mock his own self-delusion, to destroy it, to commit in fact a «sham suicide» (IV, 371)–much more sensible, and so much more efficacious, than the real thing.

Looking into the mirror, at his laughing face, Harry sees it dissolve into many faces, innumerable fragments and separate egos, a heterosexual and a homosexual self. Harry's visits to the penny sideshows of the Theater now begin with the «Automobile Hunt»; passing over various suggestively inviting prospects, he then selects «Introduction to the construction of the personality. Success guaranteed» (IV, 386). Here sits a man cross-legged, with a kind of chessboard before him; by the use of another mirror this man again breaks Harry's personality into pieces, assembles the pieces, and demonstrates the great error conventional psychology has made in assuming that these can be combined only in one valid order. It is the old error of the teachers, and there is a touch of the sarcasm of more than twenty years back in the remark: «its value lies solely in the fact that the officially appointed teachers and educators find themselves spared their labor» (IV, 387). That this is an error means of course that «insane» and «normal»[77] are highly unreliable terms; it also means that anyone who has once experienced the dissociation of his personality can reconstruct it as he likes, «and that thereby he can achieve an infinite variety in the game of life» (IV, 387–388). Life is a game, and as the chess player plays it, it reveals itself, through the analogies employed, as a musical game. As insanity (in the loftiest sense) is the beginning of wisdom, so schizophrenia is the root of art; and the handling of the personality, precisely, is «the art of living.»

In contradistinction to this learned and incisive exposition, the next booth in the Theater offers something much more Grand Guignol: «Miracle of Steppenwolf training» (IV, 389) is an ironic horror peep show in which the animal trainer, resembling Harry, trains the wolf and then gives the animal the whip hand, falls to the floor, and himself *acts* the wolf, tears the clothes off his own back with his stopped teeth, bloodily rends a rabbit and a lamb. This is the bestiality of hell, and Harry flees in terror, with a mingled taste of chocolate and blood in his mouth; 1914's «O Friends, Not These Sounds» echoes in his memory, and he has a vision of piles of mangled corpses in gasmasks. The world of the unconscious is evidently hardly paradise unalloyed, though being the home of the memory it can also offer the fragrant atmosphere of youth, longingly evoked in «All the girls are yours» (IV, 392). In this particular dream there is the boy of fifteen again, looking down from the hill upon Calw; all is alive with sense-experience as he recalls his first love for Rosa Kreisler and his mistake in failing to tell her of it, an error he puts right in the dream. In this dream the Steppenwolf lives out to the full a frustrated side of his personality, the lover within him. Hesse's work and especially *The Steppenwolf* is constantly concerned with just this rediscovery of the «shadow,» that part of the self which has been denied its rights. It is life in a magic garden, a river, «a playful, childlike swimming in the stream of sex» (IV, 398), and in this richness of self-discovery Harry even develops a belated taste for Pablo's orgies. He emerges from this immersion transformed, and the language is much like that of *Siddhartha:* «Out of the

146

infinite stream of enticements, of vices, of ensnarements I came to the surface again, quiet, silent, prepared, sated with knowledge, wise, deeply experienced, ripe for Hermine» (IV, 399).[78] What we have here is adult baptism, by total immersion.

«How to kill by love» (IV, 399)–the title of this booth-add–brings to Harry's mind Hermine's dark words about the last command she will give him, the command one day to kill her. In his pockets he rummages for fragments of his personality but finds only a knife. In the giant mirror he sees a wolf, then himself, with whom he converses. At this moment the music from the last act of *Don Giovanni,* which heralds the approach of the Commendatore, begins to be heard. Don Juan is to be called to repentance; the music of the Immortals is icy. The poem «Die Unsterblichen,» which Harry once wrote on the back of a wine card, sums up this motif:

> We however have found ourselves
> In the ice of the ether bright with stars [IV, 348].

Mozart, now materializing, points out the laughter which is in such music. A conversation about Brahms and Wagner, once held to be so different but now both of them souls in purgatory, convicted of that foul sin of the late Romantics, «thick instrumentation» (IV, 402), leads Mozart to talk of original sin, and of salvation as being attainable only in the eventual achievement of the super-personal state. Salvation is synonymous with depersonalization–and thinking of the *personal* nature of his own

78 Hesse's use of the word *«tauchen»* is interesting. We may compare, e. g., «aus diesem Augenblick einer Kälte und Verzagtheit tauchte Siddhartha empor . . .» (III, 649). The etymological relationship between *«tauchen»* and *«taufen»* seems to have been everpresent in Hesse's mind as an assonance. Figures of baptism constantly recur. So later, Goldmund «tauchte . . . in den frommen Übungen wie in einem tiefen, kühlen Wasser unter» (V, 295). Cf. also Wackenroder: «oh, so tauch' ich mein Haupt in dem heiligen, kühlenden Quell der Töne unter» (*op. cit.,* p. 131).

literary endeavors, of his endless articles and reviews, the Neo-Romantic Steppenwolf has to shudder with guilty apprehension. Depersonalization is a state of total detachment from existence, which is a symptom, of course, of acute introversion but which, in its positive connotation in Hesse's novels, is the distinguishing characteristic of successful players of the game, from the cool manipulations of the gambling Teresina to the austere and sovereign meditations of the best exponents of the Glass Bead Game. For his sins Harry Haller must go to hell—and the pointed suggestion (IV, 404) that he is not merely an epigone but a plagiarist to boot is too much for the Steppenwolf; he seizes Mozart by his pigtail, and is duly transported on this «comet's tail» just where he has always been so eager to go, outer space, the freezing vacuum in which the Immortals live. Before losing consciousness, he experiences «a bitter-sharp, steely-bright, icy serenity, a desire to laugh just such a ringing, wild and unearthly laugh as had Mozart» (IV, 404).

But he reawakes in his old miserable Steppenwolfian world, looks once more in a mirror at the dilapidated features of this fifty-year-old man, and is filled with his old self-contempt again and an upsurge of aggression. Armed with his knife he sets off in search of Hermine, finds her and Pablo together, naked and asleep, and stabs her beneath the breast. Pablo wakes up, half covers the body with a carpet, and makes a cool exit; Harry remains with the debris of what is left of all his love and happiness, of his entire life: «a little red, painted on a dead face» (IV, 407).[79] The body radiates a terrible, musical

---

79 Cf. the poem «Mit diesen Händen»:

> «Alles läßt mich im Stich,
> Jetzt ist auch meine Geliebte kaputt,
> Es war so schauerlich,
> Sie hieß Erika Maria Ruth.
> . . .

frigidity–«The cold ... was deathly and yet beautiful: it resounded, it vibrated wonderfully, it was music!» (IV, 407). Mozart (really of course Pablo–both address Harry as «Monsieur») has still to teach the Steppenwolf a lesson, and he does this by reappearing with a radio; in this instrument Handel's Concerto Grosso in F Major, broadcast from Munich, sounds like a mixture of «bronchial phlegm and chewed rubber» (IV, 408). This technical monstrosity represents the ultimate bourgeois corruption of art, «the triumph of our era, its last victorious weapon in the war of annihilation against art» (IV, 408). But Mozart points out that through all the distortion and interference the «original spirit» of this music can still be heard, and thus the radio is symbolic of the whole structure of existence, of the perpetual tension and conflict between ideas and phenomena, eternity and time, the divine and the human. That Platonic note characteristic of the finale of *The Steppenwolf* sounds here. Mozart's own detachment is dubious, his dislike of modern civilization is as intense as Harry's, but he does deliver a timely admonition: «People of your sort have no right to criticize

> Ich wollt, ich wär tot, ich wollt, ich wär
> Das Messer, mit dem ich sie totgestochen.
> . . .
> Doch von all den erloschenen Sonnen
> War kein Abendrot mehr . . .»
> (*Krisis*, p. 78).

> (Everything leaves me in the lurch,
> Now my lover is done for.
> It was so horrible.
> She was called Erika Maria Ruth.
> . . .
> I wish I were dead, I wish I were
> The knife I used to kill her.
> . . .
> But from all the dead suns
> There was no sunset any more. . . .)

Erika is the name of Harry's girl (IV, 259). Maria and Ruth may recall Maria Bernoulli and Ruth Wenger. *The Steppenwolf* also uses the sun image in this way: «Had I extinguished the sun?» (IV, 407).

the radio or life. First of all learn to listen!» (IV, 410).
To learn to listen, like Siddhartha, is the foundation for
an understanding of action. To act–especially if it means
to knife a pretty girl–is pointless and absurd. Harry's
defense–that it was Hermine's wish that he should kill
her–is a weak one, for, as he well realizes, he is unable to
distinguish at all clearly between Hermine's wishes and
his own. The murder from which Friedrich Klein shrank
back at the last moment is in *The Steppenwolf* committed
in a dream. Mozart derides what inevitably follows–Harry's offer of himself for retribution, for the guillotine, but
lets him go through with this in the hope that it may end
by instilling in him a sense of humor, «gallows humor»
(IV, 411). At Harry's «execution» judgment is first read
out: he is convicted by the Immortals of mischievous and
humorless misuse of the Magic Theater. Harry's murder
of Hermine is evidence that he has failed; he succumbs to
the illusion of Maya (that is, magic), an illusion within an
illusion, since the Theater itself is an opium dream. Although, as the tractate says, he had no theoretical objections to prostitution, he was unable «to take a tart
seriously and really look upon her as someone like himself» (IV, 236). He discovers in Maria the type of women,
naïve sensual creatures, who fulfill him in a way their intellectual predecessors in his life had never been able to do.
But all the same he remains unfree, throttled by his bourgeois conscience. His murder of Hermine is not simply
motivated by common jealousy (as Pablo, taking the long
view, vainly hopes) but is rather a disastrous reversion to
his bourgeois self, an upsurge of disgust with the sensual.

He still divides the world into irreconcilable halves. In
that the Immortals ridicule this attitude they reveal
themselves as of the same stuff as Demian,[80] acolytes of

80 *Demian* also uses the image: «the loneliness and deathly cold of
cosmic space» (III, 144); in this case it describes the condition at
the time of puberty, of the death of childhood.

Abraxas; and yet we are forced to take account of the fact that the world these Immortals inhabit is totally beyond the sensual, is that icy cosmic vastness which belongs so obviously to the emerging scientific mythology of the age, a Third Kingdom much less linked than Siddhartha's was to experience through the senses. The suspicion arises that—in spite of Goethe's toy leg—their fulfillment is somehow but a surrogate for the real thing. Here lies the root point, the problem of interpretation which the conclusion of *The Steppenwolf* presents. Harry is condemned by the court of the Immortals «to the penalty of eternal life and a twelve-hour withdrawal of entrance permission for our theater. Also the accused cannot be excused the penalty of being laughed at once» (IV, 412). He must learn to overcome his masochistic impulse to self-analysis, the descent into himself is duly forbidden him for a time, and he is introduced to the weapon of humor, the awful «laughter of the Beyond» (IV, 412). Since he was ready only for punishment full of pathos and devoid of wit, he is condemned to go on living forever and listening to the radio-music of life. Mozart now turns into Pablo, who looks so much like the chess player. Pablo scolds Harry for his indecorous violence; he has not yet learned what he must learn, «to play the figures game better» (IV, 415), the technique of the «game.»

*The Steppenwolf*, then, differs radically from *Siddhartha* in that it affirms the ultimate value and psychological necessity of the game, *in nuce* the aesthetic existence, on the spiritual level implying a condition of life in which the controlling will is all-dominant—in Hesse's terminology, therefore, a masculine bias rather than the true androgynous union. The «humor» of *The Steppenwolf* (it is after all a remarkably unfunny novel) has been variously interpreted; central must be the statement of the tractate: «Humor is always in some respect bourgeois, though the genuine bourgeois is incapable of understanding it» (IV, 239). Humor is conceived of as a state of sovereign superiority above the polar tensions of life, tending toward resolution, harmony and balance, its elevation above the melee making it all but synonymous with Romantic irony–which vertical polarity in turn implies an unresolved duality. The aim of outsiders is «to burst out into starry space» (IV, 239); a few indeed do find their way through «to the unconditional» (IV, 239)[81] and are destroyed; «for the others, however, those who remain bound ... for them a third kingdom is open, an imaginary but sovereign world: humor» (IV, 239), a sphere which embraces saint, profligate, and bourgeois in an imaginary reconciliation. Yet–somewhat inconsistently perhaps–humor is also declared to be the key to the Tao: «To live in the world as were it not the world, to respect the law and yet to stand above it, to possess ‹as though not possessing,› to renounce as though it were no renunciation» (IV, 240)–the Steppenwolf's only hope is to distill this fairy-tale «magic potion» (IV, 240) in the hell of his night-mind. Thus the meaning of Goethe's sly humor, thus Jean Paul; thus also Hesse is able to speak of «the divine humor of Asiatic yogis»[82] and in *The Nuremberg Journey* to describe humor as «a crystal which grows only in deep and lasting pain» (IV, 128).

The image of the crystal fits well into the patterns of *The Steppenwolf,* the symbolism of coldness, clarity, translucent hardness, the brightness of the musical dome of the cosmos, the luminosity of dark streets and of stars:

The Immortals, as they live in timeless space, removed, turned into images and crystal eternity poured over

81 Cf. Ziolkowski, «Hermann Hesse and Novalis» (pp. 133–134). Novalis uses this term in *Blütenstaub (Schriften,* II, 15). We may compare Hesse's comments on the nature of heroism in «On Hölderlin» (1924; VII, 279). At the end of *The Glass Bead Game,* Joseph Knecht tells Master Alexander that what he yearns for is «the unconditional» (VI, 503).
82 «Herr Claassen» (IV, 686).

them like ether, and the cool, starlike radiant serenity of this extraterrestrial world—what made all this so familiar to me?» He reflects, and he remembers the music of Bach and Mozart: «and everywhere in this music, this cool, starry brightness seemed to shine, this ethereal clarity to vibrate. Yes, this was it, this music was a sort of time frozen into space, and above it vibrated endlessly a superhuman serenity, an eternal divine laughter [IV, 347–348].

So persistent is the imagery of the cosmic dome, of eternity, time, and space in *The Steppenwolf,* that it is probably no accident that the novel actually refers to the theory of relativity and to Einstein by name; the poet's imagination has been caught and held by the scientific imagery of his own day. Depersonalization, as in Goethe's case, is achieved when the individual has passed through all the vicissitudes of common life and has burst «into the Eternal, into cosmic space» (IV, 347), where time has been redeemed, has undergone that metamorphosis of which «Old Music» had spoken in 1913, «its transformation back into space.»

*The Steppenwolf* is an optimistic work[83] and a Strindbergian catharsis of crisis years. Like his predecessor in *Inferno,* Hesse is experimenting with faith. Hermine's own philosophy is a curious mixture of transcendental optimism and death-wish, highly reminiscent of Novalis, to whom it no doubt owes a good deal. She draws parallels between her own unsought fate as a courtesan and Harry's; they both have «a dimension too many» (IV,

---

[83] As Hesse must have grown weary of protesting. Many readers failed to see «that over and above the Steppenwolf and his problematical life there rises a second, higher, immortal world.» «Postscript to *The Steppenwolf*» (VII, 413). While the novel certainly aimed to reveal the desperate problem of existence, it also sought «to give some sense nonetheless to this apparently senseless, cruel life» (*Letters;* VII, 490). It is Mozart and the Immortals «who are the real content of the book» (*Letters;* VII, 493). The message of the book is how to endure life and overcome time (*Letters;* VII, 501–502).

343); maybe outsiders—«people with a dimension too many» (IV, 344)–are themselves only epiphenomenal and will eventually vanish from the face of the earth. Meanwhile all they can call their own is death and eternity–by eternity, she says, she means what the pious call the Kingdom of God. This is defined as the world of the real and the true, of music, poetry, miracles, genuine feelings and actions, beyond time, of the communion of saints. The essential Platonism[84] of this outlook is manifest; the suggestion made in *Siddhartha* that knowledge of the One might itself be merely «a childishness of the think-people, of the think-child-people» shows that Hesse was fully aware not only of the ambiguities inherent in the term «child-person» but also of the epistemological difficulties in his concept of «magical thinking.» Whereas *Siddhartha*, in effectively moving away from the abstractions of Buddhism and of the Vedanta[85] toward the Hindu pantheon–its intellectual chaos and the earthiness of graven images[86]–partially bypassed these difficulties, *The Steppenwolf* remains seized with them, as in the last resort the thought of Novalis, with its critical heritage, also is. Hermine echoes the latter yet again: «Oh, Harry, we have to grope through so much dirt and senselessness, to reach home. And we have no one to lead us, our only guide is our home-sickness!» (IV, 346).

Thomas Mann remarked of *The Steppenwolf* that it was a book not inferior in its experimental boldness to

84 Plato is ranked with Jesus, Buddha, and Lao-tzû. «War and Peace» (1918; VII, 120).
85 Cf. Max Schmid, *Hermann Hesse: Weg und Wandlung*, p. 61: «Die Upanishad-Philosophen suchen die Einheit von Mensch und Natur. Daß sie diese Einheit wieder herstellen müssen durch das Wissen um sie, zeigt, daß sie bereits von ihr gespalten sind» (The Upanishad-philosophers seek the unity of man and nature. That they have to reconstruct this unity by knowledge of it shows that they are already cut off from it).
86 Gods and magic, we are told, may be just as necessary as «pure» teaching: Shiva and Vishnu are a requisite counterweight to Buddhism. Cf. *Letters* (VII, 616).

*Ulysses* or *Les Fauxmonnayeurs*.[87] Certainly it depends for its effect upon an artistic principle very different from that which informs *Siddhartha*. The extremely conscious structure, the massive intrusions of reflective commentary through the bourgeois narrator, through the tractate, through Harry's obsessional process of self-diagnosis, the discourses of Hermine, Pablo, and the chess player, and a speculation about music as a German heritage in which Harry's reflection all but cracks the taut framework of the novel[88]–all this shows the bent of the book. Furthermore, we have to note a good deal of political matter, an only partly integrated left-wing polemicism, predictions of war, an attack on that old *bête noire,* «world history,» and finally some pontifications *à la Demian:* Harry's memoirs, says the bourgeois narrator, are not just the fantasies of a paranoid but «a document of the age, for Haller's sickness is ... the sickness of the age itself, the neurosis of that generation to which Haller belongs» (IV, 205). The widespread use of rhetorical questions is a feature of a style which has in general a marked rhetorical nuance. The existence of at least four narrators–the young bourgeois, the author of the tractate, Harry Haller, and then by prominent implication Hesse himself–all this is ostentatious artifact. Hesse experiments in the novel in a greater degree than heretofore with montage techniques, but it is no doubt important to remember in this connection the debt *The Steppenwolf* owes to Romantic narrative art, especially the writings of Hoffmann and Jean Paul. In its very structure the book is Platonic, representing the nexus between matter and idea, life and faith, the radio and the music beyond (the analogy is apt because it requires that we should see

87 «Hermann Hesse: Einleitung zu einer amerikanischen *Demian*-Ausgabe,» *Neue Rundschau,* LVIII (1947), 248.
88 «In the German spirit matriarchy reigns» (IV, 326 ff.)–a passage reading a good deal more like Mann than Hesse and fitting none too well into the general conspectus of Harry's views on music.

the radio as the matter of the narrative and the original music as its form). The Platonic way of thinking is not, ultimately, «magical thinking,» for the latter is a genuine monism best found in the *Märchen* and *Siddhartha,* Hesse's least Platonic works. *The Steppenwolf,* one must sum up, is an act of faith imposing form on chaos, time on space, and music on life, by the sovereign *acceptance* of the old Calw dualism, by the apotheosis of irony («laughter of the Beyond»). It is indeed the eternity of the father which here finds its form; the senses are denied by the very language in which the acceptance of sensual experience is enjoined. The «depersonalized,» though they may treasure ladies' legs in caskets, must find sense experience rather difficult of access, or at any rate subordinate to that superior form of game which Siddhartha *finally* abandoned only on leaving Kamala, finding eventually that the warm, naïve experience of the «child-people» (of which, despite flickerings of it in Maria and elsewhere, there is not a word at the end of the novel) was essential to samadhi. «Eternity, eternity! The black bird sang, and his hard shiny eye gazed at us like a black crystal»–these words from an earlier story are worth quoting here once again, for the tractate ends: «We take our leave of Harry, we let him go his way alone. If he were already with the Immortals, if he were already at that place to which his *steep road* seems to lead, with what astonishment would he look upon this wild, indecisive zigzagging path» (IV, 251–252; my italics). The world of the Immortals, therefore, lies at the very end of the Way, of «The Steep Road,» where there is not merely the bird song of eternity but also cold laughter. Yet even the tractate had its reservations–perhaps after all the only Way *is* that of martyrdom, leading «to still greater sufferings, to proscription, to the last renunciation, perhaps to the scaffold» (IV, 248). Indeed, one may well feel that the vision of the scaffold is not effectively exorcised by the mockery of the Immortals.

Harry knows, at all events, that he is still far from being at one with them; another *saison en enfer* still awaits him, perhaps over and over again; *unio mystica* he may have briefly experienced, but *unio mystica substantialis* is reserved for the saint. There remains the suspicion that the point Harry Haller has now reached is not the well of space but rather only a certain mountain peak; humor, confessedly the key to an *imaginary* reconciliation, will prove an inadequate panacea. The ultimate «leap *(Sprung)* into the universe» (IV, 240), will be still to come, as inevitable as Klein's «leap into cosmic space»; and to follow the analogy a trifle further still, Harry may yet discover that it is not Mozart and Pablo but rather his own mother who awaits his eventual fall.

# 4

## ERNST A. ROSE
## THE FULNESS OF ART

With *Steppenwolf*, Hesse reached the end of his «confessional» period. The poet realized that an exclusive concern with his own soul would never lead to the desired integration of man and society. Unity could be reached only by his immersion in the full stream of life, and in his last great novels he chose to depict life as a whole. At the same time he was aware that contemporary civilization constituted a very poor parable for the envisioned unity. In each case, therefore, he selected a remote locale. The first story took place in the past, the second moved in the world of fancy, and the third portrayed a distant future. In every case he gained detachment and perspective.

Hesse's first great parable, *Narcissus and Goldmund* (*Narziss und Goldmund*, 1929–1930), was taken from medieval life. The conflict between artistic and scholarly existence, between sinful sensualism and ascetic sainthood had been a personal problem of the author from childhood and had already been employed in a medieval frame in the fragment *Berthold*, which appeared in 1908 (I, 831–883). But this conflict reflected general, no longer personal, tendencies of human life and could be understood only as a part of the immense problem of becoming and declining. A cold-blooded logical solution of the conflict was impossible. A valid artistic image of it came closer to the truth.

The conjunction «and» in the title *Narcissus and Goldmund* indicates the absence of any intention by Hesse to set up a specific example for everyone. Hesse is no dogmatist. To be sure, the vagaries of Goldmund's life are so interesting that in many chapters Narcissus plays a secondary role. Yet Goldmund cannot achieve his individual goal without the help of Narcissus and, of course, Narcissus needs his friend to round out his own life. Each is far from being ideal by himself, and although in the beginning both are disciples of the monastery school of Mariabronn, their essential differences and limitations are apparent and the antagonistic undercurrent in their friendship is very strong.

While Narcissus was dark and haggard, Goldmund was shining and blooming. While Narcissus was an analytic thinker, Goldmund seemed to be a dreamer of a child-like candor. Yet their contrasts were bridged by something they had in common: both were noble souls, both were distinguished before others by visible gifts and marks, and both had been given by fate a special warning (V, 23).

Narcissus is predestined to become a scholar. He is looking everywhere for differences and definitions; he represents the fatherly side of man. Goldmund, on the other hand, is of motherly origin and has to live in the concrete. As Narcissus tells him: «To you belongs the bounty of life, to you the juice of the fruits, to you the garden of love, the beautiful country of art. Your home is the earth, as ours is the idea. You are running the danger of drowning in sensuality, while we could suffocate in airless space. Your are an artist, I am a thinker» (V, 51).

Young Narcissus' abstract and precocious differentiations rouse Goldmund painfully from the warmth of his dreams, but they also help him realize that subconsciously he is seeking the world of his mother and that his aim can never be the priesthood. At the end of his novitiate, Narcissus takes final vows and starts his prescribed ascetic exercises. He sees ahead of himself a life of service to the spirit, although he is aware of its one sidedness.

Goldmund, on the other hand, runs away from Mariabronn, just as Hermann Hesse himself ran away from the school of Maulbronn, after which Mariabronn was fashioned. Goldmund's mother too had left her family to live her life to the full. One day, while Goldmund is gathering herbs in the fields, he meets a young gypsy, who surrenders herself to him. In order to be able to return to her, Goldmund leaves the monastery. But the woman in turn deserts Goldmund to return to her husband. Thus Goldmund's first experience in the world of the senses teaches him how unstable and fleeting it is.

Nevertheless he must continue his search for worldly satisfaction. He has an adventure with a peasant woman before he joins the household of a knight who needs help in writing his memoirs. The knight has two daughters, Lydia and Julia. Lydia falls in love with Goldmund and comes into his bed, but remains chaste. Julia, who has observed her sister's action, demands also to be taken into Goldmund's bed, unless he wants to be found out by her father. Lydia, realizing that she and her sister will no longer be able to resist their lover, confesses everything to her father, who chases Goldmund away.

On the next lap of his journey, Goldmund meets Victor, a common thief who is scheming to rob him of the goldpiece which Lydia had secretly sent after him. Goldmund catches Victor in the act of stealing and stabs him to death. He hides Victor's corpse and escapes. Now he has experienced the physical violence of the world; a world which he loves so fervently.

As he wanders on, Goldmund discovers a beautiful statue of St. Mary and is imbued with the desire to meet its creator. The artist is Master Nicholas who lives in a great city which reminds one of Basel, or Constance. Nicholas accepts Goldmund as his disciple, and the youth soon fashions a statue of the Disciple John, whose features are actually those of Narcissus. Master Nicholas realizes Goldmund's possibilities and decides to admit him to the guild and to give the young man his daughter in marriage. But Goldmund does not want to live a bourgeois life and deserts his master.

Goldmund does not find greater happiness in his new adventure, but experiences instead the world of the Black Death. He meets Robert, a vagabonding cleric, and Nell, whom Robert has saved from a pest-ridden town. For a time the three live together in a country cottage. When Nell herself contracts the disease, Robert flees, but Goldmund remains and nurses her until her death. He then burns the hut together with the corpse.

Now Goldmund returns to the city of Master Nicholas. On his journey he meets the Jewess Rebecca. Her father was burned by the Christians who blamed the Jews for the pestilence. She rejects Goldmund's advances, since she desires only to die, and he respects her wishes and leaves her alone. In the city he is informed that Master Nicholas also has fallen victim to the disease. Then Goldmund catches a glimpse of Agnes, the governor's mistress. He pursues her until she admits him into her bedchamber. But on his second visit he is seized by the watchmen who plan to put him to death the next morning.

A priest comes to give him Extreme Unction, and Goldmund considers killing him and escaping in the priest's habit. But the priest turns out to be Narcissus, who has become Abbot John. As Narcissus had promised, he has come to his friend in the hour of his direst need, when the world of the senses and the world of violence and disease threaten to engulf him and steep him in the sin of premeditated murder. Through Narcissus' influence, Goldmund's execution is prevented and he is freed from jail. Together they return to Mariabronn, where Goldmund is given a shop in which he can create sculptures.

Once again Narcissus assumes the direction of Goldmund's destiny and tells him what to do. But he assigns only congenial tasks and does not condemn Goldmund for his sins. Spiritually, Narcissus is suffering from the vileness of the world *with* his friend, but he realizes that the development of Goldmund as an artist would be impossible without his previous experience *in corpore vili:* Art has justified this adventurous and dangerous life, and Goldmund needs no other forgiveness.

Yet he cannot submit for long to the discipline of monastic life and he must run away once more into the world of the senses. Eventually he returns to Mariabronn as a tired old man whom his young apprentice can scarcely recognize. The world has become too much for him and he longs for peace, but he harbors no grudge against fate. He has no faith in a life after death, but still looks forward to dying: «I am hoping that death may be real happiness, a happiness as great as the first consummation of love. I cannot get rid of the thought that instead of death with the scythe it will be my mother who will take me by my hand and will lead me back into the innocence of non-existence» (V, 319).

Goldmund dreams that his mother is opening his chest and loosening his heart. During his whole life he has imagined that he would ultimately represent her in a creative work of art. Now he realizes that it is she who has created him, and he willingly endures her last ministrations. Will Narcissus ever find home in the same peaceful way, Narcissus who «has no mother?» (V, 322). Goldmund's last words burn in the abbot's breast «like fire» (V, 322).

The end of the novel expresses the same belief in love as the ultimate reality as does the last verse of Dante's *Divine Comedy* or those lines of Goethe's *West-Eastern Divan* where the poet is anticipating his dissolution and extinction «in contemplation of the love eternal.» Only a motherly image was able to convey such a sentiment, and Hesse chose it with an unerring artistic instinct. At the same time his choice could be defended in the light of

Jung's theories which always emphasized the female aspects of man's image of the divinity.

Yet it is clear that Hesse's turn to a motherly divinity in this novel no longer bears the earmarks of an unsolved Oedipus complex; of a violent rebellion against the world of the father. The early stories had sought release from fatherly strictness in the arms of motherly nature, and *Demian* had ended in a symbolical union with the divine mother. The fatherly world, the world of the spirit, at that time was seen as ending in «convulsions and suffering and war» (cf. the poem «Return,» V, 644).

Hesse has now come to accept the fatherly spirit as being necessary also. To be sure, Narcissus, whose very name seems to indicate an egocentric preoccupation with the mysteries of his individuality, realized his lack of creativity and his lack of love. «My life has been poor in love, I have lacked the best. ... I am not unjust against men, I am taking pains to be fair and to be tolerant towards them, but I have never loved them» (V, 316). Still, without Narcissus' roving participation there would have been no direction or purpose to Goldmund's life.[1] For just as Goethe knew that the path to the creative «Mothers» was also the path into the chaos which gave birth to everything, Hesse was aware that the artist was always in danger of losing himself in chaos.

On his journey through life's unplumbed mysteries, Goldmund is forever skirting the abyss and wooing temptation and sin. He needs Narcissus to give him tasks and measure so that he can understand his needs and appreciate his abilities. Goldmund confesses in the end that he has always loved Narcissus and that he has been searching for him through half of his life (V, 317).

It is hard to say which one of the two stands in greater need of the other, although the pointer of the scales per-

[1] The name «Goldmund» is the German equivalent of the Greek «Crysostomos,» the name of Goldmund's patron saint.

haps balances slightly toward Goldmund, who symbolizes Hesse's personal artistic approach to life. This «perhaps» is the poet's final word in the conflict between the fatherly and the motherly principles of life. Ultimately, life is a continuous oscillation between Yin and Yang, as a Far Eastern sage might express it, or between systole and diastole, as Goethe would have said. The approach of the occidental to the oriental world appears to be complete.

Yet there is no oriental stress on withdrawal from the world and on ascetic concentration upon the mystic union. Hesse has become neither a Buddhist nor a hermit. He is Eastern only insofar as the *Bhagavad-Gita* is also Eastern. The stress is still on active mastery of the world, even though this means suffering and sin and error. There is still the conviction that man has to do the work of God and has to embrace all the world with his love.

Goldmund's love is not the love of an ascetic. It is avowedly sensual and sexual. But he knows that sensual love «can become the vessel of the soul» (V, 318) and does not pursue it as an end in itself. Hesse's concern is far removed from the current preoccupation with sex to the exclusion of everything else. He has clearly broken with orthodox Christianity, and his religion can be called Christian only when one defines Christianity as a wholly undogmatic religion of love (cf. also VII, 373). Absent is the belief in the myth of Christ's life and the divinity of Jesus, in the redemption of sins through his death on the cross, and in resurrection and personal immortality. (Goldmund is not saved by Christ's redemption.)

Still, Hesse has by no means renounced the Christian spirit. He has not turned into a pagan who worships God through orgies. With him, the path of erotic art toward the inscrutable divinity is, to be sure, one way, but it is not the only way. To the same degree, ascetic dedication to the pure spirit is not the only way, although it is right for some people. For Hesse mysticism has never been an esoteric attitude confined to a few «spiritual» men. On the contrary, his «natural» men are just as fervent seekers for God as are his «spiritual» men. Both Narcissus and Goldmund have the same destination, but they reach it in different ways.

As Narcissus states at the end: «We philosophers try to approach God by divesting Him of the world. You however approach Him by loving His creation and producing it again. Both ways are human ways and therefore unsatisfactory, but the way of art is the more innocent one» (V, 300). «We two, dear friend, are sun and moon, are sea and land. Our aim is not to combine, but to realize each other and to learn to see and honor in the other what he is: one's own contrast and complement» (V, 49).

Because the theme of the novel is the development of two human beings, its narrative structure is determined by the stages of human development. But, since the two lives are inextricably interwoven, this structure is anything but simple. Narcissus is portrayed from the beginning in an advanced state of development. He has accepted the world for what it is and is consciously filling his place in it. Yet we know that in spite of his relative maturity he has by no means reached the ultimate stage of sainthood. Even in the end Narcissus has not achieved perfection; he is still on the way to it. The outward stages of his life are clearly marked, but they are of minor interest and are therefore mentioned only in passing.

In the main, Narcissus' life serves as a frame for the life of Goldmund. It is elaborated in the beginning as well as the end of the story. In between, the life of Goldmund is developed in stages, similar to those of Siddhartha. To be sure, Goldmund's innocence is not Siddhartha's childhood innocence among gentle Brahmins. It is the innocence of nature which follows its sensual impulses without restraint. One has to be free from traditional preconceptions to realize that Goldmund's first sexual experiences with the gypsy Lise are basically innocent. A different note enters only with the daughters of the knight, where the conflict between the spirit and the flesh, between what is traditionally «good» and traditionally «evil,» plays a decisive role.

The murder of Victor, although committed in self-defense, clearly marks the fall from grace. Then follows the conscious dedication to accepted evaluations of life and work under the guidance of Master Nicholas. There is just as conscious abandonment during the period of the Black Death and the episode with the governor's courtesan. Acquiescence to God's will is begun by Goldmund's return to Mariabronn, but it is not achieved without major struggles. The vision of reintegration and a regained «innocence» comes to Goldmund only in his dying hours.

One realizes that Hesse's original scheme of human development is still visible, but one also finds that it cannot be applied without bold simplifications. Ultimately Goldmund's life defies simple logic. The fabric of his soul is too rich to be dominated by a single strain. There are knots in its skein and minor weaving faults in the form of unsolved riddles and interrupted developments. To be sure, the structure is fugue-like, as the basic theme of Goldmund's relation to sensual reality is repeated in different keys, until the final repetition leads to an integration of the dissonances and their dissolution in a new harmony. But the theme of the fugue is complicated, and the ensuing variations are richly ornamented. While *Siddhartha* is characterized by an almost Gothic simplicity, *Narcissus and Goldmund* could be described as baroque. But one has to describe it as a calm and balanced baroque.

The novel is richer in colorful descriptions than most of its forerunners. *Siddhartha,* for example, clothes the real world in a haze of unreality. *Narcissus and Goldmund* brings the world of the late Middle Ages vividly alive.

It is the fifteenth-century world of Nicholas of Cusa, when unorthodox interpretations of Christianity were tolerable, although few people in that day found fault with pogroms. Hesse's picture of the Middle Ages is certainly not nostalgic. Christian cruelties against the Jews are not excused, but condemned (IV, 230–231; 274–275), and the ravages of the Black Death form an important part of the general background. However, the fascinating and elevating aspects of the Middle Ages are equally emphasized. The touching innocence of medieval men and women, the simple piety of medieval art, the unspoiled character of the medieval landscape, are present in ever changing images.

*Narcissus and Goldmund* is replete with fine descriptions of the heath and the forest, of the sun's rising and setting. The image of a village with all its shades of color and sound and odor is evoked in a few pertinent sentences:

> Already in the evening of this day he was in a beautiful village, which lay between the river and the red, sloping vineyards by the great highroad. At the gabled houses the pretty framework of beams was painted red, there were vaulted gateways for wagons and alley ways of stone stairs. A smithy threw a red, fiery glow upon the street and broadcast the bright pealing of its anvil. The curious visitor roamed around in all the sideways and byways, he sniffed at cellar doors the scent of the wine barrels and at the river edge the cool, fishy odor of the water, he observed the house of God and the cemetery and did not omit to look around for a useful barn where one perhaps could alight for the night. But first he wanted to try his luck in the parsonage with a request for sustenance (V, 150).

The picture of a fish market is sketched in a few masterly strokes and at once achieved a new, transcendental dimension:

> The next day Goldmund could not make the decision

to go into the studio. Like on other adverse days he gadded about in the town. He saw the women and the maid-servants go to the market, he particularly loitered at the well on the fish market and watched the fishmongers and their buxom wives, as they were offering their wares for sale and praising its virtues, as they tore the cool, silvery fishes from their tubs and displayed them, as the fishes with mouths gaping from pain and with golden eyes livid with fear calmly became resigned to death or were fighting it in fury and desperation. Like often before he was seized by pity for these creatures and by a sad annoyance at people; why ... did they not see these mouths, these eyes afraid unto death, these tails wildly slashing about, why not this gruesome, useless struggle of despair, why not this unbearable transformation of the mysterious, wondrously beautiful creatures, as the last, subtle tremor was rippling over their dying skins and they then lay dead and extinguished, spread out as pitiful chunks of meat for the table of the cheerful glutton? (V, 183).

In all of these repetitions there is, however, no redundancy. On the contrary, each new element of the sentence adds a nuance of perception and illuminates or widens the picture. Hesse is likewise a master of the art of visualizing places and personalities with a few, effective adjectives. There is «the haughty, cool maiden Elisabeth» (V, 186). There is gentle Nell, «a sweet playmate, shy and inexperienced, but full of love» (V, 215). There is, in the beginning of the story, the gypsy Lise, the ripe «young woman in a faded blue skirt, with a red kerchief tied around her black hair, with a brown face tanned by summer» (V, 79). There is little Marie, «a child of fifteen years, a quiet, sickly creature with beautiful eyes, but with a hip injury which made her limp.» She receives Goldmund's kiss «reverently, with closed eyes» (V, 199). There is the courtesan Agnes, «his beautiful, royal sweetheart, who looked so haughty and yet could forget herself and abandon herself so much in love» (V, 256).

Never before had Hesse attempted such full pictures of sensual union and completion. Since it is physical as well as spiritual completion, it could be described without vulgar details. Instead of the probing of adolescent curiosity we have here the joyous awareness of maturity. There remains no trace of the nervous frustrations evident in *Peter Camenzind,* in *Gertrude*, in *Rosshalde*, and even in *Demian*.

The novel is so rich in color that it can indulge in long, philosophical passages without fear of dimming its brilliance. A certain didacticism is perhaps inseparable from a novel of development. But in this case it is not obtrusive and does not jar the reader. Because of all the vivid images he experiences in the novel's pages, he accepts the philosophical remarks as a natural evidence of life's fulness. Through this combination of impressive, colorful imagery and lofty philosophy, Hesse's story is a worthy addition to the lengthy series of German novels of growing up *(Bildungsromane)*, a reassertion of the problems discussed in Goethe's *Wilhelm Meister* and Keller's *Green Henry*.

## 5

## J. C. MIDDLETON
## HERMANN HESSE'S MORGENLANDFAHRT

*Die Morgenlandfahrt* (1932) was the first narrative after «Kinderseele» (1919) which Hesse wrote undisguisedly in the first person singular. *Der Steppenwolf* (1927) was quasi-autobiographical, but, like *Hermann Lauscher* (1901), it was also mock-anonymous. Even «Kinderseele,» like *Demian*, was first published under the Sinclair pseudonym. But the distance between author and work, which these stratagems aimed to provide, was not, in *Die Morgenlandfahrt*, filled in by the first person singular. On the contrary, Hesse was here to explore the scope of a new irony. It was this irony which was now to provide greater detachment than his narratives had hitherto shown. The unmistakable H. H., who is at once narrator and protagonist of *Die Morgenlandfahrt*, may be recognized as Hermann Heilner of *Unterm Rad* (1906), or again as Harry Haller of *Der Steppenwolf*; but he is already the future ironic biographer of Josef Knecht, the serene mandarin historian of *Das Glasperlenspiel* (1943). The following interpretation of *Die Morgenlandfahrt* shows that the new irony of this work is one among many other qualities of the narrative which made it a turning-point in Hesse's work. Earlier themes and figures, it will be shown, were here assembled, recreated by integration within the new metaphor of the «voyage,» and thereby matured into the substance of Hesse's final geometric vision of things.

H. H. writes his first two chapters in retrospect upon the halcyon days of his voyage. His experiences, he explains, must remain mostly inexplicable, because he has no documents, and because the arcana of the society which made the voyage cannot be divulged (VI, 11).[1] He quotes:

Die Unerfahrenheit, ich kann mir's denken,
Wird meinem Sange wenig Glauben schenken.

Hence, if you are «unerfahren,» have no experience of the voyage yourself, then what he, H. H., now says about it you will consider absurd. Yet this is anomalous, because it will soon be found that H. H. is convinced that he is the sole surviving voyager, that «you» (i. e. «der Leser,» 11) means in a sense H. H. himself, for he can be the only understander of his work, and that this work is consequently a monologue, or, to use a title found in *Eine Stunde hinter Mitternacht* (1899), «ein Gespräch mit dem Stummen.» The ramifications of the enclosure of H. H. in himself, in solitary monologue, soon become evident. The verses quoted are also of course in part a warning to readers who are unfamiliar with Hesse's previous works, his earlier monoligic records of his voyage. Above all, however, they are a key to the echoing tunnels of association in the work, to the overtones of earlier work which here reverberate, to the network of experience which the narrative most succinctly maps out.

In his retrospect upon the society of the voyagers, H. H. explains that the route taken cannot be described in spatial terms. He relates that the journey was different from the spatial journeys Keyserling and Ossendowski made. For this voyage went «actually into the heroic and the magical.» It went moreover «ins Reich einer kommenden Psychokratie» (10). Later Klingsor will be found among the voyagers, the hero of *Klingsors Letzter Som-*

[1] Unless otherwise indicated the source of quotations and references throughout this essay is Hermann Hesse, *Gesammelte Dichtungen,* in six volumes (Frankfurt, 1952). Hereafter only page numbers will be given for references to *Die Morgenlandfahrt,* which is contained in Vol. VI.

*mer* (1919), who painted in his self-portrait the soul's realm not as an ordered place of cult and cultivation, but as an archaic chaos of formative energies. Since it is later recounted that the «Orient» meant the «unison of all times and all places» (24), it is clear that the psychocracy to come was to be composed of men who dare to penetrate chaos and hell in themselves, seeking, like Klingsor and Haller, the «golden track» of a divine cosmos in the welter of living in time. It is now also observed that the voyage was a Pilgrimage of Fools. Each voyager was impelled by his own childish aim (12). H. H. was drawn into the quest by his dream of the love of Princess Fatme (13). This is surely Hermann Lauscher's «Lulu,» the magician's daughter who, in «Iris» (1918), became Anselm's beloved, personification of the soul as divine mystery in immanence, «a fragment,» as Lauscher had speculated, «of the manuscript of the old philosopher» (I, 157). Leo, the master-voyager, we learn, joined the pilgrimage to learn the language of birds from Solomon's Key (22f.). Here too there are analogies in Hesse's earlier writings. There is the hawk-image in *Demian:* Sinclair is made to eat the hawk-image in a dream. In *Der Steppenwolf* Haller is made to eat duck by Hermine, who finally initiates him into the Magic Theatre; and just before this initiation he eats chicken for his dinner, then finally at the masquerade, in the midst of chaos, he finds that he has «lost his number» (in Jung's psychology these events would be introversion-figures expressive of a fertilization of the psyche). The bird-figure is taken up again in the story «Vogel» (in *Traumfährte*, 1932). Here Vogel is exuberant spontaneity, subject to no laws of space and time. In *Piktors Verwandlungen* (1923) and in «Iris» likewise he is a magic bird. His movements in *Piktor*—«wippte mit dem Schwanz, zwinkerte mit dem Auge»[2]—anticipate the later

2 *Piktors Verwandlungen* is not included in *Gesammelte Dichtungen*. It was originally circulated as an illustrated manuscript in Hesse's

«wie er mit dem flinken Schwänzchen auf und nieder wippend Triller schlug» of «Vogel» (IV, 552). Also in *Piktor,* Vogel's home is «das Innre der Erde»; and this is the home which Anselm seeks in «Iris»: the psyche as fountainhead of generation and regeneration. Consequently the «bird» guides Anselm to the path which leads him finally «ins blaue Geheimnis des Innern» (III, 382). Anselm then will appear among the voyagers in *Die Morgenlandfahrt*; Leo the psychocrat will whistle like a bird; and H. H. will write, «unser Morgenland war ... die Heimat und Jugend der Seele, es war das Überall und Nirgends, war das Einswerden aller Zeiten» (24).

H. H. counts himself among the faithful («Treugebliebene,» 13) who have kept the spirit of the voyage alive, though the society has dispersed. At present he cannot know the ambiguous character of this idea of himself as one who has *stayed firm* («treugeblieben») in his faith in the *voyage*. It will clarify his present state at once if we refer back to his pun on «Unerfahrenheit,» and forward to his account of this present state. He is, in fact, not voyaging, for he is sedentary, in a town, and his writing has taken «months and weeks» (54). Thus, while writing, he is conscious of that very «Zahl und Zeit» (15) which the voyage had aimed to transcend. He thinks himself the sole surviving voyager, yet knows himself to be imprisoned in number and time. He has not «lost his number,» as Harry Haller had to do before he could enter the «Magic Theatre.» H. H., while he is writing, is then, just as Haller was, enclosed in despair by egotism, but struggling by writing to extricate himself from this enclosure, and to relive the ecstatic voyage, to re-enter the society. This capsized condition he will recognize only when Leo

own hand. Bücherfreunde Chemnitz printed 700 copies for limited circulation, but not for sale, in 1925. The Suhrkamp edition of 1954 is a facsimile of the manuscript, and also includes four unnumbered pages of printed text.

retrieves him later and when he is given to understand that it was he himself, in his illusory isolation and in his *superbia,* who erred in thinking of himself as one of the faithful.

These points shed light on another aspect of the voyage as this can be seen, still in the first chapter, through the eyes of H. H. He writes: «Die ganze Weltgeschichte scheint mir oft nichts andres zu sein als ein Bilderbuch, das die heftigste und blindeste Sehnsucht der Menschen spiegelt: die Sehnsucht nach Vergessen» (12). He admits: only fragmentary memories of the voyage remain to him. Again the quandary of his self-righteousness is made clear: he is writing the history of the voyage; but history, he says, happens in time, is blindness, is the longing to forget. His very office of historian defeats his aims. Reflection upon the past breaks the shape of the past: the outsider's vision dislocates its object. Although this corruption in self-consciousness is not diagnosed until later in the book, it is plainly Hesse's intention to show this at this point; for in this first chapter a kindred situation is revealed in the account of the young man who, having renounced the voyage, is «cursed» by the «spokesman,» and suffers immediate loss of memory (18–19). It will thus be found that what makes the voyage for H. H. a dim radiance in the past is his own *superbia* and his own egotism. This is what causes his history to be, as he later comes to see it, «wie Tapeten mit anmutig sinnlosem Ornamentgewirke» (59). And as Hesse's earlier writings very often showed a coincidence of sentimental despair and ornamental language, so now will H. H. confess that he cannot recreate the essential and solid form of his experience. He writes in a state of «Verzweiflung,» which is induced by egotism, and it is «Verzweiflung» which has cut him off from the society and the voyage. Such despair induces loss of memory and loss of conscious life. Incoherence ensues. But it should be remarked at once that this «Ver-

174

zweiflung» will ultimately prove to have been a phase of the voyage, a transitional duality in an unbreakable unity. Despair is the trial of the voyager. It is a necessary darkness, without which, as his friend Lukas will later show H. H., no «voyage to the home of the light» (15) would be conceivable.

Chapter ii tells of Leo's «desertion» and its consequences. Writing when sedentary in his town, H. H. explains that only later did he see that this was not an accident, but a «link in the chain of persecutions by which the arch-enemy sought to spoil our undertaking» (28). But H. H. is still capsized. Not until the fifth chapter does he realize not only that he was himself the deserter, but also that the arch-enemy («Erbfeind») was no radical evil but a trial arranged by the society of the voyage. Leo's absence means loss of faith in the voyage as it provokes despair over oneself and drains everything of meaning (30). Leo «abandons» the group in Morbio Inferiore, a fair name for any area of hell, and each voyager begins to think that he has lost some object of value. If the lost objects are recovered, still the *Bundesbrief* cannot be found. Then confusion comes, because nobody knows what is the nature of this document. H. H. is sure that it is the «original,» not a copy of the document, which is missing (32); and he is certain that Leo has taken it. Since this document was the original, the *fons et origo* of the society, this society now lacks a center. The *idea* of the voyage is not lost, H. H. states; but the society now has neither unity nor security. It is significant that H. H. had faith in his belief that Leo had the «original»; for, in fact, the possibility of unity in the society remains until at last he loses his faith (333). At this point he translates his account of these events into terms of his personal problem as historian of the society: «Wo ist eine Mitte der Ereignisse, ein Gemeinsames, etwas, worauf sie sich beziehen, und was sie zusammenhält?»

This is the desperate question asked by all Hesse's men in monologue since Peter Camenzind: it is the cry of the *déraciné*, the outsider, the self-seeker and the God-seeker. Now memory is dismembered, experience has no coherence. The historian H. H. is now in hell, for the organism of faith has disintegrated. He is the rootless ego as Haller was, and he sees himself as a mirror in which a bursting mass of images is reflected, himself being nothing, «ein Nichts ... die oberste Haut einer Glasfläche» (35). With Leo gone, the old unity of the society breaks. «Verzweiflung» induces the awareness that «I» is «nothing.» Whence H. H. will write that «our history» is now undermined with doubt (36); for it is clear that he now sees this history as «deine Geschichte,» meaning in the monologue his own history, the ego's history, which is here without coherence in despair. Therefore H. H. writes his chronicle in Halleresque solitude: «ich stehe noch immer dem Chaos gegenüber» (36).

Chapter iii opens with a glimpse of the truth which dawns upon H. H. in chapter v. He writes now that the voyage went towards the light, that it was an unbreakable procession through darkness. He is already partly aware that his desperate egotism is itself an aspect of the voyage: this ambivalence of the voyage, light in darkness moving towards light, will soon make itself known through H. H.'s darkness, when Leo emerges from a dark house. But first H. H. has to describe how he came to find Leo's address.

It is recalled that the *idea* of the voyage is now not in doubt. What H. H. doubts is himself. His problem, as a fragmentary isolated ego, is to conquer despair and recover unity of self by recovering his faith. He knows that it is necessary to get beyond the idea, whose «grounds in the intellect» (37) have not the power of faith to unify the self which is «verzweifelt.» As the idea of the voyage replaced the faith of the voyage when Leo vanished, so now the tenuous idea is insufficient for H. H.[3] He now takes the first step towards the recovery of faith in a way which echoes Sinclair's experience in *Demian*: H. H. finds that his experience is shared by another person. His friend Lukas, who is for H. H. a light in the darkness as Lukas is the same as *lux,* tells him how he re-lived and re-united his scattered memories of the war by writing them down –which is just what H. H. has tried to do with his memories of the society. Lukas also tells H. H. exactly what he has already told himself: «Vielleicht hat der Mensch nächst dem Hunger nach Erlebnis keinen stärkeren Hunger als den nach Vergessen» (40). Lukas describes how he wrote his memoirs in grisly monologue among his remembered dead, as H. H. is also writing his, as a means to conquering despair, and to save himself from suicide: «es war die einzige Möglichkeit meiner Rettung vor dem Nichts« (40). H. H. is now ready to work on memory as a threshold of faith: «durch meinen Dienst am Gedächtnis jener hohen Zeit mich selbst etwas zu reinigen und zu erlösen, mich wieder in Verbindung mit dem Bund zu bringen» (53).

The labor of despair now finds a simple reward: Lukas looks up Leo in the telephone directory. The number of his house is 69 a. The number is a unity, divisible, but divisible only by the number 3, which is itself indivisible. Thus 69 a symbolizes the voyage in despair as a moment of division within an unbreakable unity. The number 69 also remains 69 when stood on its head; and it is thus a symbolic number for the Heraclitan conception of the voyage, towards which H. H.'s mind in its monologue is working: «The way up and the way down are one and the same»:[4] faith and despair are both predicates of the

---

3 Carlsson (in *Dank an Hermann Hesse* [Frankfurt, 1952], p. 96) proposes that H. H. finally knows in triumph the «timelessness of his idea.» But this is to introduce Hegel where he has no place.
4 Diels, *Fragmente der Vorsokratiker*, Vol. I, Fr. 60.

process called «voyage.» The letter *a* here would signify «beginning»; and Leo has, or is, the «original.» And the street where Leo lives is «Seilergraben,» the significance of which will become clear when Leo appears in chapter iv and H. H. notes that he is wearing canvas shoes with rope soles.[5]

Writing his last two chapters, not piecemeal as the first three, but at a single sitting, H. H. is no longer cut off from the society and the voyage. Chapter iv tells of his meeting with Leo two evenings before; and Chapter v recounts the consequences of this meeting. He is now writing on the day after his readmission to the society. He says: «ich weiß noch nicht, ist meine Sache ... eigentlich gefördert worden oder nicht»; and then: «vorgestern abend ist mein Wunsch in Erfüllung gegangen. Oh, und wie ist er in Erfüllung gegangen!» (43). The mixed feelings with which he ends his book show that he is not yet wholly delivered from despair; and, as his «wish» was to meet Leo again (the mood at this meeting is by no means exultant), it is not to be supposed either that this wish was a triumphal re-entry into the society, or that its fulfillment implied a complete recovery of faith. It is the crowning irony of *Die Morgenlandfahrt* that its last words are here hidden, at the beginning of the penultimate chapter: «ich weiß noch nicht, ist meine Sache ... eigentlich gefördert worden oder nicht.»

H. H. stands outside Seilergraben 69 and hears someone whistling upstairs. These birdnotes («Vogeltöne»), commonplace as they are, seem sweetness itself to him (44). An old man passes, with a sickly and sunken face, stops, listens, smiles to H. H., then passes on. Here there is an echo of *Kurgast* (1925), for H. H. listening to the

5 Seilergraben in Zürich may be the source of this street-name, as Morbio (5 km. east of Mendrisio, in Italian Switzerland) is the source of Morbio Inferiore.

whistler is the Hesse who asked there for a moment's ecstasy from his invalid body, and the old man who passes is the aging Hesse of 1932. Thus in the monologue, the moment this «old man» leaves H. H., the latter knows that this must be Leo the lithe psychocrat whistling, servant of the society, the master-voyager, the self who is fully alive and delivered from afflictions of «Zahl und Zeit.» It is twilight, and the house is unlit. Leo walks out into the gathering darkness; and H. H. now recognizes him as the comrade of «ten or more years ago,» whistling, he is now sure, the music of the pilgrimage (45). He notes: Leo walks with elastic gait, is wearing sandals or gym-shoes: yet he is «abendlich.» This light gait, and this «Abendmensch» quality, are both characteristics of Hesse himself, as works diverse as *Knulp* and *Der Steppenwolf* show, and they appear now recreated in H. H.'s Halleresque monologue, as Hesse projects himself into the antinomies of H. H. and Leo. Leo is no bright-faced Max Demian. His face is not shown at all. But here he is characteristically the man in whom light and dark are entwined, himself a personification of the ambivalent voyage. So now, as H. H. follows Leo unobserved, streetlamps are lit, and surrounding light increases (45). But under the trees in the park, where Leo halts, it is «quite dark,» except for Leo's bright grey eyes (46). This park lies near «St. Pauls Tor.» Here H. H. will now play the egotist, just as he does the next day when Leo enters the «Pauluskirche» (66). The pun on the word «Tor» here does not prove significant until, under trial, H. H. learns how ridiculous his «novice's fooleries» have been, for this is what his errors will be called; then he will see how wrong was his irreverent egotism in such proximity to the apostolic spirit, whether symbolized in the hidden Pauline sense of «Tor,» or personified in Leo as he later appears in Papal regalia.

H. H. now sees that Leo is wearing canvas shoes with

rope soles: there is now complete clarity of vision in the closed monologue. Here is signified the encounter of the divided («verzweifelt») H. H. with the single-minded Leo: for Leo not only lives in «*Seiler*graben,» he also wears shoes with *rope* soles: there is consistency of where he *stays* with what he *moves* on. This in itself would succinctly represent the conjunction of the opposites: H. H. at odds with himself, and Leo at one with himself. But there are other possible implications in this rope-imagery; they may seem far-fetched, but such remote associations are not unusual in Hesse. It may be that he is here associating Leo with the conception of the *Bhagavad Gita*, that the universe is a necklace *strung* with God. Whence Leo might be associated with the «Inner Controller» of the *Brhadaranyaka Upanishad*, that «thread who from within controls this and the other world and all beings.» Another possible implication is that idea which very often recurs in Hesse's work and which he expressed in a letter dated 1930: «wir sind Fäden im Schleier» and «wir werden gelebt.»[6] Again, Leo does now appear to be enacting Nietzsche's image in *Zarathustra*, an image which also underlay *Der Steppenwolf*: «Der Mensch ist ein Seil, geknüpft zwischen Tier und Übermensch,–ein Seil über einem Abgrunde.»[7] It is not necessary to bear these possible significations of the rope-imagery in mind, however, as long as Leo's capacity as «Inner Controller» gradually asserts itself in the narrative of H. H.'s monologue of its own accord, and as long as we recognize the emergence, at this stage in the metaphor of the voyage, of H. H.'s new conception of its meaning:

6 Hermann Hesse, *Briefe* (Berlin-Frankfurt, 1951), p. 36.
7 *Also sprach Zarathustra* (Musarion ed., XIII, 11). Nietzsche's image itself is a variation of *Bhagavad Gita*, VII, 7, and of *Brhadaranyaka Upanishad*, III, 7, 1. Homer and Plato used kindred images: see *Iliad* VIII, 18 f., *Laws*, 644 and 803–44, and *Theatetus*, 155 D. Likewise Hölderlin in the poem called «Blödigkeit.» Hesse's interest in Oriental thought dates from *Gertrud* (1910).

namely the Taoist concept of *yu*, which is «a spiritual not a bodily journey.»[8]

Leo seems not to recognize H. H. When H. H. says that he was a musician, but sold his violin, Leo remarks that this could only happen in despair, and that he is reminded of the story of Saul and David (47–48). H. H. does not recognize that Leo's words echo the story he has told already himself, of the young man who was cursed by the spokesman. For now, like Saul, H. H. lies under a curse, the curse of despair: he only hopes that Leo will deliver him, as David with his harp delivered Saul from the evil spirit (cf. «Erbfeind,» 29). On this level of the monologue, then, Leo and H. H. personify Hesse's faith and despair respectively. Thus, when Leo gets up to go, he still does not recognize H. H., for the latter has still no faith in him: H. H. remains cursed, «verzweifelt,» as he expressly states (49). He is rejected by Leo, as he is rejected by the dog which Leo summons out of the darkness, because he has rejected Leo, and because he has no faith in him. He says he is too weary to «stroll through the night,» as Leo proposes. This fatigue springs from his fear of humiliation (51). But if the proud and desperate egotist goes home refusing humiliation, at home his despair rises to such a pitch that he writes to Leo his full confession (53). Once his despair has reached that depth at which it bursts through into penitence, engaging the whole self, Leo the next morning comes of his own will into the room where H. H. is sleeping. He is now ready to learn of the ambivalence of the spiritual journey, for he has traversed despair, and has got beyond the brittle realm of ideas. Yet, even at the end of the fourth chapter, H. H. is still thinking of the voyage as time past. In the fifth chapter, therefore, he must suffer an increase of self-knowledge. Before he can re-enter the realm of faith, he

8 A. Waley, *Three Ways of Thought in Ancient China* (London, 1946), p. 61.

has to descend deeper into the shaft of his memory. Soon in his monologue he will look into the dark archive of his memory and find there the voyage as a perpetual process. He will look into the last recess, where Leo, the «Inner Controller,» and H. H. stand undivided, the one receiving fullness and form from the other.

It is the egotist H. H. who is awakened the next morning by Leo's entering his room: «Man erinnerte sich meiner, man rief mich, man wollte mich anhören, mich vielleicht zur Rechenschaft ziehen ... Ich war bereit ... zu gehorchen» (54–55). Later called the «egotism of impatience» (66), this mentality clings to H. H. as Leo guides him to the headquarters of the society. He is kept waiting when Leo goes to pray in the Pauluskirche, the route they take seems unnecessarily devious, for, he says: «alles stand für mich auf dem Spiel, mein ganzes künftiges Leben würde sich entscheiden, mein ganzes gewesenes Leben würde jetzt seinen Sinn erhalten oder vollends verlieren» (55). This agitated self-concern persists when they enter the society's buildings: they see Klingsor at work but, H. H. writes: «ich wagte ihn nicht zu begrüßen, dazu war noch nicht die Zeit, ich war erwartet, ich war vorgeladen» (56). The spirit of selflessness, however, which rules the society, is evident the moment Leo and H. H. arrive on the top floor: «Niemand kümmerte sich um uns, alles war lautlos beschäftigt» (56). It is recalled that Leo, when H. H. found him, was living at the top of a house (his whistling came from an upstairs window). In his case it might appear that the top of a building represents, in the monologue, a residence of «higher powers,» just as in this present case of the headquarters of the society. In Leo's case, it is the power of joy, elasticity, ecstasy; in the second case, it is the power of judgment, particularly of self-judgment. The meaning is found earlier also in Hesse, namely in «Kinderseele»: «Unten in unsrer Wohnung waren Mutter und Kind zu Hause, dort wehte harmlose

Luft; hier oben wohnten Macht und Geist, hier waren Gericht und Tempel und das Reich des Vaters» (III, 437). So now, as H. H. realises that he is in the registry of the universe, as Leo sings, as the vast silent archive dissolves and becomes a hall of judgment, as Leo vanishes, H. H. is left in solitude to face his judges, and he is called a «self-accuser» (57).[9]

The purpose of the trial which now ensues is to show H. H. the vanity of egotism. He is allowed to continue writing his history of the society, and given access to the archives; but when he finds his own manuscript there he is utterly dismayed, for in it the fragmentary ego stands revealed as inadequate to its task; in the imagery of erasure, correction, and meaningless ornament he finds how wrong he has been. But now at least he is able to refer to the «original,» to the *Bundesbrief*, because, in the monologue, his egotism is undergoing purgation and is in decline. He finds the document in the «Chrysostom File, Cycle V, Strophe 39, 8.» But the script is unintelligible. It is unintelligible as was Sinclair's dream of incest in *Demian*, and Haller's neon-sign between the church and the clinic in *Der Steppenwolf*: in all three cases the inability to grasp the meaning of the «original» in memory, or in the imagery which the protagonist projects upon the cavern wall of his monologue, is due to insufficient self-knowledge. Thus now H. H. will accuse himself afresh, of having tried to write the history of the society while he remained in ignorance of himself: «mich selber nicht begreifend» (62). Only by self-judgment then can he ar-

9 It is appropriate that Albertus Magnus should number among H. H.'s judges. His Neoplatonism stressed the kenotic «Entwerdungs-mystik» of Augustine, and his commentaries on Dionysius the Areopagite were treasuries for early Swabian religious thinkers (cf. H. O. Bürger, *Die Gedankenwelt der großen Schwaben* [Stuttgart-Tübingen, 1951], pp. 71 ff.) Himself a Swabian, Hesse writes of the conquest of the empirical ego in its theological context in a letter dated Jan. 1933: das Sichweggeben oder, wie die deutschen Mystiker es einst nannten, das «Entwerden» (*Briefe*, p. 102).

rive in the monologue at the recognition that it is his «Verzweiflung» which has separated him from his «Inner Controller» by splitting his individuality. Only now in the monologue can he humbly hear Leo pronounce forgiveness for his sins: and Leo now appears to him in Papal regalia, which recalls his role as servant, since «Servant of the servants of God» has been a Papal title since Gregory the Great. Leo explains that H. H. is still in the midst of despair (68), but that this despair must be overcome if the soul is to be «awakened» (68). And here one recalls Leo's reference to the story of Saul and David, and that the «evil spirit,» which afflicted Saul, was «from God» (I *Sam.* XVI, 23).

From Leo's words it may now be deduced how the *Bundesbrief* came to be in the Chrysostom File. We may now even translate »Zyklus V, Strophe 39,8» into «*Gesammelte Dichtungen*, V, 308»: for it is here in *Narziss und Goldmund* that Narziss realises that Goldmund has traversed hell without losing sight of God. In the terms of *Die Morgenlandfahrt*: it is possible and necessary to traverse despair («Verzweiflung») without losing faith in the society («Bund»). Implicit here is H. H.'s understanding this. It is the principle of the monologic form that all events in the narrative are events in the psyche of the protagonist. Thus H. H. looks for the original *Bundesbrief*, the document of unity and faith, in the Chrysostom File, his self-projecting author, Hermann Hesse, having deliberately put it there.

The burning of the papers which now follows consequently signifies H. H.'s readiness at this stage to look through the forms of purgatory into the realities they contain. The forms here, as they were to Anselm in «Iris,» and as they were to Haller in *Der Steppenwolf* up to the moment when he took the image for the reality, are the envelopes of essences, not the essences themselves. H. H. announces that he is prepared to «ask the archive about himself.» Now begins his last «Blick ins Chaos,» the last stage of this quest of his identity. So he recognizes the chaos implicit in the three unreconcilable accounts of Leo's desertion in Morbio; and then he approaches a dark recess in the «Hesse Archive» («Chattorum res gestae»). He descends, as once Sinclair had done, into his ancestral memory.

Here he finds an image: it is a double figure with a single back, «eine alt und mitgenommen aussehende Plastik aus Holz oder Wachs, mit blassen Farben, eine Art Götze oder barbarisches Idol» (75). From what he has read in Leo's archive, the formula «Archiepisc. XIX. Diacon. D.VII. *cornu Ammon. 6*» (my italics), we should already be prepared here for a final representation of the spiritual continuum of the voyage, its primitive and pre-Christian content, as well as its function in a Christian civilization. The image which H. H. now discerns is indeed this final representation. He lights a candle, and he sees that the image is, on the one hand, an image of corruption and transience, while on the other hand it is firmly colored and formed as far as concerns the «other figure» (75). This «other figure» he recognizes as Leo. He lights a second candle and sees that the surface of the double figure is transparent, and that there is a gradual process of transsubstantiation from the one figure into the other. It is recalled that he had earlier written of his «Ich» as «die oberste Haut einer Glasfläche» (35). But now this image is transformed in the light of his new knowledge. This same «Ich» is no longer sheer fragile surface reflecting dismembered illusions; it is a transparent envelope of the Janus-like unity of the double figure: the unity of the ego and the *imago* of the «Inner Controller.» The connection between the two aspects of the figure, it might be added, recalls the process of individuation which Hesse has elsewhere called «Seelengestaltung.» H. H. thus now sees, «daß mein Bild im Begriffe war, sich mehr und mehr an Leo hinzugeben und zu verströmen, ihn zu nähren und zu stärken ... Er mußte wachsen, ich mußte abnehmen» (76). Trying to understand this process, H. H. recalls an earlier saying of Leo's, that poets transfuse their life into their creations as mothers transfuse theirs into their unborn children. By this is meant, in other terms, that despair may have its place as a fructifying force, however humble and insecure, in the hierarchy of faith. The image would thus endorse Nietzsche's axiom: «Ein höheres Wesen, als wir selber sind, zu schaffen ist *unser* Wesen. Über uns hinaus schaffen!»[10]

H. H. then goes to find a place where he can sleep. Thus he ends his fifth chapter as he ended his fourth, in sleep, so indicating that the desperate insomnia of unremitting and sterile reflection, from which Haller suffered, is at least for the present ended, even if his fate must remain for the time being undecided. For, he has already concluded, «ich weiß noch nicht, ist meine Sache dadurch eigentlich gefördert worden oder nicht.»

In the foregoing analysis I have tried to show how, in *Die Morgenlandfahrt,* Hesse was recreating themes and figures out of his earlier writings into a concise verbal representation of the essentials of his own mental history. To achieve this end, he used a form of symbologistic monologue (a form whose scope he had already begun to explore in *Demian,* and which he had developed extensively for *Der Steppenwolf*), and he used a metaphor (that of the voyage) to substantialize the rarest regions of his thought.[11] In a letter dated 1935 he called the book an articulation of faith.[12] But his narrative exhibits also an enaction of that conflict between faith and unfaith which Goethe judged to be the crucial theme of history.[13]

10 *Die Unschuld des Werdens* (Leipzig, 1931), II, 446.
11 An account of the evolution of the monologic from in Hesse's writings is given in the present writer's dissertation, *Hermann Hesse as Humanist* (Diss. D. Phil., Oxford, 1954).    12 *Briefe,* p. 170.
13 *Noten und Abhandlungen zum West-Östlichen Diwan,* Jubiläums-Ausgabe, V, 247–8.

This faith is not merely that of a literary man in search of a religion. The special, symbologistic form of monologue shows that *Die Morgenlandfahrt* was Hesse's *anima poetae* in a stricter sense; and it is clear that this faith means an unshakable awareness of relations existing between the whole being of the individual and the holy. Thus in a letter of 1932 Hesse discourses on what he calls «das Heilige» in his book, meaning by this «the possibility of human society and its real meaning.»[14] Though he treated of these relations here only within the scope of an imagined hierarchy of human beings, the «Bund,» Hesse does by implication articulate a faith in an inner coherence among human beings of all sorts. He does this by showing for ordinary things or events corresponding psychic events, the correspondences being established in the monologic form. For the world of this monologue is as it is manifest in the psyche. All that the narrative exhibits is at once psychic and phenomenal. The conflict of which the book tells thus concerns the desperations of solipsism, and the struggle to arrive at authentic vision by cleansing the gates of perception. It is the struggle to arrive at the substantial and sacred grounds of being. In Hesse's later writing, as in Rilke's, all things do seem to turn upon an awareness of an order in things devolving from their sacred center, which is called «invisible.» Leo thus has this in common with the Angel of the *Duineser Elegien*, that he stands for his creator's awareness of a relation with this «invisible.» So is Hesse's H. H. lost in rootlessness the moment he «clings to the visible,» as Rilke has it in the letter to von Hulewicz. And as Rilke knew the «terror» of the Angel, so has Hesse known the tempter «despair» which besets the creative imagination in an age of unbelief. The monologic form of *Die Morgenlandfahrt* was appropriate, for the book was Hesse's final exploration of the world of despair. *Das Glasperlenspiel,*

14 *Briefe*, p. 73.

in which Leo is transformed into Josef Knecht, was to be a book of faith in the invisible. Thus Hesse wrote at the head of *Das Glasperlenspiel*: «nichts entzieht sich der Darstellung durch Worte so sehr und nichts ist doch notwendiger, den Menschen vor Augen zu stellen, als gewisse Dinge, deren Existenz weder beweisbar noch wahrscheinlich ist, welche aber eben dadurch, daß fromme und gewissenhafte Menschen sie gewissermaßen als seiende Dinge behandeln, dem Sein und der Möglichkeit des Geborenwerdens um einen Schritt näher geführt werden.»

# 6

JOSEPH MILECK

DAS GLASPERLENSPIEL

Genesis, Manuscripts, and History
of Publication

To argue that the genesis of a literary work of art is
indispensable for its understanding is to suggest that art
cannot quite speak for itself. On the other hand, to give
no heed to the genesis is to ignore what could upon occasion be a significant aid in dealing either with form or
with substance. This is most certainly true of Hermann
Hesse's enigmatic *Glasperlenspiel*.

The sporadic publication of various segments of the
novel from 1934 to 1942 left the critics rather puzzled.
The finished novel, which appeared in 1943, proved to be
equally perplexing. Hesse's own frequent references in his
published letters to the genesis of the novel and his sug-
gestions as to its interpretation have tended, if anything,
to add to the general perplexity.[1] Perhaps it has been this
very factor that has kept the critics fascinated over the
years. At any rate, since 1946, when *Das Glasperlenspiel*
first became readily available in Germany, enough has
been written about it to fill a half dozen or more sizable
volumes.[2]

This mass of secondary literature, mired in controversy

1 *Briefe*, Erweiterte Ausgabe (Frankfurt a. M.: Suhrkamp, 1964), pp.
89–90, 105, 111, 126, 128, 129–130, 132, 147, 201, 204, 205, 206–209,
211–212, 227, 236, 241–242, 247, 265, 274–275, 286–288, 293–294,
320, 339, 409, 418, 435–439, 457, 473, 531.
*Blätter vom Tage* (Zürich: Gebr. Fretz, 1948), 16 pp.: »Brief einer
Schülerin über Josef Knechts Tod und Antwort des Autors« (Nov.
1947), pp. 3–6; «Antwort an einen Studenten der mit dem *Glasperlenspiel* nichts anfangen kann . . .» (May 1948), pp. 7–8.
Portion of a letter to his sister Adele Gundert (1934), *Prosa aus dem
Nachlaß* (Frankfurt a.M.: Suhrkamp, 1965), pp. 604–605.
2 See Otto Bareiss, *Hermann Hesse. Eine Bibliographie der Werke
über Hermann Hesse* (Basel: Karl Maier-Bader & Co. Teil I, 1962,

189

from the outset, proposes a multitude of severely conflicting interpretations, compositional observations, and value judgments.3 In the hope of resolving some of this controversy, critics have begun in more recent years to concentrate on the novel's genesis, seeking either a better point of departure for their studies or external supportive evidence for their interpretive and structural observations.4 Their intentions have been good but their efforts somewhat premature. The genesis of *Das Glasperlenspiel* is complex; attempts to reconstruct it based exclusively on Hesse's often oblique and cryptic published letter references could only add error to controversy. This need no longer be the case. Revealing facts are now at the critic's disposal. The manuscripts, memoranda, and unpublished letters in the Hesse-*Nachlaß* have finally made possible a functional reconstruction of the genesis.5 Though this reconstruction is neither ideally detailed nor itself beyond dispute (bold speculation had to be substituted occasionally

118 pp. [Bücher, Dissertationen]; Teil II, 1964, 228 pp. [Zeitschriften- und Zeitungsaufsätze]).

Helmut Waibler, *Hermann Hesse. Eine Bibliographie.* (Bern & München: Franke, 1962), 350 pp.

3 See Joseph Mileck, *Hermann Hesse and His Critics. The Criticism and Bibliography of Half a Century* (Chapel Hill: The University of North Carolina Press, 1958), pp 178–192.

4 Theodore Ziolkowski, *The Novels of Hermann Hesse. A Study in Theme and Structure* (Princeton: Princeton University Press, 1965), pp. 283, 294–301, 307–309, 337.

Mark Boulby, «Der vierte Lebenslauf as a Key to *Das Glasperlenspiel*,» *Modern Language Review*, 61 (1966), 635–646.

Theodore Ziolkowski, «Hermann Hesse: Der vierte Lebenslauf», *The Germanic Review*, 42 (1967), 124–143.

Mark Boulby, *Hermann Hesse. His Mind and Art* (Ithaca: Cornell University Press, 1967), pp. 262–267, 312–314.

5 The Hesse-*Nachlaß* was deposited in the Schiller-Nationalmuseum, Marbach a.N., in the autumn of 1964. The Hesse-*Archiv* was officially opened on Feb. 23, 1965.

Two studies, both based upon manuscripts in the Hesse-*Nachlaß*, appeared after this article was written:

Roger C. Norton («Variant Endings of Hesse's *Glasperlenspiel*,» *Monatshefte*, 60 [1968], 141–146) finds supportive evidence for a very positive interpretation of the novel's cryptic conclusion in the manu-

where information was inadequate) it should provide new insights into both the substance and the form of *Das Glasperlenspiel* and will make possible a broader and more informed scholarship.

## The Beginnings

Reflecting upon the genesis of *Das Glasperlenspiel* in a very significant letter (January 1955) to Rudolf Pannwitz, Hesse remarks:

> In den Jahren, die zwischen der ersten Konzeption und dem wirklichen Beginn der Arbeit am Buche lagen und in denen ich noch zwei andre Aufgaben zu erfüllen hatte, hat die Dichtung ... mir in wechselnden Gestalten vorgeschwebt. ... Es waren für mich Jahre leidlichen Wohlergehens nach einer ernsten Lebenskrise ... (*Briefe*, p. 437)

Since the two other tasks and the severe crisis could only refer to *Narziß und Goldmund* and to the difficult *Steppenwolf* period, and since this crisis was over by the end of 1926[6] and *Narziß und Goldmund* was begun in the middle of 1927,[7] it is reasonable to conclude–assum-

script fragments «Schluß» and «Ende des Ludi magister» (see Prosa Manuscripts *b* and *j*).

G. W. Field («On the Genesis of the *Glasperlenspiel*,» *The German Quarterly*, 41 [1968], 673–688) is less interested in an extensive genesis of the novel than in its very interesting but more confined evolution under the impact of political events. He draws attention to some of the unpublished manuscripts and memoranda relevant to the novel's genesis–to Hesse's initial autograph plans for his work, to his memoranda of 1934, to «Schluß,» «Ende des Ludi magister,» and to «Ende des Magister Musicae» (see Prose Manuscripts *a*, *f*, *b*, *j*, and *n*, respectively)–then concentrates on the textual differences between the third and the final version of the «Einleitung» and the first and the printed version of Knecht's «Rundschreiben.»

6 According to unpublished letters (*Schweizerische Landesbibliothek*, Bern) to Helene Welti (Sept. and Dec. 1926), *Der Steppenwolf* was begun in 1924 and the first draft was finished in Dec. 1926.

7 According to an unpublished letter (*Schweizerische Landesbibliothek*, Bern) to Helene Welti (Dec. 19, 1928).

ing that his memory served him well–that Hesse first began to think about his novel early in 1927.

In this same letter to Pannwitz, Hesse elaborates upon his initial thoughts. It had occurred to him that reincarnation could be an excellent symbol of the element of stability existing in the midst of life's flux and of the continuity of tradition and things intellectual. Then one day he envisaged a type of biography which could be both personal and timeless, the story of an individual who in several reincarnations experiences the great epochs of human history.[8] These were the seeds of thought from which Hesse's novel was to sprout.

In a brief typescript memorandum of June 1934 (see Prose Manuscripts f), Hesse notes: «Die Dichtung, in deren Mitte die Idee des Glasperlenspiels steht, hängt mit der *Morgenlandfahrt* zusammen, ihre ersten Anfänge stammen aus dem Jahre 1930/31.» The second version of this memorandum (June 1934) reads «stammen vom Ende des Jahres 1930.»

In a letter of October-November 1934 (*Briefe*, pp. 129–130), Hesse mentions that he began to occupy himself with his new project after he had put the finishing touches to his *Morgenlandfahrt*. The latter was completed in April 1931.[9]

On the reverse side of a letter from Gebr. Fretz A.G., Zürich (April 30, 1931), Hesse refers to or briefly outlines five »Lebensläufe« (see Prose Manuscripts *a*). The undated document was actually drawn up in two stages. The initial plan in ink consists only of biographies I, II, and IV. Biographies III and V were added in pencil presumably a few days or at most a few weeks thereafter. Hesse's vision of 1927 was assuming shape. As yet, these

8 Hesse gives expression to similar thoughts in his letter of 1934 to his sister Adele Gundert, *Prosa aus dem Nachlaß* (1965), p. 604.
9 See Hesse's remarks on the typescript of the tale in the Leuthold-Hesse-Collection, *Eidgenössische Technische Hochschule*, Zürich.

biographies have no titles and their hero is known only as X. The first of them was obviously to become «Der Regenmacher.» The second is too briefly outlined to permit meaningful conjecture. The third is vaguely suggestive of «Der Beichtvater.» The fourth might have become Hesse's own story and that of the twentieth century; perhaps the «feuilletonistisches Zeitalter» of the novel's introduction is all that came of this intended reincarnation. The fifth biography is unmistakably that of Knecht and Castalia, the embryo of what was ultimately to become the novel proper. The name Castalia does not yet appear and the hero is still only known as X, but the nature of the «Perlenspiel» and its *Blütezeit* and *Verfall* and reasons for its decline are already clearly defined. The detailed exposé of this fifth biography also suggests that the «Perlenspieler» and their realm had already become Hesse's major preoccupation. The other biographies were indeed soon shelved in its favor.

On the reverse side of a letter from the *Neue Rundschau* (June 22, 1931, see Prose Manuscripts *b*), Hesse next outlined a possible conclusion for his fifth biography (undated typescript). His hero is now called Knecht and the «Perlenspieler» have become «Glasperlenspieler.» Reference is made to an important conversation between Knecht and the «Führer der Diktatur,» to Knecht's refusal to place himself and his institution at the disposal of the state, to his final Game, and to his death. Knecht's last Game reflects his undying conviction in the ultimate victory of *Geist* over evil worldly powers. Hesse never made use of this conclusion. He was to insert contemporary German politics briefly into the third version of this introduction, but in the manner of social comment and not of a dramatic physical confrontation.

In summary: thoughts related to *Das Glasperlenspiel* arose in Hesse's mind as early as 1927; but they did not engage him seriously until he had finished his *Morgen-*

*landfahrt* in April 1931. Initially one tale and two re-incarnations were to demontrate Hesse's belief in the ever-never-changing nature of human life. Plans for two more reincarnations were added almost immediately, and the last of these, Knecht and a glass-bead-game, began at once to absorb Hesse. It seems that Hesse's new project at this early stage was simply to comprise a series of Novellen, clearly linked thematically yet merely jux-taposed compositionally. Nothing as yet suggests the closer-knit structure of the finished novel.

Hesse's plan of 1931 had hardly been conceived before it started to change. When the bead-game tale moved rapidly into the foreground of his interest and in plan assumed unanticipated proportions, it gradually became divorced from the initial project and seemed destined to become a separate book publication. It is specifically to this tale and not to his multistory project that Hesse refers when he mentions a new book in letters of January and July 1933 to Gottfried Bermann and Thomas Mann (*Briefe*, pp. 90, 105). The first three versions of the in-troduction (1931–33) were also specifically intended for this bead-game book; no mention is yet made in these of any writings by Knecht, nor are any other provisions made for the inclusion or attachment of other tales. A letter to Thomas Mann written toward the end of 1933 suggests that another change of mind must have brought the bead-game tale and the other biographies together again sometime after July. This letter indicates that an eighteenth-century tale was likely to be added to the project Hesse alludes to his absorption with biographies of eighteenth-century Pietists and then adds: «Dabei wächst die Vorstellung von meinem seit zwei Jahren vor-handenen Plan (dem mathematischmusikalischen Geist-Spiel) zur Vorstellung eines bändereichen Werkes . . .» (*Briefe*, p. III). The bead-game tale seems now not only to have been reunited with the other biographies but structurally to have assumed a central, dominant position; the parenthetical remark equates the bead-game tale with the whole project. This departure from an original only loosely juxtaposed series of stories marks the emergence of the more complex structure of Hesse's finished novel.

It is undoubtedly this new structure that Hesse had in mind when in his preface for «Der Regenmacher» (sent to the *Neue Rundschau* on Feb. 20, 1934) he explains that the tale is but part of «eines weit größeren Ganzen.» It was also this new structure which compelled Hesse to discard the third version of the introduction for his bead-game tale. From one of many biographies, this bead-game tale was to become the structural backbone of Hesse's *now* envisaged novel, and the remaining stories were to become appendages. The third version of the introduction had to be rewritten accordingly. This was done between March and September of 1934. A Castalian narrator of the year 2400 was introduced so that Knecht's story could be told in distant retrospect, permitting a convincing inclusion of his extant manuscripts.[10] The biographies were simply to be incorporated as Knecht's manuscripts. According to an autograph fragment of early 1935 (see Prose Manuscripts *h*) these biographies were at first assigned, as school exercises, to Knecht's Waldzell years. When Hesse decided also to ascribe poems to Knecht (about May 1935), he shifted the prose to the later *Studienjahre*.

According to Boulby's conjectured genesis, *Das Glasperlenspiel* had its origin in the not entirely successful marriage in 1933 of two originally separate themes: the «transtemporal biography» of the late Twenties and the Castalia-utopia conceived by the end of 1931. The novel's

10 The narrator in the preceding versions is not a Castalian. He tells his story in 2197 and is more or less a contemporary of Knecht's. The name Castalia appears for the first time in Chapter 1 («Die Berufung»); in the printed introduction, reference is still only made to «unsere Provinz.»

internal compositional inconsistencies are attributed to this original bifocality of theme.[11] According to the initial stages of the novel as traced above, compositional flaws are more accurately to be ascribed to Hesse's regrouping in 1933–34 of thematically related tales which he had linked structurally in 1931 to demonstrate a thesis of 1927.

Ziolkowski's contention, too, that the most serious of the novel's compositional flaws are to be attributed to Hesse's shift in the course of writing from detached aestheticism to responsible social involvement fails to accord with the demonstrated facts of the genesis.[12] Hesse's rejection of a Castalia-utopia which has become socially irresponsible in its aestheticism is already present in his initial exposé (1931) of the fifth biography. It is not Hesse but only Knecht who shifts his ideological allegiance in the course of composition–a shift occasioned by a change in the relationship between author and hero. It is to this change in Hesse's relationship to Knecht that Ziolkowski's structural flaws might better have been ascribed: a change from objective depiction of a representative of a decaying realm–an exemplary Magister Ludi not to be identified with the author–to self-projection. In this identification, Knecht becomes ideologically what Hesse was from the beginning, and with this identification, ultimate defection became a likelihood.[13] The reference to friction between Knecht and Castalia introduced in the fourth version of the introduction (1934) marks the beginning of this change in Hesse's relationship to his hero.[14] That

11 Boulby, op. cit., pp. 264–267.
12 Ziolkowski, op. cit., pp. 283, 294, 334.
13 In this regard it may be noted that in the most personal of the four biographies, the eighteenth-century fragment with which Hesse was preoccupied when he wrote the fourth version of the introduction, the hero also defects. Knecht's defection from the Castalian hierarchy is clearly anticipated in Josef's abandonment of the church hierarchy for greater self-realization as a simple church organist devoted to his music.
14 *Gesammelte Schriften* (Frankfurt a.M.: Suhrkamp, 1957), VI, 82.

Knecht's quarrel with Castalia is here only hinted at, and that no specific mention is made of his ultimate defection (flaws singled out by Ziolkowski), is merely indicative of plans not yet worked out in detail and should not be construed as proof of Hesse's lingering aestheticism. This does not, of course, alter the fact that Knecht's life is indeed not adequately anticipated in the introduction, a blemish which Hesse might well and could easily have removed in the book publication of his novel.

## The *Einleitung*

Die Einleitung, die ich als Kuriosität hier zur Aufbewahrung gebe, wurde dreimal geschrieben. Die hier vorliegende ist die dritte Fassung, sie wurde im Frühsommer 1932 beendet, nahezu ein Jahr vor den deutschen Ereignissen vom März 1933. Da diese Einleitung heute in Deutschland nicht gedruckt werden könnte, habe ich im Mai und Juni eine vierte zum Teil veränderte Fassung vollendet. (Montagnola im Juni 1934)

Since the autograph first version of the introduction (see Prose Manuscripts *l*) and the typescript copies of versions two, three, and four are undated (see Prose Manuscripts *d*), this typescript memorandum assumes considerable importance and merits careful examination (see Prose Manuscripts *f*).

According to an undated remark jotted down in pencil on the first sheet of «Versuch einer Geschichte des Glasperlenspiels. II. Fassung,» a typescript copy of this version was sent to Gottfried Bermann. It is undoubtedly to this manuscript, which lacks the Latin translation of the motto, that Hesse makes reference in a letter to Bermann, January 28, 1933 (*Briefe*, p. 89). It must have been mailed to Bermann in the autumn of 1932 before Hesse received Franz Schall's Latinized version of the motto in a letter dated November 29, 1932 (Hesse-*Nachlaß*). In this letter of January 28, 1933, Hesse alludes to an expanded second version: «Hinzugekommen sind seit der Niederschrift des Vorworts einige Details zu diesem Vorwort, sowie die lateinische Wendung des Mottos . . .» The «einige Details» actually consist of three inclusions: a one-page autograph on verso of a letter dated July 16, 1931, and two pages of typescript, one of which (Hesse's caustic sociopolitical comment which was omitted from the final, printed version) is on verso of a letter dated August 1, 1932. In a typescript note to his wife, January 19, 1933 (Hesse-*Nachlaß*), Hesse calls this expanded second version «die dritte, vielleicht annähernd endgültige Fassung» and states that it was completed that very day. In view of the above evidence, the third version proper, which is the expanded second version revised and again expanded, could only have been written after January 1933[15] and not «im Frühsommer 1932,» as Hesse states in his memorandum of June 1934.

It must certainly be to this third version, and not to the first, that Hesse alludes in his letter of January 1955 to Rudolf Pannwitz:

> In meinem ersten Manuskript gab es einige Abschnitte, namentlich in der Vorgeschichte, die mit Leidenschaft gegen die Diktatoren und die Vergewaltigung des Lebens und Geistes Stellung nahmen: diese in der endgültigen Fassung größernteils gestrichenen Kampfansagen wurden in meinem deutschen Freundeskreise heimlich abgeschrieben und verbreitet. (*Briefe*, p. 438)

It was because he knew full well that this direct, caustic comment on the political situation in Germany would preclude eventual publication and because his modified plans of 1933–34 called for a revision of the introduction that Hesse discounts this third version in his letter to his sister Adele, March 1934:

15 The third version must have been written soon after January. «Der Regenmacher» had still to be tended to in 1933, and in the autumn Hesse became engrossed in the eighteenth-century biography.

Denn wenn auch die Einleitung zum Glasperlenspiel unmöglich und wertlos geworden und noch durch keine andre ersetzt ist, so sind die Gedanken dran doch weiter gegangen, und ein Bruchstück ist auch geschrieben worden, das ich Dir einmal zeigen werde.[16]

The «Bruchstück» here referred to is probably the beginning of the fourth version, which was to omit politics and to provide for his new alignment of the biographies, and which, according to Hesse's memorandum of June 1934, was written in May-June 1934. If the expression «zum Teil veränderte Fassung» of this memorandum is to be taken literally, Hesse must have continued to revise his fourth version during the summer months, for there is considerable difference between the third version and the version sent to the *Neue Rundschau* on September 8, 1934.

In the middle of July 1933, Hesse wrote Thomas Mann that the «Vorwort» of his new book was written more than a year ago (*Briefe*, p. 105). Since the third version must have been written after January 1933, Hesse could only have had the first or the second version of his introduction in mind. If the former is the case, then it may be assumed that the first version, begun in the summer or autumn of 1931, was completed in the spring of 1932 and the second some time before the autumn of 1932 when a typescript copy was sent to Bermann. On the other hand, if this letter reference is to the second version, then it may be concluded that the first version was completed in late 1931 or early 1932 and the second version followed in the spring of 1932.

In summary: the first version of the «Einleitung» was completed in late 1931 or early 1932, the second before the end of November 1932, the third after January 1933, the fourth in June, or at the latest, by September 1934. The evolution of this introduction is remarkably similar

16 *Prosa aus dem Nachlaß* (1965), p. 604.

to the very Game it describes. What was a sociopolitical comment with specific contemporary dates and allusions to specific political and academic figures, political ideologies and events, becomes a philosophical observation. The abstract evolves from the concrete. What was anchored in time is elevated to myth.

## The *Lebensläufe*

For want of information, little can be said about the genesis of «Der Regenmacher.» It is obvious from Hesse's exposé of 1931 (see Prose Manuscript *a*) that he had already given considerable thought to this biography. It is probable that the tale was more or less finished when Hesse turned his attention to his eighteenth-century biography toward the end of 1933. It is possible that Hesse was able to find some time for «Der Regenmacher» while preoccupied with the first three versions of the introduction for his Castalia-tale (1931-33), but more probable that he put it aside until he had completed the last of these (early part of 1933). It is most likely, therefore, that «Der Regenmacher,» conceived in 1931, was finally written in 1933. At all events, according to Hesse's Records of Publications, the story was sent to the *Neue Rundschau* on February 20, 1934.[17] It appeared in print two months later.

Having completed or almost completed his «Regenmacher» by late 1933, Hesse began to steep himself in German Pietism of the eighteenth century. This diversion very quickly suggested a new possibility for his novel, another «Lebenslauf.» In a letter (end of 1933) to Thomas Mann, Hesse writes: «Ich lese, soweit die Augen es erlauben, pietistische Biographie des 18. Jahrhunderts,

17 Since Hesse customarily sent his manuscripts to publishers almost immediately after completing them, it is possible that he did not put the finishing touches to «Der Regenmacher» until Feb. 1934.

und weiß gar nicht mehr, was Produktivität eigentlich ist» (*Briefe*, p. III).

Hesse elaborates upon this new interest in his letter of March 1934 to his sister Adele:

> Eine der späteren Existenzen wird die eines schwäbischen Theologen aus der Zeit Bengels und Oetingers sein, daran, bin ich seit Monaten, d. h. erst an Vorbereitungen, zur Zeit habe ich aus einer Zürcher Bibliothek sämtliche Bände von Spangenbergs Leben des Grafen Zinzendorf bei mir ... auch ein württembergisches Gesangbuch vom Jahr 1700. ... .[18]

It is quite obvious that this eighteenth-century biography had become all-absorbing and that it had not yet begun to assume shape.

Hesse's next reference to his eighteenth-century biography in a letter of October-November 1934 adds little that is new:

> Studien habe ich manche getrieben, um meinen Plan zu nähren ... es gehörte dazu viel Lektüre aus dem 18. Jahrhundert, wo mir namentlich der schwäbische Pietist Oetinger sehr gefiel, auch Studien über klassische Musik, bei denen mir ein Neffe [Carlo Isenberg] half. ... (*Briefe*, p. 130)

No further allusions to this eighteenth-century biography appear in Hesse's published letters until 1955. Now, in his letter to Pannwitz (January 1955), Hesse finally fills out the genesis of this tale and accounts for its fate:

> Es gab übrigens in meinem Plan noch einen weiteren Lebenslauf, ins 18. Jahrhundert als die Zeit der großen Musikblüte verlegt, ich habe auch an diesem Gebilde nahezu ein Jahr lang gearbeitet und ihm mehr Studien gewidmet als allen andern Biographien Knechts, aber es ist mir nicht geglückt, das Ding blieb als Fragment liegen. Die allzu genau bekannte und allzu reich dokumentierte Welt jenes Jahrhunderts entzog sich dem

18 *Prosa aus dem Nachlaß* (1965), p. 604.

Einbau in die mehr legendären Räume der übrigen Leben Knechts. (*Briefe*, p. 436)[19]

Not one, but two versions of the eighteenth-century biography were attempted. These untitled and undated autograph fragments (see Prose Manuscripts g) were published posthumously as «Der vierte Lebenslauf» in *Prosa aus dem Nachlaß* (Frankfurt a. M.: Suhrkamp, 1965). This was followed by a separate book publication: *Der vierte Lebenslauf Josef Knechts* (Frankfurt a. M.: Suhrkamp, 1966), 163 pp.

On a scrap of paper (see Prose Manuscripts g) with autograph remarks about his eighteenth-century biography, Hesse noted that it was «Lebenslauf III.» This designation persuaded Ninon Hesse to conclude that Hesse intended the eighteenth-century biography to follow «Der Regenmacher» and «Der Beichtvater» in the finished novel.[20] Such was not the case. The III used by Hesse did not relate to the internal biographies of the novel but to Hesse's work schedule. The eighteenth-century biography was simply the third (following the Castalia-tale and «Der Regenmacher») of his «Lebensläufe» to receive his attention. Had it been incorporated in the novel it would have become the fourth internal biography, representing, as it does, the stage most immediately preceding Castalia and its glass-bead-game. Hesse indicates as much in his reference to it in the «Studienjahre» chapter of the novel,[21] and states as much on another scrap of paper (undated autograph in the Hesse-*Nachlaß*), the remains of a purple envelope which once must have contained these fragments: «2 Fassungen des nicht vollendeten *vierten* (Hesse's italics) Lebenslaufes.» The eighteenth-century biography was of course published

19 Hesse has his narrator give a similar account of the eighteenth-century biography in Chapter 3 («Studienjahre»). *Gesammelte Schriften*, VI, 192–193.
20 *Prosa aus dem Nachlaß* (1965), pp. 603–604.
21 *Gesammelte Schriften*, VI, 192.

as «Der vierte Lebenslauf,» and correctly so, but for a wrong reason. Unaware of her husband's intent, Ninon Hesse decided to call it the fourth simply because «Indischer Lebenslauf» had become the third in the finished novel.

«Der Beichtvater» may have had its origin in the third biography of 1931 (Christ, Ritter, Mönch). An undated autograph sketch of the tale on verso of a letter sent to Hesse by the Verlag Ullstein, November 9, 1931 (see Prose Manuscripts c), suggests that the story may already by the end of 1931 have been thought out in broad outline. Hesse customarily used newly arrived commercial mail for such purposes. It is very likely that these plans were then put aside in favor of the Castalia-tale, «Der Regenmacher,» and of the eighteenth-century biography, and that Hesse did not return to them until late 1935 or perhaps even early 1936. Hesse's Records of Publications indicate that «Der Beichtvater» was sent to the *Neue Rundschau* on May 28, 1936. It appeared two months later.

There is a remote possibility that «Indischer Lebenslauf» may in its genesis return to the second biography of 1931 (Wiedergeburt als Enkel oder Urenkel, Held. Gründet Reich der Welt). However, without any other evidence that Hesse was already busy with the tale at this early date, it can best be assumed that he began it only after having finished «Der Beichtvater» (May 1936). It was probably written some time between June 1936 and April 28, 1937, the date it was sent to the *Neue Rundschau*. It was published three months later.

### Chapters 1 to 12

It was not until after he had completed the three satellite biographies (April 1937) that Hesse finally returned to the Castalia-tale which according to his modified plans of 1933–34 was to become the body proper of his novel.

From the day Hesse sent the fourth version of the introduction to the *Neue Rundschau* (September 8, 1934) to the time he turned his attention to the first chapter of Knecht's life (as early as May 1937 or as late as the beginning of 1938), vague plans must have become a detailed outline. Knecht's brilliant career, his defection, and legendary end are already anticipated on the first few pages of Chapter 1. Thought out, the novel had now only to be written.

Chapters 1 to 6 were written after the completion of «Indischer Lebenslauf» (April 1937) and before «Magister Ludi» was submitted to the *Neue Rundschau* (September 1940). «Die Berufung,» «Waldzell,» and «Zwei Orden» were sent to *Corona*, May 28, 1938, Aug. 18, 1938, and February 1939 respectively; «Studienjahre,» «Die Mission,» and «Magister Ludi» to the *Neue Rundschau*, August 29, 1939, April 16, 1940, and September 12, 1940 respectively. With two exceptions, each of these chapters was probably finished two or three weeks, at most, before its submission. According to Hesse's Records of Publications, both «Waldzell» and «Studienjahre» (Chapters 2 and 3) were ready to be submitted to *Corona* on August 18, 1938. Assuming that Chapters 1, 2, and 3 were written in sequence, and there is no evidence to the contrary, and remembering that Chapter 1 was sent to *Corona* on May 28, «Waldzell» must have been finished by the end of June, and «Studienjahre,» the longer of the two chapters, must have been written during the remaining six to eight weeks before August 18. Hesse gives no reasons for withholding «Studienjahre» in 1938 and not submitting the chapter to the *Neue Rundschau* until August 29, 1939.

Chapters 7 to 10 («Im Amte,» «Die beiden Pole,» «Ein Gespräch,» and «Vorbereitungen») were not published separately before the novel appeared in book form. They were probably written in that order between September

1940, when Hesse finished Chapter 6, and late 1941, when he began Chapter 12.

The genesis of Chapter 11 («Das Rundschreiben») is reflective of the degree to which Knecht's story was thought out even before the first chapter was in print. Knowing that Chapter 1 was submitted on May 28, 1938, one can determine from an undated typescript memorandum (see Prose Manuscripts *k*) that the first version of «Das Schreiben des Magister Ludi an die Erziehungsbehörde» (see Prose Manuscripts *j*) was written as early as 1938, immediately after or perhaps even before the completion of the first chapter. A copy of «Das Schreiben...» was sent to Peter Suhrkamp in September of that year. It was probably Suhrkamp's extremely negative reaction to Knecht's letter that decided Hesse against an eventual separate publication.[22] Both the paper and the handwriting of the first version of the reply made by the *Erziehungsbehörde* suggest that it, too, was written in 1938 (see Prose Manuscripts *j*). Chapter 11–the final version of these letters plus a connective introduction and conclusion–must have troubled Hesse almost to the day the book went to press. Suhrkamp's wish of February 19, 1943 (unpublished letter in the Hesse-*Nachlaß*) to see the «neue Fassung des Abschiedsbriefes» suggests that Hesse was still revising at the outset of 1943.

Chapter 12 («Die Legende»), begun in late 1931, finished on April 29, 1942, was sent to the *Neue Rundschau* in May and published in July-August. The last portion of the chapter–Knecht's departure from Castalia, his visit with the Designoris, and his death–meaningful

---

22 «Es sind Äußerungen eines Aufgestörten. Der Schreibende hört auf ein Weiser zu sein. Er ist nicht mehr der Glasperlenspielmeister. Ich weiß nicht ob er der Lehrer sein kann, in dem er weiterhin seinen Beruf sieht. ... Ich würde eine Veröffentlichung im Zusammenhang des Ganzen durchaus vertreten. Es dürfte aber auf keinen Fall als Stück für sich publiziert werden, da es dann zu leicht mißverständlich ist.» Unpublished letter (Oct. 7, 1938) in the Hesse-*Nachlaß*.

only in terms of the novel as a whole, was omitted from this separate publication.

## The Poems

Knecht's thirteen poems were composed from December 1932 to May 1941, and all were published separately or in clusters from December 1934 to June 1942 (see Poetry Manuscripts and Poetry Publications). But for «Stufen» (May 3, 1941), all were in print even before Hesse had finished the first chapter of Knecht's life (May 1938). There is no specific mention of poetry in the final version of the introduction (September 1934). At the time, only three of Knecht's poems had been written («Doch heimlich dürsten wir ...,» December 1932; «Das Glasperlenspiel,» August 1, 1933; «Klage,» January 1933), and it probably had not yet occurred to Hesse that these and others could eventually become part of his novel. In 1935, four poems («Buchstaben,» February; «Dienst,» April; «Toccata u. Fuge,» May 10; «Nach dem Lesen in der Summa contra Gentiles,» June 9) were added to the original three and together they were submitted to *Corona* on May 21 as «Die Gedichte des jungen Josef Knecht.»[23] This is the first indication that poems were to be ascribed to Knecht.

It is clear from the title of this poem cluster and the date of its submission that Hesse had decided by May 21, 1935, to relate Knecht's poems to the novel in the same manner in which he had decided earlier in 1935 to incorporate the *Lebensläufe* (see Prose Manuscripts *h*). This meant that his plans for the Waldzell chapter as reflected in the autograph fragment of early 1935 (see Prose Manuscripts *h*) had to be changed accordingly: the poems

23 Actually only six poems were sent to *Corona* on May 21. The seventh («Nach dem Lesen in der Summa contra Gentiles») was sent soon after its composition (June 9).

were assigned to Waldzell and the *Lebensläufe* were shifted to Knecht's *Studienjahre*.

The very arrangement of the poems in this cluster is
quite revealing. It is neither chronological according to
dates of composition, nor random, but a deliberate sequence progressing, albeit haltingly, from lament, doubt,
and despair to faith and dedication to the Castalian
ideal. From this it may be concluded that Hesse's carefully arranged sequence became a formative factor in the
writing of the Waldzell chapter in which these poems and
their progression from doubt to faith are commented on,[24]
or more likely, that the Waldzell chapter was already at
that time more or less clearly envisaged and determined
this arrangement of the poems.

When «Die Gedichte des jungen Josef Knecht» were
supplemented in Hesse's *Neue Gedichte* (Berlin: S. Fischer,
1937) by four poems («Ein Traum,» July 1936; «Entgegenkommen,» November 20, 1936; «Beim Lesen eines
alten Philosophen,» November 24, 1936; «Seifenblasen,»
January 14, 1937), and in the publication of the novel
(1943) by two more («Der letzte Glasperlenspieler,» November 1937; «Stufen,» May 4, 1941) the new poems
were not simply appended chronologically to the original
sequence but carefully inserted in it, disturbing the original progression from doubt to faith as little as possible.

### The Book

Hesse's correspondence with his publisher Peter Suhrkamp reveals that he was becoming somewhat anxious,
already as early as late 1938, about an eventual publication of his stil far-from-finished *Glasperlenspiel*.[25] His
contract with the S. Fischer Verlag was about to expire

---

24 *Gesammelte Schriften*, VI, 182.
25 Unpublished letters in the Hesse-*Nachlaß*. Suhrkamp took charge
of the S. Fischer Verlag when Gottfried Bermann-Fischer emigrated in
1936.

(1939) and he had misgivings about renewing it, for it
hardly seemed likely that S. Fischer would be spared the
fate of other Jewish publishing houses much longer. However, after negotiating for a while with a number of German publishers, Hesse decided to remain with S. Fischer,
notwithstanding.

Hesse's own position in Germany at the time was relatively secure. He had been denounced a rank Jew-lover
and a traitor to the Nazi cause by Will Vesper's *Neue
Literatur* in 1935–36, but despite Vesper's determined efforts he had not been placed on the *Schwarze Liste*.[26]
Indeed, Hesse was not only not proscribed, but was subsequently completely exonerated by an official circular
addressed to all book-dealers by Goebbels' own *Propa-
gandaministerium*.[27] With this official sanction, Hesse's
books continued to be published freely and to sell relatively well.[28] When, in February 1942, Suhrkamp applied to
the *Reichsschrifttumskammer* for permission to print *Das
Glasperlenspiel*, he fully expected that this permission
would be forthcoming after the usual protracted formal-
ities. Such was not the case: permission was withheld.
Paper had become extremely scarce for new publications
by authors not beyond all suspicion, and Hesse had, since
his clearance of 1937, become somewhat suspect in the
eyes of officialdom. Even now, however, Hesse was not
put on the *Schwarze Liste*. New printings of his old book

26 See «Unsere Meinung,» *Die neue Literatur*, XXXVI (1935), 685–
687; XXXVII (1936), 58; XXXVII (1936), 239–242.
27 «Entgegen anderslautenden Meldungen stelle ich ausdrücklich fest,
daß ich im Einvernehmen mit dem Herrn Reichsminister für Volks-
aufklärung und Propaganda und der Parteiamtlichen Prüfungskom-
mission zum Schutze des NS-Schrifttums aus bestimmten Gründen die
Ansicht vertrete, daß der Schriftsteller Hermann Hesse zukünftig keinerlei Angriffen mehr ausgesetzt und daß demnach die Verbreitung
seiner Werke im Reich nicht behindert werden soll.» Auszug aus den
vertraulichen Mitteilungen der Fachschaft Verlag, Nr. 23 vom 27. Mai
1937.
28 See [Horst Kliemann], «Ernst Wiechert und Hermann Hesse,»
*Prisma*, II, No. 17 (1948), 41.

publications continued to appear until the end of 1943, and newspapers did not stop printing Hesse until early 1945.

After *Das Glasperlenspiel* had been rejected in Germany, Hesse submitted it in November 1942 to the Fretz & Wasmuth Verlag of Zürich. It appeared exactly one year later. Suhrkamp was not permitted to import copies for the German book market.

In the autumn of 1945, Suhrkamp applied for and received permission from the occupation authorities to rebuild the Fischer-Suhrkamp Verlag. His first postwar publication was to be *Das Glasperlenspiel*. Paper was located by January and the book appeared in August 1946. The first printing was sold quickly and a second followed in December. Since 1946 new printings and editions have appeared regularly (see Book Publications). Combined, these must number over 300,000 copies. The novel has also been published in eight translations.[29]

Though graced by the Nobel Prize in November 1946, *Das Glasperlenspiel* has not and is not likely ever to become a best seller. It promises, however, to become a classic.

## MANUSCRIPTS

### Prose

Except for item *l*, all of the manuscripts, memoranda, and miscellany listed are in the Hesse-*Nachlaß*, Marbach a.N. Dates in brackets do not appear on the documents in question; they are dates supplied by Hesse elsewhere or deduced dates. Words in italics were underlined by Hesse.

*a* Undated initial autograph plans for the novel on verso

---

29 English (1949), Spanish (1949), Swedish (1952), French (1955), Italian (1955), Serbo-Croatian (1960), Korean (1961), English (1969).

of a letter (April 30, 1931) sent to Hesse by Gebr. Fretz AG.

Published in abbreviated form in G. W. Field's «On the Genesis of the *Glasperlenspiel*,» *The German Quarterly*, 41 (1968), 673–674.

*5 mal* wird X geboren [the hero is still without a name].

I Regenmacher bei Müttern?

Primitives Leben. Endet freiwillig, kleiner Häuptling, als Opfer nach Dürre oder Seuche oder Erdbeben. Geht in den Wald (der Seelen), entschlossen, sich als Sohn eines Sohnes oder Enkels wiedergebären zu lassen.

II Wiedergeburt als Enkel oder Urenkel, Held. Gründet Reich der Welt.

III Christ, Ritter, Mönch.

IV Wiedergeburt als jetziger X, der die Geschichte erzählt:

Die Sage von X.

Ende in Mechanei. Wird (will) *nicht* wiedergeboren werden.

Deshalb stirbt aber Reich u. Erde nicht aus. In die Körper seiner Enkel wird nicht Er mehr einkehren, sondern andre Wesen, Dämonen, vielleicht werden diese fremden Enkel einst eine neue Weltjugend schaffen.

V Zukunft. Noch weniger Wirklichkeit, noch mehr Phantasie. Höchste Kultur: Das Perlenspiel in vielen Kategorien, umfaßt Musik, Geschichte, Weltraum, *Mathematik*. X ist jetzt höchster Perlenspieler, spielt die Weltsymphonie, wandelt sie nach Plato, nach Bach, nach Mozart, drückt das Komplizierteste in 10 Zeilen Perlen aus, wird von 3 oder 4 ganz, von 1000en halb verstanden.

Aber die Notleidenden u. Kulturlosen haben genug, sie schlagen (mit Recht) alles zusammen, die Perlenspieler sind ihnen lächerlich u. verhaßt.

Die Geistigen haben aufgehört Bücher zu schreiben, statt

dessen Perlenspiel. Sie haben ebenso auf Wohlleben und Erfolg verzichtet, u. leben höchst genügsam u. bedürfnislos ihrem schönen lebenslangen Spiel.

Schilderung des Spiels: «nicht leicht anschaulich zu beschreiben, da so kompliziert u. außerdem ja noch gar nicht erfunden.»

This document was drawn up in two stages. The initial outline in ink consists only of three biographies (see above, I, II, IV). Biographies III and V were added in pencil. At the same time, Hesse crossed out the «drei» of «dreimal» in the heading, and wrote a 5 above it, added a possible title for the first biography (Regenmacher bei Müttern?), and changed the original biography III to IV. These changes were also made in pencil.

*b* Schluß [1931]. Undated one-page typescript on verso of a letter (June 22, 1931) sent to Hesse by the *Neue Rundschau.*

Published in Roger C. Norton's «Variant Endings of Hesse's *Glasperlenspiel*,» *Monatshefte*, 60 (1968), 143.

Das große Gespräch über Geist u. Politik zwischen Knecht und dem Führer der Diktatur, der ihn dafür gewinnen will, das Gl.Spiel in den Dienst des neuen Staates zu stellen, andernfalls muß seine Partei gegen die Glspieler ebenso rigoros vorgehen wie gegen alles ihr reaktionär scheinende, die Bünde auflösen, das Spiel verbieten und zerstören, seine paar Führer und Wissenden töten.

Der Versucher spricht recht klug und beinahe geistig, Knecht gibt höflich und bescheiden Auskunft, macht keinerlei Versuch sich zu retten. Er weigert sich, auf den Vorschlag einzugehen, d.h. sein Institut dem Staat zu unterstellen und die ihm vom Staat überwiesenen jungen Leute im Spiel auszubilden, damit so der Geist mit der Politik und Aktion verbunden werde. Er sagt: es wäre auch ganz wertlos, wenn er aus irgend w. Gründen sich bereit erklären würde Ja zu sagen: denn wer sich gewissenhaft und nach allen Regeln jahrelang dem Erlernen des Spiels widme, und dabei etwas erreiche, der sei für immer verdorben und verloren für jedes ausüben von Macht, für jedes materielle Streben. Es würden also, selbst wenn er den Versuch machen wollte, doch nur jene Schüler, die zum Spiel untauglich sind, nach der Ausbildung zum Staatsdienst zurückkehren.

Also: er sagt Nein, und willigt in den Untergang. Doch erbittet er Erlaubnis und Frist zu einem letzten Spiel. Das bereitet er sorgfältig vor und endet mit ihm sein Tun und Leben, es ist sein Abschied. Thema dieses letzten Spieles ist: Kampf der unreinen streberischen Mächte gegen den reinen Geist, scheinbare Fortschritte der Macht, Politik etc., die sich aber langsam als lauter Auflösungen erweisen, und zuletzt, wo das ursprüngliche Geist-Thema sich zum Machtthema umgekehrt hat, erweist sich Alles als vom Geist verwande[lt] und durchsetzt.

c Zwei Heilige (eventuell als Schluß eines Knecht-Lebens?). Unpublished autograph on verso of a letter sent to Hesse by the Verlag Ullstein, November 9, 1931.
Initial outline for «Der Beichtvater» (submitted May 28, published July 1936).

d Versuch einer Geschichte des Glasperlenspiels. II. Fassung [late 1931 or early 1932]. Unpublished typescript, 15 pp., and five loose typescript sheets which were incorporated in the next version.
Das Glasperlenspiel. Versuch einer allgemeinverständlichen Einführung in seine Geschichte. Unpublished typescript, 23 pp.
«Die hier vorliegende ist die dritte Fassung, sie wurde im Frühsommer 1932 [sic] vollendet...» (a typescript memorandum, see f below).
Das Glasperlenspiel. Versuch einer allgemeinverständlichen Einführung in seine Geschichte [Sommer 1934].

Fourth and final version, sent off September 8, and published in December 1934. Typescript, 29 pp.

«Es ist unsre Absicht in diesem Buch...» and «Das Gl.Spiel nun entstand in Deutschld....» Two unpublished, untitled, four-page autograph fragments which lie textually between the third and fourth versions of the introduction.

e  Der Regenmacher [1933]. Published typescript, 39 pp.

f  «Die Dichtung, in deren Mitte die Idee des Glasperlenspiels steht....» An unpublished, untitled memorandum (Montagnola im Juni 1934) in which Hesse dates the third and fourth versions of the «Einleitung.» Typescirpts (two versions), 1 p.

g  [Manuscript I, 1934]. Autograph, 121 pp.

Also, Schwäb[ischer] Theologe im 18. Jahrhundert, a two-page typescript summary of the latter part of Knecht's life.

Manuscript II des nicht vollendeten 4. Lebenslaufs [1934].

Autograph, 59 pp.

These are the first and second versions of «Der vierte Lebenslauf»; both were published for the first time in *Prosa aus dem Nachlaß* (Frankfurt a.M., 1965).

Lebenslauf III. One-page unpublished autograph remarks about this fourth biography.

h  «Es war ihm nicht unbekannt, daß im Lauf der 5jährigen Waldzeller Studienzeit...» [1935]. An unpublished four-page autograph fragment. Parts of this were incorporated in each of the first three chapters. According to this fragment, Hesse initially assigned the biographies to Knecht's Waldzell years and not to the *Studienjahre* which follow. Some time after writing the fragment, Hesse crossed out the word «Lebensläufe» in the last paragraph and substituted «Gedichte.» This suggests that the autograph was written before Hesse decided to add poems to the novel and emended after this decision. The decision was probably made only shortly before Hesse submitted «Die Gedichte des jungen Josef Knecht» to *Corona* on May 21, 1935.

*i* Dasa. Eine indische Legende [1937]. Typescript, 39 pp. Only the first paragraph differs from the printed «Indischer Lebenslauf» (submitted April 28, published July 1937).

*j* Das Schreiben des magister ludi an die Erziehbehörde [1938]. First version. Autograph, 36 pp.
Das Schreiben des Magister Ludi an die Erziehungsbehörde.
Printed version. Typescript, 13 pp.
Die Erziehungsbehörde an den Mag. Ludi [1938]. Briefer version than the printed text. Autograph, 2 pp.
Ende des Ludi magister. One-page undated autograph reference to Knecht's last bead-game, to his reasons for leaving the province to serve in a humble capacity, perhaps as a musician, in the outside world, and to his departure. Knecht is not heard from again. This is probably Hesse's initial plan for Chapters 11 and 12. Published in Roger C. Norton's «Variant Endings of Hesse's *Glasperlenspiel*,» *Monatshefte*, 60 (1968), 142.
Three unpublished, undated autograph fragments relating to «Das Schreiben des Magister Ludi»: a two-page segment (earlier than the printed version) of the letter on verso of a letter sent to Hesse by the Querido Verlag of Amsterdam, dated March 11, 1938; a one-sentence reference (on a postcard) to Knecht's discussion of the matter with Tegularius; Knecht and Tegularius discussing the matter (one page).

*k* «Die utopische Erzählung von Josef Knecht...» [1938]. Unpublished one-page typescript outline of the novel. Hesse's remarks indicated that «Das Schreiben des Magister Ludi an die Erziehungsbehörde» was written by May 1938.

*l* Das Glasperlenspiel. 29. April 1942. Autograph in the

Bodmer-Hesse-Collection (Hans C. and Elsy Bodmer, deceased friends and patrons of Hesse; their collection is now in the possession of their sons, H. C. and Peter Bodmer, Zürich, Switzerland).

This autograph includes the unpublished first version of the «Einleitung.»

Missing: Knecht's poems.

*m* [Das Glasperlenspiel]. Mitt. 29. April 1942 wurde J. Knecht vollendet. Published typescript.

Missing: «Einleitung,» «Joseph Knechts hinterlassene Schriften.»

*n* Miscellany. Unpublished and undated fragments.

«Aus einer Schrift Jos. Knecht's: Merkwürdig ist es ja....» One-paragraph typescript on verso of a letter sent to Hesse by the *Mannheimer Tageblatt*, May 11, 1932.

«Designori: Mein Großvater besitzt eine grosse Bibliothek...» Two-page autograph on verso of a financial statement of 1936 and of a letter sent to Hesse by the Erich Reiss Verlag, January 4, 1936. Designori and Knecht in conversation about «Mutter» and «Müttern.«

Die Verschleierten. One-paragraph autograph referring to Knecht's association with women (on verso of a financial statement sent to Hesse by the S. Fischer Verlag, November 19, 1932).

Ende des Magister Musicae. One-page autograph reference to the old Magister's resignation, to his subsequent humble service as an organist and to his death at the age of seventy-nine.

Published in abbreviated form in G. W. Field's «On the Genesis of the *Glasperlenspiel*,» *The German Quarterly* 41 (1968), 683–684.

«Es heißt vom Musikmeister....» One-paragraph autograph reference to Carlo Ferromonte's later years.

«Ideen sterben nach Verwirklichung....» One-page autograph remark about *Das Glasperlenspiel*.

«Knecht erklärt u. a.: Spielen hat mehrere Bedeutungen. . . .» Two-paragraph typescript account by Knecht of the art of playing. Published in abbreviated form in G. W. Field's «On the Genesis of the *Glasperlenspiel*,» *The German Quarterly*, 41 (1968), 685–686.

«Meister Jakobus hat einmal gesagt: Wie wird unsre Generation Probe halten. . . .» One-page typescript.

«Zu Knecht's letztem Glasp. Spiel: Er beginnt, wie das bei feierlichen Spielen. . . .» One-paragraph typescript.

Four one-paragraph autograph references to the novel (on four scraps of paper): «Leben ist ein Dynamisches. . . .»; «Knecht sagt: wir sind nicht . . .»; «Wenn wir an Knechts Schriften. . . .»; «Den Plato schmeiß an die Wand. . . .»

A folder with working notes reflecting Hesse's research in music: two autograph leaves dealing with the Fugue; typescript remarks about Händel and improvisation on verso of a letter dated July 16, 1934; three typescript leaves with references to music of the seventeenth and eighteenth centuries, to Bach and to Luther's hymns; typescript remarks (a single paragraph) about variations in music on verso of a letter dated August 11, 1934; autograph remarks about harmony on verso of a letter dated August 10, 1934. See also letters addressed to Hesse by Karl Isenberg (April 16, 24, and May 7, 1934), Carlo Isenberg (March 18 and April 16, 1934) and Kurt Haering (March 26, 1934).

Two pen sketches of the school Escholz described in «Die Berufung,» Chapter 1.


Poetry

To draw attention to dates of composition, reference here need only be made to Hesse's initial autograph recording of each of the *Glasperlenspiel* poems and not also to the many autograph and/or typescript variants which followed in every case. Each of the references is therefore a first version autograph. All but item *m* (in the possession of Martin Hesse, Bern) are in the Hesse-*Nachlaß*, Marbach a.N. Titles in brackets mean that the poems in question had not yet been given titles. The dates appear in Hesse's handwriting on the autographs.

*a* [Doch heimlich dürsten wir . . .]. December 1932.

*b* Das Glasperlenspiel. August 1, 1933.

*c* [Klage]. January 1934.

*d* [Buchstaben]. February 1935.

*e* [Dienst]. April 1935.

*f* Toccata u. Fuge. May 10, 1935. = Zu einer Toccata von Bach.

*g* [Nach dem Lesen in der Summa contra Gentiles]. June 9, 1935.

*h* Ein Traum. July 1936.

*i* [Entgegenkommen]. November 20, 1936.

*j* Beim Lesen eines alten Philosophen. November 24, 1936. = Beim Lesen in einem alten Philosophen.

*k* [Seifenblasen]. January 14, 1937.

*l* Der letzte Glasperlenspieler. November 1937.

*m* Stufen. May 4, 1941.

## PUBLICATIONS

Prose portions published before the book appeared:

*a* «Der Regenmacher. Erzählung,» *Neue Rundschau*, XLV, i (May 1934), 476–512 (submitted February 20, 1934).

*b* «Das Glasperlenspiel. Versuch einer allgemeinverständlichen Einführung in seine Geschichte» («Einleitung»), *Neue Rundschau*, XLV, ii (December 1934), 638–665 (submitted September 8, 1934).

*c* «Der Beichtvater,» *Neue Rundschau*, XLVII, ii (July 1936), 673–701 (submitted May 28, 1936).

*d* «Indischer Lebenslauf,» *Neue Rundschau*, XLVIII, ii (July 1937), 7–40 (submitted April 28, 1937).

*e* «Die Berufung. Aus dem ‹Versuch einer Lebensbeschreibung Josef Knechts,›» *Corona*, VIII, iii (1938), 223–270 (submitted May 28, 1938).

*f* «Waldzell,» *Corona*, VIII, iv (1938), 341–370 (submitted August 18, 1938).

*g* «Zwei Orden. Aus dem ‹Versuch einer Lebensbeschreibung Josef Knechts,›» *Corona*, IX, i (1939), 54–91 (submitted February 1939).

*h* «Studienjahre. Aus dem ‹Versuch einer Lebensbeschreibung Josef Knechts,›» *Neue Rundschau*, L (October 1939), 320–335 (submitted August 29, 1939).

*i* «Die Mission. Aus dem ‹Versuch einer Lebensbeschreibung Josef Knechts,›» *Neue Rundschau*, LI (July 1940), 317–329 (submitted April 16, 1940).

*j* «Magister Ludi. Aus dem ‹Versuch einer Lebensbeschreibung Josef Knechts,›» *Neue Rundschau*, LI (December 1940), 577–589 (submitted September 12, 1940).

*k* »Die Legende. Aus dem ‹Versuch einer Lebensbeschreibung Josef Knechts,›» LIII (July-August 1942), 316–323, 359–363 (submitted May 1942).


Poetry published before the book appeared:

*a* «Das Glasperlenspiel» (August 1, 1933), *Neue Rundschau*, XLV, ii (December 1934), 637.

b «Buchstaben» (February 8, 1935), *Neue Zürcher Ztg.*, February 24, 1935, No. 320.

c «Zu einer Toccata von Bach» (May 10, 1935), *National-Ztg.* (Basel), May 26, 1935, No. 238.

*d* »Nach dem Lesen in der Summa contra Gentiles» (June 9, 1935), *National-Ztg.* (Basel), July 7, 1935, No. 306.

*e* «Die Gedichte des jungen Josef Knecht,» *Corona*, V, iv (1935), 390–398 («Klage,» January 1934; «Doch heimlich dürsten wir...,» December 1932; «Buchstaben,» February 1935; «Zu einer Toccata von Bach,» May 10, 1935; «Dienst,» April 1935; «Nach dem Lesen in der

Summa contra Gentiles,» June 9, 1935; «Das Glasperlenspiel,» August 1, 1933).

*f* «Ein Traum» (July 1936), *Die Zeit* (Bern), IV, iv (September 1936), 144.

*g* «Seifenblasen» (January 14, 1937), *National-Ztg.* (Basel), January 24, 1937, No. 38.

*h* «Entgegenkommen» (November 20, 1936), *National-Ztg.* (Basel), February 28, 1937, No. 96; *Neue Rundschau*, XLV iii (February 1937), 190.

*i* «Beim Lesen in einem alten Philosophen» (November 24, 1936), *Neue Rundschau*, XLVIII (February 1937), 191.

*j* «Der letzte Glasperlenspieler» (November 1937), *National-Ztg.* (Basel), December 12, 1937, No. 577.

*k* «Die Gedichte des jungen Josef Knecht,» *Neue Gedichte* von Hermann Hesse (Berlin: S. Fischer, 1937), pp. 65–83 («Klage,» January 1934; «Entgegenkommen,» November 20, 1936; «Doch heimlich dürsten wir...,» December 1932; «Buchstaben,» February 1935; «Beim Lesen in einem alten Philosophen,» November 24, 1936; «Zu einer Toccata von Bach,» May 10, 1935; «Ein Traum,» July 1936; «Dienst,» April 1935; «Seifenblasen,» January 14, 1937; «Nach dem Lesen in der Summa Contra Gentiles,» June 9, 1935; «Das Glasperlenspiel,» August 1, 1933.

*l* «Stufen» (May 1941), *Neue Rundschau*, LIII (June 1942), 289.

## Book Publications:

*Das Glasperlenspiel*. Versuch einer Lebensbeschreibung des Magister Ludi Josef Knecht samt Knechts hinterlassene Schriften. Herausgegeben von Hermann Hesse. Zürich: Fretz & Wasmuth, 1943. Vol. 1, 452 pp.; Vol. 2, 442 pp. 8°. «Den Morgenlandfahrern.»

Vol. 1: Einleitung: Das Glasperlenspiel. Versuch einer all-

gemeinverständlichen Einführung in seine Geschichte–Die
Berufung–Waldzell–Studienjahre–Zwei Orden–Die Mission–Magister Ludi–Im Amte–Die beiden Pole.

Vol. 2: Ein Gespräch–Vorbereitungen–Das Rundschreiben
(Das Schreiben des Magister Ludi an die Erziehungsbehörde, Nachschrift)–Die Legende–Josef Knechts hinterlassene Schriften: Die Gedichte des Schülers und Studenten
(Klage, Entgegenkommen, Doch heimlich dürsten wir . . .,
Buchstaben, Beim Lesen in einem alten Philosophen, Der
letzte Glasperlenspieler, Zu einer Toccata von Bach, Ein
Traum, Dienst, Seifenblasen, Nach dem Lesen in der
Summa contra Gentiles, Stufen, Das Glasperlenspiel); Die
drei Lebensläufe: Der Regenmacher, Der Beichtvater, Indischer Lebenslauf.

*a* Berlin: Suhrkamp, August 1946. Vol. 1, 409 pp.; Vol. 2,
403 pp. 8°. *Gesammelte Werke.*
New printing, December 1946; 11.–20. Tsd., 1937; 21.–
35. Tsd., 1949.

*b* Berlin und Frankfurt a.M.: Suhrkamp, 1951, 771 pp. 8°.
*Gesammelte Werke.*
36.–46. Tsd., 1951; 37.–53. Tsd., 1952; 54.–59. Tsd.,
1953; 60.–65. Tsd., 1954; 66.–71. Tsd., 1956; 72.–
76. Tsd., 1956; 133–138. Tsd., 1958; 139.–143. Tsd.,
1959; 144.–149. Tsd., 1961; 150.–156. Tsd., 1962.

*c* *Gesammelte Dichtungen*, 1952, VI, 77–687.

*d* Berlin und Frankfurt a.M.: Suhrkamp, 1957, 617 pp. 8°.
Suhrkamp Hausbuch.
77.–132. Tsd.

*e* Berlin: Aufbau Verlag, 1961, 604 pp. 8°.
With a Nachwort by Hans Mayer: «Hesses Glasperlenspiel oder die Wiederbegegnung,» pp. 575–600.

*f* Frankfurt a.M.: Suhrkamp, 1963, 617 pp. 8°. Unge-
kürzte Sonderausgabe. 157.–183. Tsd., 1963; 184.–194.
Tsd., 1963; 195.–199. Tsd., 1965; 200.–204. Tsd., 1966.

*g* Berlin, Darmstadt, Wien: Deutsche-Buchgemeinschaft,
1964, 479 pp. 8°.

*h* Frankfurt a. M., Hamburg: Fischer Bücherei, 1967,
446 pp. 8°.

*University of California, Berkeley*

I am deeply indebted to Dr. Bernhard Zeller, Director of the Schiller-
Nationalmuseum, for permission to print Hesse's hitherto unpublished
plans, fragments and memoranda, and the excerpt from Peter Suhrkamp's letter.

# 7

## CHRISTIAN I. SCHNEIDER
## HERMANN HESSE'S «GLASPERLENSPIEL»
### Genesis, Structure, Interpretation

*Das Glasperlenspiel (Magister Ludi)*, Hermann Hesse's
Nobel Prize winning novel, is considered by many of his
critics as the poet's *magnum opus* not so much because
it is the most voluminous and difficult, but because it
represents a unique synopsis–based on poetic intuition
and scholary insight–of spiritual values of all times and
many nations. Above all, it is Hesse's last great book,
the summary of his thought and life which points back-
ward and forward in both a personal and transpersonal
sense. The problems of self-identity, fate and the individual, outsider and society, the conflict between *vita
contemplativa* and *vita activa*, spirit and nature, and the
polarity and unity of universal laws are subjectively retrospective themes the poet raised and discussed in detail
in *Peter Camenzind, Demian, Siddhartha, Der Steppenwolf, Narziss und Goldmund*, yet perhaps brought to a
final synthesis for the first time in *Das Glasperlenspiel*.
It is objectively retrospective regarding the connecting
lines which can be drawn between Hesse's last novel and
other *Bildungsromane* in German literary history. It
transcends, however, the modern German genre *Zukunfts-
roman* as well as most of Hesse's own works–at least in
its multivalence and significance for future generations.
Therefore, an analysis of the development and structure
of the book promises to present more definite results than
an interpretation which must remain more or less relative,
subject to contemporary points of view.[1]

1 In the following, the Roman numbers I–VII refer to Hermann
Hesse's *Gesammelte Dichtungen*, vols. I–VII (Frankfurt am Main
1957, Suhrkamp Verlag); the Arabic numbers indicate the pages.

# I. Genesis

The genesis of the *Glasperlenspiel* has long been a matter of controversy among Hesse critics. This is due to the complexity of the work itself as well as to the absence of manuscripts and material which has not yet been published. Hesse's often cryptic letter references are another source of errors and more or less misleading speculations. However, the manuscripts, memoranda and unpublished letters in the Hesse-*Nachlaß* (in the *Schiller-Nationalmuseum*, Marbach a. N. since 1964) have made possible at least a satisfactory «functional» reconstruction.[2]

The conception of the book might date back as far as the late nineteen twenties, maybe 1927. Long before the actual work began, the poet had «the vision of an individual but transtemporal biography of a man who lived on earth at different periods.»[3] The result of the vision are five fictitious autobiographies (*Lebensläufe*) which were briefly outlined on the reverse side of a letter, April

2 Mark Boulby, on the basis of recently discovered letters and other material, gives a more comprehensive genesis than has hitherto been realized. Cf. M. Boulby, *Hermann Hesse. His Mind and Art* (Ithaca, New York 1967), pp. 262–267. Another Hesse scholar, G. W. Field, does not present an extensive genesis of the entire novel but dwells upon its evolution under the impact of political events. He also draws attention to Hesse's initial autograph plans for his work and concentrates on the textual variations of certain chapters. Cf. G. W. Field, «On the Genesis of the *Glasperlenspiel*», in: *The German Quarterly* 41 (1968), pp. 673–688. The most important contribution to the problem of the genesis of the *Glasperlenspiel* is Joseph Mileck's article: «*Das Glasperlenspiel*. Genesis, Manuscripts and History of Publication,» in: *The German Quarterly*, 43 (1970), pp. 55–83. Based on hitherto unpublished plans, fragments and memoranda, Mileck wrote a carefully documented history of the beginnings, the *Einleitung, Lebensläufe*, poems and the various editions of the book. The following is indebted to a great extent to Mileck's findings.
3 See H. Hesse, *Briefe. Erweiterte Ausgabe* (Frankfurt a. M. 1964), p. 436: letter to Rudolf Pannwitz, and the letter to Hesse's sister, Adele (1934), in: H. Hesse, *Prosa aus dem Nachlaß* (Frankfurt a. M. 1965), p. 604.

30, 1931. The hero–then still without a name–is born five times (I) as a «rainmaker with the mothers»; (II) as the rainmaker's «grand- or greatgrandson» who founds a «realm of the world»; (III) as a «Christian, knight, monk»; (IV) as the hero «X» who is now telling the story; and finally (V) in the future as the highest *«Perlenspieler»* who plays the «world symphony» and expresses the most complicated things in «ten lines of beads.»[4] The sketches of these five *Lebensläufe* can be regarded as the seeds from which the entire novel grew. It seems as if Hesse's project at this early stage was a series of novellas linked together thematically yet not compositionally. In a letter from the *Neue Rundschau* (June 22, 1931), Hesse next gave an outline of a possible conclusion for the fifth biography in which the hero is now called *«Knecht»* and the *«Perlenspieler»* have become *«Glasperlenspieler»*. We also hear of an important conversation between Knecht and the «leader of the dictatorship», of Knecht's refusal to place himself and his institution at the disposal of the state. In the following years, Hesse's plan of 1931 has changed continuously as it is shown by several significant remarks in his letters to Gottfried Bermann and Thomas Mann in January and July 1933. Hesse begins to think of the loosely juxtaposed series of novellas in terms of a «voluminous work» which gradually gains the complex structure of his finished novel.

In the years between the first conception and the real commencement of the *Glasperlenspiel*, Hesse was also concerned with *Narziss und Goldmund* and *Die Morgenlandfahrt*–two books which have in content and form much in common with Hesse's last novel. Especially *The Journey to the East* can rightly be understood as a preamble to the *Glasperlenspiel*. It is particularly the idea

4 My translation of the Hesse autographs printed in Mileck's article: *«Das Glasperlenspiel*. Genesis, Manuscripts and History of Publication», *ibid.*, pp. 56 f., 71 f.

of service, no longer the preoccupation with his ego with which Hesse deals in both books. Testimony for the slow process of growing and ripening of the *Glasperlenspiel* are the following lines of Hesse's idyllic poem *Stunden im Garten* (1936). While the poet stirs his garden fire and meditates upon the transformation of the plurality into the unity.

> ... there begins within me/a game of thoughts that I have been practicing for years,/called Glass Bead Game, a nice invention,/whose framework is music and whose basis is meditation./Josef Knecht is the master to whom I owe my knowledge of this/lovely exercise of the imagination. In times of joy/it is game and pleasure, in times of sorrow and distress/it is consolation and reflection for me ...[5]

The words ‹consolation› and ‹reflection› are significant for the shifting focus from the series of reincarnations in the past to the biography of Knecht in the future. Hesse, in the meantime, had to take the Nazi movement seriously and felt compelled to summon up all his energy to confront the deplorable present with a utopian kingdom of the spirit.

The introduction *(Einleitung)* exists in four different versions, the first of which was completed in late 1931 or early 1932, the fourth in June, or at the latest, by September 1934. Hesse's conception of the *Glasperlenspiel* had changed fundamentally in the course of the composition from «objective depiction of a decaying realm–an exemplary Magister Ludi not to be identified with the author–to self-projection» (Mileck). The motif of Knecht's defection must have been in his mind as early as in 1935 or even 1934, which would indicate that Hesse's work was fully formed about the time when the introduction was completed.

As for the incarnations, there is little information

---

5 From V, 348 f. translated by Theodore Ziolkowski, *The Novels of Hermann Hesse* (Princeton, N. J. 1965), p. 44.

available about the first, *Der Regenmacher*, except that it was more or less finished when Hesse became preoccupied with his eighteenth-century biography which since has become known as *Der vierte Lebenslauf*—mistakenly, for the poet himself obviously intended this biography to follow *Der Regenmacher* and *Der Beichtvater* in the finished novel. Hesse, however, gives in the novel only a brief sketch of this ‹fourth› biography (VI, 192f.), though he had dedicatetd a great deal of time to absorbing studies of Swabian pietism and German baroque music among other subjects.[6] *Der Beichtvater* may originate in the third biography (*«Christ, Ritter, Mönch»*) and *Indischer Lebenslauf* (*«Wiedergeburt als Enkel oder Urenkel, Held ...»*) outlined on the letter from 1931. The fifth autobiography (*«Zukunft. Noch weniger Wirklichkeit, noch mehr Phantasie ... Das Perlenspiel in vielen Kategorien ...»*) can be considered to be the main novel, that is the twelve chapters of Knecht's biography as written by the anonymous Castalian, the various stages of which encompass the years between 1931 to 1942.

Like the *Einleitung* (1934), *Der Regenmacher* (1934), *Der Beichtvater* (1936), *Indischer Lebenslauf* (1937), eight chapters (except 7 to 10: *«Im Amte»*, *«Die beiden Pole»*, *«Ein Gespräch»*, *«Vorbereitungen»*) and all of the thirteen poems ascribed to Knecht's *Studienjahre* were published separately (mainly in *Neue Rundschau, Corona*) before the novel appeared in book form. They were finally integrated in the novel, not simply in chronological order, but carefully inserted in such a way that «the original progression from doubt to faith» (Mileck) was disturbed as little as possible.

In the middle of World War II, on April 29, 1942, *Das Glasperlenspiel* was finished. For seven months the man-

6 The two different versions of *Der vierte Lebenslauf* were published posthumously in H. Hesse, *Prosa aus dem Nachlaß*, ibid., pp. 441 to 593.

uscripts waited in Berlin, where Hesse's friend and publisher, Peter Suhrkamp, had applied to the *Reichs-schrifttumskammer* for permission to print them. Though Hesse was not put on the *Schwarze Liste* and had completely been exonerated by an official letter addressed to all book-dealers by Goebbels' own *Propagandaministe-rium*, the permission was withheld. After it had been rejected in Germany, Hesse submitted the manuscripts in November 1942 to *Fretz & Wasmuth Verlag* in Zurich, Switzerland. *Das Glasperlenspiel in toto* came out there one year later, and the first postwar publication not until August 1946 in the *Suhrkamp Verlag*.

Since that time new printings and editions have appeared not only in the *Suhrkamp Verlag* but also with other German publishers, the last one in the *Fischer Bücherei,* Frankfurt a. M. and Hamburg in 1967. It has also been translated into English, Spanish, Swedish, French, Italian, Japanese, Serbo-Croatian, Korean, and is at the present time distributed in approximately 300,000 copies or more all over the world.[7]

## II. Structure

Hesse himself was aware that a book compiled over a period of eleven years might well have some structural defects.[8] Its balance, therefore, appears to be less organic than ‹architectonic›, contrary to Thomas Mann's novel *Doktor Faustus* with which *Das Glasperlenspiel* has so often been compared.[9] Both novels deal with the dangers

7 For more details, see among others Bernhard Zeller, *H. Hesse in Selbstzeugnissen und Bilddokumenten* (Reinbek 1963), p. 130; J. Mileck, «*Das Glasperlenspiel.* Genesis, Manuscripts and History of Publication», *ibid.,* pp. 71, 79 f.
8 Cf. the letter to Siegfried Unseld (1949/50), in VII, 701 f.
9 For a more detailed comparison of the *Glasperlenspiel* with other German novels, see Th. Ziolkowski, *The Novels of H. Hesse, ibid.,* pp. 282–287; Joseph Mileck, *H. Hesse and His Critics* (Chapel Hill,

of an excessive aestheticism and are to a certain extent
*romans à clef (Schlüsselromane),* referring to significant
figures in the cultural history of Germany. Both authors,
moreover, make extensive use of the montage technique
by which quotations, reflective and didactic passages are
blended into the fictional text. Closer to Hesse's novel,
however, seems to be the third volume of Hermann
Broch's *The Sleepwalkers* which Hesse read and reviewed
in 1932. Both works contain a range of techniques lacking
in *Doktor Faustus,* for example the movement from total
objectivity of the abstract essay to the absolute subjectiv-
ity of lyric poetry. After all, the most fruitful *tertium
comparationis* is another novel for which both Hesse and
Broch revealed a specific interest: Goethe's *Wilhelm Meister* (particularly *Meister's Travels*), the classical master-
piece of the German *Bildungsroman* to which Hesse is
more or less indebted, as are most of the German novelists
since Goethe.[10] As a utopian novel, *Das Glasperlenspiel*
stands also within the German literary tradition, in particular that of the postwar era, where we find other such
conspicuous examples as Franz Werfel's *Star of the Unborn* (1946), Hermann Kasack's *City beyond the River*
(1947), and Ernst Jünger's *Heliopolis* (1949).

The disposition of the *Glasperlenspiel* consists prin-
cipally of three distinctive parts: the «Attempt at an In-
troduction into the History of the Glass Bead Game
Intelligible to All» (VI, 79–116); the «Biography of the
Magister Ludi Josef Knecht» (VI, 117–543); and «Josef
Knecht's Posthumous Writings» (VI, 544–685).

The introduction combines almost all characteristics of

N. C. 1958), pp. 97–100; Inge D. Halpert, *H. Hesse and Goethe with
particular reference to the relationship of Wilhelm Meister and Das
Glasperlenspiel* (Doct. diss. Columbia Univ. 1957).

10 See Winfried Pielow, «Hesses ‹Glasperlenspiel› und die Tradition des Bildungsromanes seit Goethe,» in W. Pielow, *Die Erzieher-
gestalten der großen deutschen Bildungsromane von Goethe bis zur
Gegenwart* (Doct. diss. Univ. of Münster, 1951), pp. 101–133.

a typical essay. It begins with a Latin quotation of a fictitious treatise with Knecht's handwritten translation into German, which we may understand as a sort of aphorism including the mysterious concept of the Bead Game *in nuce*. The following is an attempt to explain the Bead Game within the context of the novel's development. It is the intention of the narrator (an anonymous Castalian always speaking in the collective we-form), «to collate the small amount of biographical material that we have been able to gather concerning Josef Knecht, or Magister Ludi Josephus III as he was known to the archives of the Bead Game.»[11] (VI, 80) In keeping with the author's historic and didactic impulse, the ‹material› is presented in a highly ‹objective› way as is evident in the rest of the essay in which the history of the Bead Game is both narrated and critically commented. This «parodistically flavoured chronicle style» of the biographer has been the reason for many animadversions among Hesse's critics.[12] However, the commentary on the problem of sources, the pretense of authentic documentation, the reflections about the difficulties of the biographer and the fact that this style is specifically designed to appear professional and self-ironizing at the same time—all these techniques are particularly justified in the introduction if we understand it as that which it is: a satire—similar to the ‹treatise› in *Der Steppenwolf*—on the «Age of Feuilleton», our present age, a term which (together with Robert Musil's «Kakania») has since become a slogan in German literature. As a counterpoint to the satire appear the writer's serious endeavors «to place before the eyes of men certain things the existence of which is neither provable nor probable» (VI, 79), that is the

11 Translated by Mervyn Savill, H. Hesse, *Magister Ludi* (New York 1949), p. 13. In the following, the English quotations from the *Glasperlenspiel* refer to this translation, if not marked otherwise.
12 See e. g. Werner Kohlschmidt, *Meditationen über H. Hesses Glasperlenspiel*, in *Zeitwende*, XIX (München 1947/48), p. 164.

existence of Castalia and the Bead Game. In order to capture the reader's attention for so difficult a task, the author, besides fictitious names and allusions to quasi-historical events, skillfully introduces figures and movements primarily in the history of music. Thus, the juxtaposition of quotations from the chapter on music in Lü Bu We's «Spring and Autumn» and phrases of Josef Knecht upon the essence of classical music (with which the essay concludes) constitute the balance of historical and fictitious elements in the introduction. This prelude, all in all, is perhaps the most problematic piece of the whole novel. It need not necessarily serve for a clearer comprehension of the Glass Bead Game, at least not before you have read the book through.

The main part, the «Biography of the Magister Ludi Josef Knecht», is a thoroughly consistent composition in which all twelve chapters, like the pillars in a Gothic cathedral, are necessary for the adequate balance in the construction of Knecht's life. Nevertheless, a close analysis shows that there are important differences in texture and style of each chapter.[13] In the first three chapters (The Call, Waldzell, Apprenticeship) the development of the incidents of Knecht's life is almost programmatically determined by the hierarchical organization of Castalia. Apart from expressively reflective passages such as the one on Castalian morals (VI, 186) and the quotation from a letter of the Old Music Master (VI, 193), the narrative moment is predominant. In chapters four and five (Two Orders, The Mission), where the tension between theory and actuality is depicted, the narrative flow freezes somewhat in the growing psychological, musicological and historic dissertations expressed in Knecht's cursory judgment on his friend Tegularius. (VI, 226f.) We find the same type of narrative in the conversations be-

13 Discussed in detail by Th. Ziolkowski, *The Novels of H. Hesse,* *ibid.,* pp. 324–333.

tween Knecht and Pater Jakobus, which strongly resemble the Platonic dialogue in form. Chapters six, seven, and eight (Magister Ludi, In Office, The Two Poles) depicting Knecht's return to Castalia and his years as Magister Ludi, are exemplary for the increasing essayification of the novel which finds its culmination in chapter nine (A Conversation) and eleven (The Circular Letter). In contrast to chapter ten (Preparations), written again in a more narrative style, the surrounding chapters to a great extent consist of theoretical discussions in which even Knecht's ideas about his office are frequently not given by himself, that is through a ‹direct› reconstruction by his biographer, but by means of reasoning and quotations (VI, 329, 252ff.). What seems to be an exception, the «circular letter«, can indeed be understood–as, in fact, it is by its addressee, the *Ordensleitung*–as an essay on the rise and decline of Castalia rather than a ‹personal› request by which Knecht tries to explain his reasons and asks permission for leaving his office. The twelfth and last chapter (The Legend), the story of Knecht's brief excursion into the world and death, is the most lyrical one of the entire biography, Knecht «himself»–at least according to the reports written by a few favorite disciples of the Magister Ludi (VI, 479)–gives an interpretation of his poem *Steps* (one of the most famous of all Hesse poems). He also recites a hymn by Paul Gerhard (VI, 523) and copies another poem by Friedrich Rückert (VI, 530). It is above all in this legend where Hesse once again makes use of his subtle art of handling the symbols of nature as a reflection of Knecht's mood and presentiment of his all but ‹sudden› death. Thus, the poetic grandeur of the *coda* of the *Glasperlenspiel* can structurally well be understood as the counterpart to the scholarly introduction. There is another structural principle by which all these chapters are related to each other: it is the observation that, whether Hesse consciously followed Jakob

Burckhardt or not, his Josef Knecht traverses the same three areas of human activity with which the Swiss historian was concerned: religion, culture, and state in their manifold interactions.[14]

Knecht's «Posthumous Writings», the «Poetic Fragments from Knecht's Student Days» and the «Three Incarnations» are expressed in a clearly lyrical and epical form. However, as documents of the hero, they can also be defined as essayistically conceived elements of the entire novel. Similar to Jean Paul's appendices, the three conjectural autobiographies add no foreign material to the novel, but represent necessary variations of the main theme. They are transpositions of Knecht's story into former times. In these autobiographies, by the way, the poet's concept of reincarnation corresponds only loosely to its Hindu counterpart. Knecht's poetic exercises take up the old tradition of didactic poetry as practiced by Walther von der Vogelweide, Friedrich Schiller, Wolfgang von Goethe, and Stefan George. Both the poems and the incarnations demonstrate the timeless tradition of human existential thought and show that present, past, and future always coexist in man's soul.[15]

Due to the essayification, as I take it, Hesse's language in the *Glasperlenspiel* has often been criticized as being too abstract, incomprehensible, «lacking the poetic nuance», or on the contrary, of being too clear, «without any deep dimension». Particularly the narrative style of

---

14 See Jakob Burckhardt, *Weltgeschichtliche Betrachtungen* (Stuttgart 1949), Chapter 2, «Von den drei Potenzen», Chapter 3, «Die Betrachtung der sechs Bedingtheiten». For the original quotations taken from J. Burckhardt and built into the novel, cf. G. F. Hering, *Burckhardts Worte im Glasperlenspiel*, in: *Die Zeit*, Nr. 28 (Hamburg, July 10, 1947), p. 6.
15 Cf. among other critics W. Kohlschmidt, *Meditationen über Hesses Glasperlenspiel*, *ibid.*, p. 218; Wolfgang von Schöfer, *H. Hesse, Peter Camenzind und das Glasperlenspiel*, in *Die Sammlung*, 3 (Göttingen 1948), pp. 597–609; Oskar Seidlin, *H. Hesses Glasperlenspiel*, in *Germanic Review*, 23 (1948), pp. 263–273.

the conversations is called «commonplace», and the poem *Stufen* as «little more than an arabesque around a platitude». Other critics single out too allegorical, playful, even «senile» features of the form in which the novel was written.[16] There is, nonetheless, substantial defense against many of the above criticisms. Whoever labels essayism as the main reason for the stylistic defects of the *Glasperlenspiel* is most likely unaware of the fact that essayism is a characteristic of almost all modern novels as it can easily be discovered also in the works of A. Chechov, L. Tolstoy, Th. and H. Mann, H. Broch, A. Gide, J. Steinbeck, V. Woolf and other writers. Moreover, it has been documented recently, that not only the modern but many great novels of world literature throughout the centuries are permeated with essayistic elements.[17] The really objective reader will soon realize by himself the deplorable one-sidedness of all such pseudo-critical observations as the above «either-or» statements, or of unlimited eulogies, too. For it is true that there are many allegorical features in the novel which have not yet become transparent, such as the employment of the motifs of the «I Ching Book» and the episode of Bertram, the deputy of Thomas von der Trave, in which—spoken in terms of C. G. Jung—the «shadow motif» finds its ultimate restatement.[18]

Hesse's play with names, which almost all have counterparts in the author's own life, transcends the framework of the novel as in *The Journey to the East*. For example, Latin equivalents for German names are «Chattus» and «Albertus Secundus» for Hesse himself; «Clangor» and «Collofino» for his friends, the classical

16 Cf. Ernst Rose, *Faith from the Abyss*. H. Hesse's Way from Romanticism to Modernity (New York 1965), pp. 134, 139 f.
17 See Ludwig Rohner, *Der deutsche Essay* (Neuwied 1966), pp. 51, 573. About specifically essayistic elements in the *Glasperlenspiel*, cf. *ibid.*, pp. 346, 351, 443, 572–575.
18 Cf. M. Boulby, *H. Hesse, His Mind and Art, ibid.*, p. 300.

philologists Schall and Feinhals; «Carlo Ferromonte» refers to Hesse's nephew, the musicologist Carl Isenberg; «Bastian Perrot» (the ‹inventor› of the Bead Game) to Heinrich Perrot, the owner of the machine-shop in Calw, where Hesse worked in 1894/95 as an apprentice. A special tribute is given to Jakob Burckhardt (1818–1897) in the figure of the Benedictine monk Pater Jakobus, and to Hesse's peer and friend, Thomas Mann (born on the River Trave) in Knecht's predecessor, the Magister Ludi Thomas von der Trave.[19]

With the same justification and for quite similar reasons one can criticize Goethe's mature style in *Wilhelm Meister's Travels:* his allegories and playful elaborating of details often mar the continuous flow of the «story». It is up to the gerontopsychologists to determine why and to what extent it is natural for the aging writer to become more and more interested in the allegorical and symbolical aspect of things rather than in their factual description. More than in Goethe's *Wilhelm Meister*, it seems to me, this mode of style is appropriate for Hesse's *Glasperlenspiel* and its character of game playing as the very subject. Therefore, those readers who have a definite feeling for art, especially the art of music, will probably be more sensitive to Hesse's mature style which is so closely related to the art of Glass Bead Playing itself.[20]

## III. INTERPRETATION

### 1. The Glass Bead Game as Idea and Reality

*Das Glasperlenspiel* is dedicated to the «Eastern Wayfarers» as we know them from Hesse's ‹narrative tract› *Die Morgenlandfahrt*, dealing with the ‹League› of all

19 See Joseph Mileck, *Names and the Creative Process. A Study of the Names in H. Hesse's «Lauscher,» «Demian,» «Steppenwolf,» and «Glasperlenspiel».* In: *Monatshefte für den deutschen Unterricht*, 53 (1961), pp. 167–180.
20 As a possible argument against the allegedly weak or senile features stressed by certain critics, there is the observation of others

those individuals who are always searching for an ‹idea›
in which they believe to find the ultimate fulfillment of
their self-identity. In their understanding the Glass Bead
Game belongs to the things

> ... the existence of which is neither provable nor prob-
> able, but which, for this very reason, pious and scholar-
> ly men treat to a certain extent as existent in order
> that they may be led a step further towards their be-
> ing and their becoming. (VI, 79)

The rather mysterious words in the dedication, nevertheless, make clear enough that the Bead Game falls
under the category of such games which (in terms of
J. Huizinga) are distinguished by their «holy seriousness»
as it is inherent in all sacred rituals, lithurgies, sacra-
ments.[21] Its esoteric character is furthermore underlined
by the very name of the place where it is played: Castalia, derived from the Castalian Spring in Delphi, the
‹Fountain of the Muses›, where the pilgrims used to purify themselves before they stepped into the sanctuary of
the god Apollo. The expression «Pedagogic Province» for
Castalia was openly borrowed from Goethe's *Wilhelm
Meister's Travels* (VI, 134).[22] In so far as the Castalian
Province tends toward Alexandrinism, it also recalls
F. Nietzsche and the polemics of *The Birth of Tragedy*.[23]

that several passages in Hesse's *Glasperlenspiel* strongly remind of
the style used in his early works. Cf. Martin Pfeiffer, *Inhalt und Stil
der Sprache H. Hesses*. In: *Sprachpflege*, 6 (Berlin 1957), pp. 82–84.
21 Cf. Johannes Huizinga, *Homo ludens* (Reinbek 1956), pp. 25–28.
22 See H. H. Groothoff, *Versuch einer Interpretation des Glasperlenspiels*. In: *Hamburger Akademische Rundschau*, II (1947/48), p. 274.
23 «Thou must know . . ., that we are here on the borders of a province, which I might justly call a Pedagogic Utopia. In the conviction that only one thing can be carried on, taught, and communicated
with full advantages, several such points of active instruction have
been, as it were, sown over a large tract of country. At each of
these places thou wilt find a little world, but so complete within its
limitation, that it may represent and model any other of these worlds,
nay, the great busy world itself.» *The Complete Works of J. W. v.
Goethe*, translated by Thomas Carlyle (New York, without year),
vol. VIII, p. 129 (Wilhelm Meister's Travels).

Castalia is conceived as one of several such which came into existence after the decline of twentieth-century-civilization which Hesse also calls «The Age of Wars» (VI, 474). Castalia was constituted and supported by the political authorities of the ‹World› as an institution for the purification and uncontaminated transmission of spiritual values, particularly the service of truth, the loss of which is said to have been a major cause of the decline of the West. It is situated «anywhere in the same country», that means symbolically, in every country of the world including our own. For the time being, however, Castalia is only on the way to its «realization» and will reach its heyday not before the year 2000.[24] The Castalian academies convey the knowledge of the sciences and arts primarily for their own sake, their uninterrupted tradition and reevaluation, but they are also utilitarian in their training of teachers for the outside world. *«Gignit autem artificiosam gentem Cella Silvestris»* (but Waldzell produces the artists of the Bead Game), is the motto of Waldzell and the *Vicus lusorum* (Village of the Bead Game Players), the senior élite school which specializes only in the education of future Glass Bead Players (VI, 155). The topography of Waldzell reminds of both Maulbronn and Tübingen, especially the *Tübinger Stift* with its aesthetic eccentrics and genial scholars. Similar to *Unterm Rad* and *Narziss und Goldmund,* the poet goes back to his own experience in a monastery-like boarding school. Constitutionally, the ‹Pedagogic Province› is a hierarchically organized and autonomous ‹state within the state› comparable to a monastic order. All participants are subject to an ascesis which—with some modifications—corresponds to the three basic commandments of

24 In the first publication of the «Introduction» in *Die neue Rundschau,* vol. 45, Nr. 2 (Berlin 1934), p. 638, Hesse himself gives the year 2400 as the date, when the biography was written. At that time, however, the Castalian Province is supposed to be already in a state of decline.

the Benedictine Order: poverty, celibacy and obedience. Since the Castalian Order aims at being a spiritual nobility through education rather than by birth (VI, 256), its academies are accessible only to a student élite which is most carefully selected by the different *Magistri* who undertake regular travels through the country for that purpose. If a student (still in his high-school years) has had the honor of becoming a ‹novice› in the Castalian Order, he has complete freedom to live and study in the province forever or to return into the ‹World› and take a profession there. In case he stays in Castalia, he is not even expected to become an outstanding Glass Bead Player—of which only the ‹élite of the élite› is capable anyway—but he is free to pursue whatever scholarly aim he likes. He may, for instance, spend his entire life, such as the ‹strange› Chattus Calvensis II who wrote four volumes about «the pronunciation of Latin in the Universities of Southern Italy towards the end of the twelfth century», a work which was originally planned to be the first part of a «History of the Pronunciation of Latin from the Twelfth to the Sixteenth Centuries» (VI, 137). As in a monastery, the Castalian need not worry about making his living. Every necessary thing (no luxury, of course) is provided for him. He is only expected to follow the basic rules of the order and his «superiors», whenever these call him to a certain place in the hierarchy, where they think he as an individual can best be of service to the whole Castalian community. At the top of the hierarchy stands the «Pedagogy» *(Erziehungsbehörde)*. It consists of twelve *Studiendirektoren* or *Meister* (including e. g. the *Magister musicae,* the *Magister mathematicae,* the *Magister grammaticae)* and the Magister Ludi.[25] His main duties are organization and technique of the

25 Cf. VI, 132–138. Nowhere in the novel do we hear of the »twelve music masters of the order«, mentioned by E. Rose, *Faith from the Abyss, ibid.,* p. 127 f.

Bead Game. He also has to ‹compose› the Glass Bead
Games which are annually performed under his direction
on the occasion of the famous *Ludus solemnus* in which
not only the Castalians themselves but–on the basis of a
sufficient ‹grade› (VI, 400)–intellectuals and artistic
people from the outside world are permitted to take part.
Without worshipping a specific god within one of the
historically known confessions, this ‹celebration› of the
Glass Bead Game as well as the priest-like Magister Ludi
are surrounded by a cult-like atmosphere.

The name ‹Glass Bead Game›–inappropriate for such
a lasting and important organization–comes originally
from a «transitory incident»: The inventor Bastian Perrot
. . . constructed for himself, upon the model of a simple
abacus for children, a frame with a dozen wires across
it upon which he could string glass beads of different
sizes, shapes, and colors. The wires represented the lines
of the music, the beads the note values, etc. etc. With
his beads he built up musical citations or invented
themes, which he varied, transposed and developed, re-
versed or opposed to each other. (VI, 102f.)

A «manual» of the Bead Game does not exist and will
never be written, according to the poet himself. Therefore, the rules of the Bead Game can be learned in the
usual prescribed ways only («the result of many years'
experience»), and none of the ‹initiated› is interested in
making its rules easier to master. At a closer look, however, these rules represent «a type of highly developed,
secret language, in which several sciences and arts, in
particular mathematics and music, play their part, and
which are capable of expressing the contents and results
of nearly all the sciences and of placing them in relation
to each other» (VI, 84). The Bead Game adept will play
upon this ‹colossal material› of spiritual values ‹as an
organist plays upon his organ›–an instrument of ‹in-
credible perfection›: «Its keyboards and pedals register

the entire cosmos, its stops are almost innumerable, and in theory this instrument allows the entire spiritual world to be reproduced in play.» (VI, 84) Not in a simile, but by means of rather concrete details, the poet explains to us at another place, that the Bead Game (such as the ‹classical› one invented by Josef Knecht himself),

... was based upon the pretty concept of taking for its structure and dimensions the building of a Chinese house according to the old Confucian ritual scheme—the orientation in accordance with the cardinal points, replete with the gateways, walls to keep out the spirits, and observing the relations and requirements of the buildings and courtyards, their arrangement to the planets, the calendar, family life, and also to symbolism and rules of style obtaining in the garden. (VI, 337)

Here, the meaning of ‹symbol› (as in general) is composed of both rational and irrational elements, and a merely ‹intellectual› comprehension is neither adequate nor possible at all. Nevertheless, the question can be raised: What does the Bead Game as a symbol actually stand for?

In the course of its history, as we hear, the ‹game of games› under the «changing hegemony of now this, now that, science or art has developed into a kind of universal speech, through the medium of which the players are enabled to express values in lucid symbols and to place them in relation to each other». (VI, 111) At all times the game was closely connected with music; its ‹themes› were similarly played and varied as e.g. the theme of a fugue or a concert piece. With the adaptation of Eastern meditation techniques and a turn towards religion, the game has finally become what it is supposed to be still to-day: «... the totality of the spiritual and the musical, the sublime cult, the Unio Mystica of all separate limbs of the Universitas Litterarum.» (VI, 109) In its function as a type of world speech for intellectuals, the game, therefore, creates an atmosphere of harmony between them, and represents «a select, symbolical form of the quest for perfection, a sublime alchemy, a self-approach to the inherent spirit beyond all images and pluralities–and thus to God.» (VI, 112) Here, at the very core, the Bead Game proves to be another symbol for Hesse's particular *Weltanschauung* underlying most of his major works. It is the idea of the unity of all world-opposites which by no means stems from Hesse's own imagination, as a concise review of its historical development will show.[26]

One of the oldest manifestations of the unity idea seems to be the ancient monotheism of primitive nations which later found its refined expression in the religious teachings of Buddha (Upanishads), the Old Testament, and also in the classical Chinese philosophy of Lao Tsu (around 300 B. C.). It can be traced in the fragments of Heraclitus (ca. 450–480 B.C.) and throughout the Middle Ages, e. g., in the writings of Nikolaus von Cusa (1401–1464), who spoke of the *coincidentia oppositorum*, the coincidence of all opposites in God. Paracelsus Bombastus von Hohenheim, the famous physician (1494–1541), developed his ideas of the ‹efficient elements›, their transformation and healing forces, because he was convinced that all life processes of man (whom he thought of as a microcosm) are in a state of harmony with the substances and laws of the macrocosm. (Modern physiologists have indeed proved that entities, fragments, and traces of all elements participate in the construction of the human body.) For the *philosophus teutonicus*, Jakob Böhme (1575–1624), God is the *Urgrund* of all being, including evil which is necessary for the creation of good. In much more rational a way Wilhelm Leibniz (1646–1716) con-

26 Cf. Otto Engel, *H. Hesse. Dichtung und Gedanke* (Stuttgart 1948), pp. 80–84; extensive studies on the same subject were done by Gerhart Mayer, *Die Begegnung des Christentums mit den asiatischen Religionen im Werk H. Hesses* (Bonn 1956); Rudolf Pannwitz, *H. Hesses west-östliche Dichtung* (Frankfurt a. M. 1957).

cerned himself with the invention of a ‹universal speech› expressed in certain mathematical formulas. The most systematic concept of the unity idea, however, is the philosophy of G. W. F. Hegel (1770–1831) and his new logic of the contradiction, according to which the struggle between ‹thesis› and ‹antithesis› always results in a final ‹synthesis›. All in all, both the traditional philosophic and religious aspects of the unity idea deeply influenced Hesse from his early youth to his old age. Thus, the Glass Bead Game as his last und highest idea and realization of this concept of ‹world unity› is in its kind a similarly daring and genial attempt to bring together the spiritual forces of our complicated and devided earth, as Werner von Heisenberg's ‹world formula›, in which this scientist tries to prove the electrical character of all natural phenomena. Now we understand better, too, why Hesse prefers to explain his Bead Game in musical terms: It is perhaps the main function of music to express opposite ‹thoughts› in form of a unity and simultaneity. Each composition consists of polar forces, of subjects and counter subjects, consonance and dissonance, high and deep tones; each fugue, each sonata exists by virtue of its contradictory themes which, nonetheless, form a resonant unity. From music we may also draw parallels to other arts and sciences. In order to write music down, we need ‹formulas› closely related to mathematics which is also as basic a constituent as measure and rhythm. The tones themselves, their different vibrations, the musical instruments and their resonance are dependent on physical laws. Synaesthetical analogies between certain keys, colors and emotions have always existed.[27] For a Glass Bead

27 For example, Johann Sebastian Bach carefully selected major and minor keys and certain musical figures in order to express different emotions in his cantatas and organ preludes destined for specific occasions of the church calendar. See the chapter on *Wort und Ton bei Bach*, in Albert Schweitzer, *Johann Sebastian Bach* (Leipzig 1954), pp. 398–425.

Player, all arts and sciences as the highest spiritual values created by men, have become transparent like glass beads and are made meaningful above all by the intrinsic unity which they symbolize each in their own way. For it would be a misunderstanding, if one assumed that a Glass Bead Player had to study all disciplines so that he, in the final analysis, would become nothing but a universal dilettante. On the contrary, Hesse points out very precisely that each Castalian should have only t w o  i d e a l s :

> ... to achieve the utmost possible perfection in his subject, and to keep both his Faculty and himself, living and elastic, so that he may know himself to be permanently bound to all other subjects and inwardly on good terms with all of them. This second ideal, the idea of the inner unity of all intellectual effort, the thought of universality, has its perfect expression in our illustrious Game. (VI, 324)

Therefore, the Castalian Order as the community of all those who know about the thought of a universal unity and are capable of expressing it in «magic» formulas, is in reality «neither a dream of the future nor a postulate, but an eternal, Platonic idea, which, in diverse grades of realization, has already often become visible on earth.»[28] Closely examined, however, the novel depicts three visions of Castalia: the utopian spiritual realm described in the introduction; the Alexandrine republic of aesthetics and scholarliness which both the biographer and (through him) Knecht sharply criticize; and finally a more balanced synthesis of spirit and life represented by the narrator, whom we may understand as the ‹moderating› voice of the poet himself.[29]

28 My translation of the passage in Hesse's letter from February 1944 «about the Bead Game» (VII, 641).
29 Cf. Th. Ziolkowski, *The Novels of H. Hesse, ibid.,* pp. 301–307.

## 2. The Magister Ludi Josef Knecht

Similar to the idea of a threefold Castalia, the biography of Josef Knecht has more than just one dimension. It is first of all a «secularized hagiography» in which the traditional form of the saintly *vita* is adapted to the pattern of the Castalian hierarchy; a second, parallel line refers to the ‹outsiderdom› of the true saint, his second soul, so to speak, which becomes the leading force once the Magister Ludi has realized the limitations of his own office; and a third line of Knecht's life appears to be much more obscure and is revealed only occasionally as in certain still unexplored passages of the autobiographies, Knecht's most personal documents.[30] In approaching Knecht's biography, however, the following questions have become more eminent in this framework: What is the development of an individual life within the Castalian Order? Is it possible at all? And what are its final consequences?

Whoever expects in Knecht's biography a compensation for the many theoretical passages on the Bead Game with which the novel is permeated, will most probably be disappointed, for the author—unlike in *Siddhartha, Der Steppenwolf, Narziss und Goldmund*—is no longer interested in a detailed description of a second ‹libertinistic› life with which to compare Knecht's strongly ascetic inclinations. Though being a highly problematic character of many talents and drives predestined not to fit into any category of a regulated life, Knecht, nonetheless, does not appear as a ‹split personality› but as one who has reached a remarkable degree of integration from the very beginning. Nor do we hear anything ‹spectacular› of his origin. «Like many other élite pupils he had either lost his parents at an early age or else been taken from them owing to their unfavorable circumstances and adopted by the

30 Cf. M. Boulby, *H. Hesse. His Mind and Art*, ibid., p. 277.

pedagogy.» (VI, 117) Knecht was spared the burden of the generation problem, the conflict between school and home—main themes in the self-developement of Peter Camenzind, Hans Giebenrath, Emil Sinclair. Of course he had «like every man of significance his δαιμόνιον and *Amor fati*, but the latter appears to us to have been singularly free from gloom or fanaticism.» (VI, 117) The confrontation with the other sex (as demonstrated almost *ad absurdum* in *Der Steppenwolf* and *Narziss und Goldmund*) has become irrelevant for Josef Knecht. «The Castalian student knows neither marriage, with its enticements and dangers, nor the prudery of many former epochs which constrained the student either to sexual abstinence or drove him into the arms of more or less venal women and prostitutes.» (VI, 188) In other words, there exists for him nothing of the attendant morality of love, and since he has no money, the venality of love does not exist either. If he likes, he may choose a temporary sweetheart among the «daughters of the townsfolk» (to whom «in the years before marriage the students and teachers seem ... particularly desirable as lovers»), and it has happened on occasions «that an élite student has returned to the world through the door of bourgeois marriage ..., but these few cases of apostasy in the history of the school and of the Order can only be regarded as curiosities.» (VI, 188 f.) This is almost all the author tells us about Castalian love, apart from a few innocuous sexually tinted wish-dreams in Knecht's «Indian Life» (VI, 651, 664). The fact that women do not play any major rôle in the novel, has become the reason for many reproachful remarks and wild speculations among Hesse critics and readers. They forget (or overstress) again that the *Glasperlenspiel* is the work of an aging poet, and aging means, according to Goethe, a «gradual stepping back from the world of phenomena», whereas the motto of youth had been: «Feeling is everything.» Without any doubt, we may find—as in Hesse's earlier novels—many autobiographic features in the figure of the Magister Ludi, features which are natural to a really mature personality, corresponding to C. G. Jung's last stages of the human way of individuation, when man is supposed to have recognized and integrated all female parts of his psyche and the mature woman the male parts. Therefore, the poet writes in reply to a letter from a «scholarly lady» who had asked why there are only élite schools for men and not for women in Castalia:

If a piece of poetry deals only with men, this should not be understood by women as an anti-female attitude. Namely a woman, who really has learned how to read and who has the prerequisites for a Castalian life ... will rather take part in the spiritual and trans-sexual of such a book without resentment. And if she has the desire, she will write a book in which she portrays the same problem from the female side ... [31]

Among the Castalians, the surrogate for sexual love is f r i e n d s h i p , which in certain cases is not quite free from (in theory at least) homoerotic features, such as we find in Knecht's sympathy for Anton (VI, 242), and in his last «love» for his pupil Tito, who appears to Knecht shortly before his death as a kind of young god or Hermes Psychopompos, similar to the final scene between Aschenbach and Tadzio in Th. Mann's novella *Der Tod in Venedig.* (VI, 539 f.) Most of all, however, it is the Platonic love for the spirit, for mutual learning and growing which draws Knecht to his students and friends: the musicologist Ferromonte, the hyperintellectual «only-Castalian» Tegularius, the scholarly monk-historian Pater Jakobus, and above all Plinio Designori, the «auditor» who returns to the outside world when his studies in Castalia are ended. He and Pater Jakobus are the embodiments of the extra-

[31] My translation of the letter in H. Hesse, *Eine Handvoll Briefe* (Zürich 1951), p. 47.

Castalian world which for Knecht (contrary to the average Castalian) becomes more and more the supplemental, ripening force in his life.

Three persons have special functions in Knecht's self-development within the Castalian Order. They are the Old Music Master, The Elder Brother, and Master Alexander. All three are portrayed not so much as men of flesh and blood with their weaknesses and peculiarities (as Knecht observes and criticizes so sharply in Tegularius), but far more as representatives of spiritual values which tempt Knecht to stay forever in Castalia. Of all three without any doubt, the O l d  M u s i c  M a s t e r has the most important influence on Knecht. He is (like Demian for Sinclair) the ‹hierophant› who initiates Knecht into the secrets of music and meditation; he is his guardian during the years of crises and doubt in the meaningfulness of the Bead Game, and attends in person the investiture (as Magister Ludi) of his «favorite pupil», in order to give him not only «a pleasant surprise» but also to offer him perhaps «a little advice» (VI, 317). As «the great Would-be-Little» *(große Gerneklein)* he becomes the widely emulated example of selfless service to the spirit of his discipline, a human symbol of music itself, its all-embracing harmony and serenity. He finally teaches Knecht (like Siddhartha his friend Govinda) without words or even music, simply through his ‹beatific smile›– a truly Castalian «saint» (VI, 352–357).[32] The E l d e r B r o t h e r in the bamboo grove, who devoted himself to oriental studies to such a degree that he became almost Chinese himself, introduces Knecht into Chinese language and literature, particularly into the Confucian *I-Ching*. One oracle in this «Book of Changes» also seems to transfigure the enigma of Knecht's end: In the sign Mong as

32 See Inge D. Halpert, *The Altmusikmeister and Goethe.* In: *Monatshefte für den deutschen Unterricht,* LII (Madison, Wisc. 1960), pp. 19–24.

the symbol of mountain and water which appears when Knecht's future is questioned, the presage of the scenery of his death may be seen.[33] His studies in classical Chinese civilization, as it seems to me, are far more than a mere «chinoiserie» or «Chinese mask» which «enriches» the *Glasperlenspiel* with a further «ironic and graceful adornment». Knecht's knowledge of the symbolism expressed in the famous Book of Oracles, of Lao Tsu's philosophy, replace in Hesse's *Bildungsroman* to a great extent the traditional ‹classical› Greek and Latin elements, and (together with his insights into Chinese music) essentially contribute to the rounding of Knecht's personality, his cosmopolitan *Weltanschauung*.[34] Master A l e x - a n d e r , at first Knecht's yoga teacher and as the ‹president› of the ‹pedagogy› his collegial friend, takes over at the end the rôle of a father confessor and judge, to whom the Magister Ludi tries to explain for the last time his reasons for abandoning his office. That Alexander dismisses him without ‹absolution› and handshake is a typical example of Castalian morals according to which friendship has to be put aside or even sacrificed, if official duties require it (VI, 319). It could be questioned, after all, which of his friends and teachers had the strongest influence upon his life. No one seems to be superfluous. Each of them revolves around Knecht like a planet at a larger or closer distance.

That he feels «chosen» to serve and master both worlds, the Castalian and the outside, can be regarded as the guiding principle of his being, as it is suggested—*nomen est omen*—by the double nature of his very name: «Josef», similar to the biblical figure, designates the «favorite son» and predestined master, whereas «Knecht» (servant)

33 Cf. J. C. Middleton, *An Enigma Transfigured in H. Hesse's Glasperlenspiel*. In: *German Life and Letters*, X (1956/57), pp. 298–302.
34 Therefore, I cannot agree with M. Boulby's statements. See M. Boulby, *H. Hesse. His Mind and Art, ibid.*, p. 286.

points to a life of obedient, renunciative service.[35] Moreover, «Knecht» in German means more than «menial servant». Through its etymological connection with «knight» (as in *Knecht Ruprecht*), it also carries the connotation of «noble faithfulness».[36] Thus, not for the sake of making a brilliant career, of obtaining material prosperity and transitory «fame» as soon as possible, nor driven by any «will-to-power» (as those ambitious but petty scholars, poets, doctors, and the average «educated» people of the ‹Age of Feuilleton› whom Hesse satirizes in the introduction: VI, 105f.), Knecht climbs step by step the ladder of the Castalian hierarchy until he finally reaches the top position as Magister Ludi; rather he is always cognizant of the rule: «The higher the office the heavier the bondage. The greater the official power, the stricter the service». (VI, 487) Since self-knowledge for Hesse is the first law of life, Knecht at the moment when he feels himself challenged by the «call» from the outside world is prepared to resign from his office. In spite of the frequency with which he expresses his gratitude and reverence to Pater Jakobus and his teachings, the historical reasons for his final leaving of the order should not be overestimated.[37] His decision is due far more to his insight into the different stages he has reached in the process of his continuous individuation, of which he becomes aware through the experience he calls «awakening» *(Erwachen)*. (VI, 490 f.) Nor does he resign from his office in order to gain more personal freedom or to indulge in the pleasures of the world outside (as Goethe's *Faust* did after he had denounced his purely «contemplative» existence). He still regards himself as the Magister Ludi, yet now in the original meaning of the word which is simply «school-

35 Cf. Inge D. Halpert, *Wilhelm Meister and Josef Knecht.* In: *The German Quarterly,* 34 (1961), pp. 11–20, esp. p. 11 f.
36 Cf. E. Rose, *Faith from the Abyss, ibid.,* p. 139.
37 As Hesse's own rebuke of R. Faesi's assumptions shows (VII, 636 f.).

master» *(Schulmeister)*. As such he becomes engaged in a new form of «active» service as the private teacher of Tito, the spoiled but promising son of Plinio Designori, his patrician friend. However, shortly after Knecht has left Castalia, and begun to get acquainted with his new pupil, he drowns in a mountain lake, following Tito's call for a swimming competition.

Few passages of modern German literature have given cause to so much controversy as this ending of the *Glasperlenspiel*. Much of it is simply passionate, superficial and ill-founded, even if it is based on Hesse's own view expressed in a letter of February 22, 1944:

Knecht's death may naturally have many interpretations. For me the central one is that of sacrifice, which he bravely and joyfully fulfills. As I take it, he has not given up his task of educating the youth, but he has fulfilled it.[38]

The poet's self-interpretation, highly as it should be respected, is only partial and scarcely consonant with the facts gleaned from a close analysis of the text, particularly of the last chapter.[39] In recent publications much attention (perhaps too much) has been given to the *Lebensläufe*, especially the fourth one, which seems to con-

38 My translation of VII, 640.
39 For details, see Hilde Cohn, *The Symbolic End of H. Hesse's ‹Glasperlenspiel›*. In: *Modern Language Quarterly*, Nr. 11 (1950), pp. 347–357; Kenneth Negus, *On the Death of J. Knecht in H. Hesse's Glasperlenspiel*. In: *Monatshefte für den deutschen Unterricht*, 53 (1961), pp. 181–189; C. I. Schneider, *Der Tod als dichterisches Grundmotiv und Existenzproblem bei H. Hesse* (Doct. diss. Univ. of Calif. at Santa Barbara 1968), pp. 353–391 (Der Tod Josef Knechts). Roger C. Norton, on the basis of a typescript (on *verso* of a letter of June 22, 1931) and an untitled memorandum of Hesse's (Montagnola, *im Juni 1934*), gives some evidence for a strongly positive interpretation of the enigmatic conclusion, insofar as the theme of Knecht's «last game», dealing with the struggle of the ‹impure powers› (i. e. «*scheinbare Fortschritte der Macht, Politik etc.*») against the ‹pure spirit›, ends with the final victory of *Geist*. Cf. R. C. Norton, «Variant Endings of Hesse's *Glasperlenspiel*. In: *Monatshefte für den deutschen Unterricht*, 60 (1968), pp. 141 to 146, esp. p. 143.

tain more possible answers for the ‹symbolic› end of Knecht's life than had hitherto been noticed.[40] Again, the source is a remark by Knecht's biographer, who regards the autobiographies (at least three of them) as «perhaps the most valuable part of the entire book» (VI, 192). These «Incarnations» reflect Knecht's thoughts about intellectual responsibility. The idea of service, symbolized by the very names «Knecht», «Famulus» (the Latin word for «servant»), and «Dasa» (servant in Sanskrit), generally represents a central theme. At the end of all three autobiographies the central figure (the rainmaker, the father confessor, the yogin) have found a successor. From there, it has been concluded, Knecht's precipitate death becomes a powerful educational influence on Tito, turning this unruly youth inward and accomplishing in an instant what otherwise would have taken years of education. Thus the transmission of responsibility is completed symbolically as Tito picks up the cloak of his Magister and dries and warms himself with it—another successor in the cycle of master and pupil (VI, 311). Since Tito promises to become «a future master, destined to be a social and political figure for country and people, an example and a leader» (VI, 536), Knecht seems to have fulfilled his last ‹call› entirely, for it is at least possible that Tito in his future life might achieve a more successful synthesis between Castalia and the ‹World› than his father and Knecht himself were able to do. Knecht's death, however plausible it may appear, leaves many other problems open. Therefore, the reader is encouraged to meditate upon his own ‹solution›, which seems to be precisely the intention of the poet, as he expresses in the answer to a letter from a startled young reader:

40 Cf. M. Boulby, *Der vierte Lebenslauf as a Key to Das Glasperlenspiel*. In: *Modern Language Review*, 61 (1966), pp. 635–646. Sidney Johnson, *The Autobiographies in H. Hesse's Glasperlenspiel*. In: *German Quarterly*, 29 (1956), pp. 160–171.

Finally, it is not important at all, whether you understand and approve Knecht's death intellectually. It left (as in Tito) a thorn in you, an admonition you will never forget ... which will still be effective after you have forgotten my book and your letter. Keep listening to this voice which now no longer speaks out of a book but from your own self, it will guide you further.[41]

If we try to summarize Knecht's development as a whole, it strikes us as a continuous transcending of life–stages, each of which «attains its prime and cannot last for ever» (VI, 555). Or, as it is expressed in the «Legend»:

They had been only major and minor steps on an apparently direct path, and yet he found himself, at the end of this path, by no means at the heart of the world and in the centre of truth, and saw also that his present awakening was only an eye opening, a reorientation and an adaptation to new conjunctions ... (VI, 489)

Knecht's life, therefore, never reaches a final stage in either world, and, even transcending death, progresses to a new metaphysical openness, as we may conclude from the lines of the poem *Stufen*: «... Maybe death's hour will send us out/new-born toward undreamed-of lands, maybe/life's call to us will never find an end ...» (VI, 556)[42]

The development to which the novel leads at the end, clearly demonstrates that the representation of the Bead Game and Knecht's autobiography inseparably belong together; for in an isolated study many problems would remain open, which now become more or less self-explanatory. Similarly, the above questions concerning the consequences to which an individual life in Castalia might

41 My translation of H. Hesse, *Ein Briefwechsel*. In: *Die neue Rundschau*, X (1948), pp. 244 f.
42 The idea that man must step from one life into the other is also clearly expressed in Gotthold Ephraim Lessing's treatise on *The Education of Mankind*. Cf. *Lessings Werke in einem Band* (Salzburg/ Stuttgart, without year), pp. 1016–1033.

lead contain their own answers. The simple solution naturally lies b e y o n d  C a s t a l i a. In other words: Hesse proves to be the liberating critic of his own Castalia, our knowledge of this province so far having been limited to its utopian aspect. Why, for instance, did the poet need to exemplify (or rather disguise) his thoughts in the representation of a utopian province at all? Wouldn't he have been more successful if he had chosen our ‹real› political situations and institutions for a thorough critique and revision?

We have finally arrived at the last critical point of our interpretation, which will conclude with some remarks about the crucial question: What does Hesse's *Glasperlenspiel* mean for our present time and specifically to each individual?

## 3. Hesse's *Glasperlenspiel* and its Relevance for Our Time

As mentioned above,[43] Hesse worked on the *Glasperlenspiel* during World War II, that is at the time when a poet was expected to concern himself far more with subjects taken from the «realistic» world rather than with fiction, especially of such a type which is all but merely entertaining. It is true that, having lived in Switzerland since 1912, Hesse was not immediately struck by the horrors of war and the tortures inflicted by the Nazi regime. Nevertheless, he understood the «poisonous gas» and the dethronement of truth as a personal threat to the very existence of any poet of the German language. In this situation, therefore, he could do nothing better than to make use of his special talent, to express himself through his productions, by which he hoped to save for himself and the world all the spiritual values that were then being destroyed. By writing his *Glasperlenspiel* he tried to

43 p. 3.

achieve mainly two goals: to build a spiritual realm in which he himself could «live and breathe» in spite of the poisoning of the world around him, and to strengthen the resistance of his German friends against the barbaric powers under which they had to suffer. In order to create this spiritual realm, however, it was not sufficient to conjure up any past situation or to write desperately about the present, but it became necessary to project his ideas into the future, when the intolerable present would have been overcome and regarded as the past.[44] Thus the utopian character of the novel arose from the roots of an existential need in a specifically disastrous period of the history of mankind which is now over. Why did the *Glasperlenspiel* not also lose much of its original impact on the younger generations?

There is hope that we have indeed overcome the Nazi movement. Yet now as ever, truth and the individual who is actually responsible for it, are endangered by political movements all over the world, which are threatening to overthrow both the spirit of truth and the individual freedom to serve it. To be a modern Castalian, so to speak, has never lost its meaningfulness. His strength and mission consist in his ability not to get totally absorbed by the tempting insinuations of any radical party whatever its program may be. He should not strive to govern only for the sake of power, for Hesse does n o t share Plato's opinion that the »philosophers« should rule in a state (VI, 465).

Modern Castalians rather are (or should be):
... specialists in research, dissection and measurement; the preservers and perpetual verifiers of all alphabets, multiplication tables and methods, and above all the gaugers of the spiritual weights and measures ... our primary and most important function, on account of

44 Cf. the letter to Rudolf Pannwitz (1955), in: B. Zeller, *H. Hesse in Selbstzeugnissen und Bilddokumenten, ibid.*, p. 130 f.

which people need and support us, always remains the same—that of the sanitation of all sources of knowledge. In trade, politics, and in fact anywhere where an accidental achievement or act of genius is possible an X may be turned into a Y and vice versa, but never with us. (VI, 466)

In the understanding of Hesse, the modern Castalians or «intellectuals» are those who make use of their spiritual freedom, who do not remain neutral at all costs, but are «people with insight» (in the original meaning of the Latin verb *intellegere*), active servants in the name of truth for which they would even sacrifice their lives, if necessary.

This, however, is only *one* aspect of the Castalian ethos. Another one is demonstrated in the figure of the Magister Ludi Josef Knecht, who had a distinct notion of the dangers which arise when the «republic of the spirit» has become a «state in the state» and is no longer in contact with the «world outside», or if both realms neglect their historical connection and interaction: «We should not flee from the vita activa into a vita contemplativa, nor vice versa; rather, we should be alternately in both, at home in both, participating in both.» (VI, 329) Therefore, Knecht, by giving up his office, does not give up the Castalian spirit at the same time, but restitutes a live connection between the Pedagogic Province and the outside world at the very roots. He no longer teaches the intellectually most advanced students and colleagues in the élite school, but a young intelligent individual who promises to further the growth of the spiritual realm not so much in Castalia, where it is abundant, but in the «World», where it is lacking most. At the end of his career, the Magister Ludi does not appear as a scholarly professor, but rather as a *Schulmeister*, that is, as a high- or grade-school teacher (who are perhaps needed most in our present age, indeed). In this «transfiguration of teacher and teaching», as one critic puts it, Hesse's last novel can rightly be considered as «a bridge from the aestheticism of his (the author's) own generation to the existential engagement of the next.»[45] Moreover, Knecht's decision to become a teacher outside Castalia and to dedicate himself to the young to whom he long felt attracted, appears to be the fulfillment of the «classical» moral which–based on Immanuel Kant–was most strikingly formulated in Friedrich Schiller's *Letters on the Aesthetical Education of Man*, culminating in the ideal that the intellectual man should strive to l i v e the virtues, truth, and happiness in which he believes, and by doing so reconcile both his «moral» duties and individual inclinations.[46]

However, Hesse, in all his previous books and above all in the *Glasperlenspiel* does n o t «teach» that you should not study at all, do (if possible) nothing, commit yourself to nobody except to your own personal freedom, and take toward modern society and the present political situation at best a negative, criticizing or principally passive attitude. In other words, Hesse (as it can be expected from one of the most scholarly and tradition-conscious poets of the German language) presents himself in the final analysis as a doubtful, only half or most likely totally misunderstood «Saint of the Hippies.»[47] Or, as it was just recently pointed out sharply by a critic: «Some Hesse-philes say that we should rejoice to see «youth» reading such inspiring literature, but Hesse himself would probably have hated the kind of adulation his novels

45 Cf. Th. Ziolkowski, *The Novels of H. Hesse, ibid.*, p. 283.
46 «. . . the intellectual man has the ideal of virtue, of truth, and of happiness, but the active man will only practice virtues, will only grasp truths, and enjoy happy days. The business of physical and moral education is to bring back this multiplicity to unity, to put morality in the place of manners, science in the place of knowledge . . .» *The Complete Works of F. Schiller* in 8 vols. (New York MCMII), vol. 8, p. 81 (Letter XVI).
47 See Th. Ziolkowski, *Saint Hesse among the Hippies*. In: *American-German Review*, vol. 35, Nr. 2 (New York 1969), pp. 19–23.

have received.»[48] Especially those who read Hesse more for the sake of his ideas than as literature will hardly be able to appreciate what really matters in the long run: What the poet has to say as poet in his own language. Therefore, Hesse, whom the late President of the German Federal Republic, Theodor Heuss (himself an eminent scholar and artist) once praised as writing «the most beautiful German among the contemporary German authors»,[49] loses much of his original thought and artistry if read in translation. As all works of Hesse, the *Glasperlenspiel* is in fact untranslatable. Each translator stands before the alternative of cutting the rhythmical flow of the naturally long German sentences into pieces, or (if he tries to stick closer to the original), of risking an exaggeration of the difficulties innate to German.[50] Of course, Hesse's ideas, too, are relevant to modern readers—old and young—if they recognize the truly humanistic nature of his advocated «revolution» never intended as a change by means of violence. What he really stands for (similar to J. J. Rousseau in his time), is an inner revolution, characterized by Knecht's unprejudiced outlook toward the Castalian institution, which he can no longer serve in the traditional way, when he realizes that following his new «call» means nothing but honestly being himself. It is perhaps mainly this honesty toward both himself and modern society, which will remain the shining symbol in all of Hesse's works and which seems to be understood by most of his contemporary readers, indeed.

In terms of modern Depth Psychology, the *Glasperlenspiel* is an archetypal symbol of completeness *(Ganzheitssymbol)*. The glass bead itself recalls the mythical Greek

48 Henry S. Resnik in his article: *How H. Hesse Speaks to the College Generation.* In: *Saturday Review* (Oct. 18, 1969), p. 36.
49 Th. Heuss quoted from B. Zeller, *H. Hesse. Eine Chronik in Bildern* (Frankfurt a. M. 1960), p. 187.
50 Neither M. Savill's nor Richard and Clara Winston's translations of the *Glasperlenspiel* are completely free of these shortcomings.

god Sphairos as well as the globular shape of Plato's «perfect» man. It resembles further a mandala symbol and seems to fall under C. G. Jung's interpretation of the «Unidentified Flying Objects» which he regards as projections of the subconscious in search of «roundness» or completeness like those four hundred years ago, when similar «objects» were allegedly sighted.[51]

The search for meaning and integration of the individual is due partly to the problems arising out of the population increase, which an out-dated moral order can no longer solve, partly to the destructive criticism and rejection of traditional values which could still tie mankind together. Or, as Josef Knecht judges our present age from his ‹future› point of view (which gives us some hope that human life in a few centuries could still be possible):

> The misfortune of that age was that no one had any moderately resolute moral code to oppose the unrest and dynamism of the monstrously rapid increase in populations, and whatever critical faculties he still had were forced into line by the prevailing slogans. (VI, 459)

Therefore, the *Glasperlenspiel* still keeps its psychological validity for our time, where «completeness» in both a universal and individual sense is needed more than ever before. In order to prevent further catastrophies in the history of mankind, primarily the following three values in Hesse's novel should not be neglected: tolerance, meditation, and piety.

T o l e r a n c e is the basic commandment of humanity, through which the plurality of opinions in spiritual and practical life is balanced, and which prevents an open war. Josef Knecht shows this virtue especially in the confrontation with Pater Jakobus, the representative of ‹the other order›, and toward his patrician friend, Plinio Designori.

51 See Carl Gustav Jung, *Ein moderner Mythus* (Zürich 1958), p. 99.

Meditation—and closely connected with it, music—benefits the individual ‹psychohygiene›, clarifies and harmonizes human drives and inclinations which are contradictory by nature. With the help of meditation, its concentrating and purifying force, Josef Knecht overcomes all the major and minor crises in his physical and psychic life.[52]

Piety, or to be more concrete, religious belief (which Hesse himself retained throughout his life), is the less rational but intuitive conviction in each truly «intellectual» person, that the development of his individual life as well as the history of mankind «makes sense» or proceeds according to a meaningful design, for which man is not responsible alone. In the *Glasperlenspiel*, this idea is expressed in the belief in the principle of unity over multiplicity of world phenomena. It is true that Josef Knecht, as Pater Jakobus tells him rather reproachfully (VI, 246), does not believe in the existence of a specific ‹transcendental› god. However, as a deeply religious character, he leaves the question open, where the «call of life» will lead him after death. Hesse preserves at least the possibility of a metaphysical dimension, thus decidedly challenging our epoch of the supposed «Death of God» and of the decline of morally obliging religion.

Insight into the existential importance of these three spiritual values finally leads to the Castalian *Heiterkeit* and valiance, embodied in the figure of the *Altmusikmeister* and his beatific smile. *Heiterkeit* has little to do with «irony», as it has recently been overstressed as a basic structural principle and method of interpretation for this novel.[53] For irony (and closely related to it, sar-

---

52 Hesse gives particular meditation instructions in a letter in H. Hesse, *Eine Handvoll Briefe, ibid.*, pp. 22–24.
53 See M. Boulby, *H. Hesse. His Mind and Art, ibid.*, p. 272: «An ironical institution, the Glass Bead Game has an ironical history.» Remarks such as these we find almost too frequently in this otherwise very interesting and illuminating study. Cf. *op. cit.*, pp. 245, 249, 250, 257, 277, 280, 316, 321.

casm and cynicism) wants to triumph, is an attitude of absolute superiority over all possible human conditions. Such an irony, as it seems to me, is not compatible with the spirit of the *Glasperlenspiel*. The *Heiterkeit* achieved by the Old Music Master and Knecht himself, is much more closely related to *Humor* which, according to a psychological understanding, suggests that everything in this world is more or less incomplete, at least in relationship to the absolute, to God. However, in spite of these shortcomings, this world is worthy of being loved.[54] With this *Heiterkeit* in mind, we can better appreciate, too, Hesse's remarks about the decline of the West and of his own Castalia. For they are not simply an expression of pessimism, but far more a contemporary reflection on the Book of Proverbs and the idleness of all human creation and endeavors. This call of a *memento mori* in modern form should result in a new realization of human life and history *sub specie aeternitatis*. Whoever takes into consideration also the transitory aspect of all our efforts and work has really achieved maturity and wisdom. Thus Josef Knecht appears to us at the end not so much as the illustrious Magister Ludi nor as a simple school-master, but as an example for a true «Master of the Game,» life itself.

Finally, it does not seem superfluous to say, that the *Glasperlenspiel* as a whole belongs to those ‹old-fashioned› books which–in spite of modern practices–provide the most rewarding understanding and appreciation if read slowly and repeatedly. We have studied it this way several times over the last twenty years with ever new results, and still have the feeling that we are just beginning to recognize in full the intricacies and world-wide meaningfulness of the really inexhaustible work.[55]

54 Cf. the definitions of *Humor* and *Ironie* by Philipp Lersch, *Der Aufbau der Person* (München 1956), p. 301.
55 For further literature about the *Glasperlenspiel*, see e. g. Helmut Waibler, *H. Hesse. Eine Bibliographie* (Bern/München MCMLXII), pp. 280–286.

# 8

## JOSEPH MILECK
## THE POETRY OF HERMANN HESSE

Hermann Hesse's poetry falls into three distinct periods.[1] Each of these periods reflects a different stage in the course of the author's struggle with himself and with life at large, and represents a correspondingly different phase in both the substance and form of his verse.

The first of these three periods begins in 1895 and terminates with Hesse's psychological crisis of 1916–17. Of these earlier years the most representative poetic form is a three-quatrain poem, folk-song-like both in the simplicity and in the lyrical quality of its expression, e. g.:

> Es nachtet schon, die Straße ruht,
> Seitab treibt mit verschlafenen Schlägen
> Der Strom mit seiner trägen Flut
> Der stummen Finsternis entgegen.
>
> Er rauscht in seinem tiefen Bett
> So wegverdrossen, rauh und schwer,
> Als ob er Lust zu ruhen hätt',
> Und ich bin wohl so müd wie er.
>
> Das ist durch Nacht und fremdes Land
> Ein traurig Miteinanderziehen,
> Ein Wandern stumm und unverwandt.
> Zu zwei'n, und keiner weiß wohin.
> (*Nachtsang*, p. 133)

Decided preference is given to iambic tetrameter, and of diverse rime schemes, the alternate prevails. Imagery is as unsophisticated as form, syntax, and language. In the tradition of Romanticism, nature prevails, mirroring Hesse's own mood and providing an appropriate setting for

1 *Die Gedichte*, Zürich, 1947, 456 pp.

his reflections. Late summer with its tired breezes, its wilted gardens and slowly wandering clouds, is nearly spent; autumn with its gloomy skies and mists, rawer winds and falling leaves, spreads its pall; roads by night and in rain are bare and lonely, villages remote and unfamiliar, and houses with their moon-lit gables sleepy. An autumnal spirit of fatigue and melancholy pervades the atmosphere, and the prevailing silence is broken only by the murmur of a little stream, the dim ring of a distant bell, or the bark of a dog.

It is in the introductory stanza of a poem that this nature-setting is presented. Tersely sketched and faint, these descriptions are much less pictorial than evocative. The nostalgia and the weary mood of gloom evoked, are heightened by the preponderance of the faint and shadowy colors (*hell, bleich, blaß, dunkel, blau, schwarz*), by the many languid adjectives (*allein, traurig, schwer, müde, fern, fremd*), by the prevalence of such emotionally suggestive verbs as *wandern, erinnern, leiden, weinen, fühlen, träumen,* and by Hesse's constant allusions to *Jugend, Heimweh, Sehnsucht, Einsamkeit, Tod, Nacht.* The preponderance of long vowels in these adjectives, verbs, and nouns, Hesse's preference for verbs of description rather than of action, and his very frequent use of the verb «to be,» tend to retard the flow of the verse and to leave its rhythm slow and solemn, its tone modulated —quite in accord with the mood of the setting.

Before the second stanza has concluded, Hesse himself appears upon the scene: a weary wanderer, a nostalgic observer, a lonely dreamer. He moves across the dim landscape like the leaves before the wind (*Das treibende Blatt,* p. 69). His friends are unknown kindred outcasts, like himself solitary sufferers of the spirit (*Einsame Nacht,* p. 122). Just as theirs, his wandering is an endless quest for *Heimat* (*Abends auf der Brücke,* p. 145): a refuge where he might merge and experience a sense of belonging. To the oblivious innocence and harmony of childhood there is no return (*Wende*, p. 83), and with the intimacy of love and the fellowship of close friendship denied him, life has become little more than memory (*Schlaflosigkeit*, p. 203) and faint hope (*Über die Felder*, p. 62). It is in this agitation that Hesse concludes and acknowledges the ultimate loneliness of the individual (*Im Nebel*, p. 151), becomes painfully aware of transition (*Kind im Frühling*, p. 161), begins to feel that life has shortchanged him (*Wie kommt es*, p. 60), and that his thoughts turn to and almost morbidly linger over death. Perhaps only death would afford the *Heimat* life denied (*Abends auf der Brücke*, p. 145).

Until the concluding years of the First World War, neither Hesse's way of life nor his poetry could have been considered exceptional. Others had been rebellious youths, romantic outsiders devoted to beauty, only in due time to conform and to seek an asylum in marriage and a bourgeois way of life, and others long before him had established the Romantic tradition of lyrical poetry. Hesse's work might possibly have continued in this traditional vein, had accumulating tensions not reached a head and changed the entire course of his life. The disrupting effect of the war, the serious illness of his youngest son, his father's death, the growing estrangement between himself and his mentally ill wife, his own frail health and prolonged psychoanalytical treatment, combined to bring to an impasse the bourgeois way of life which had never actually afforded the security Hesse had hoped it might. In desperation Hesse finally withdrew to his hermetic retreat of Montagnola, there, in the hope of rehabilitation, to probe into the basic problems of human existence, and to pursue his long shunned *Weg nach Innen*.

In both substance and form, the poetry of the second period (1917–26) contrasts just as strongly with that of the first as does Hesse's new approach to life and its problems with the old. The plaintive yearning of a nostalgic wanderer becomes the determined quest of a distraught seeker, feeling gives way to thought, self-consciousness to self-awareness, and form experiences a corresponding change.

While mood and sentiment had found ready expression in fixed stanzas, metric patterns, and rime schemes, intellectual experience and emotional distress were not to be contained by any traditional poetic restraints. The folksong-like poem, characteristic of the years preceding 1917, now yields its place to a restive prose verse. Accordingly, of the 125-odd poems written in the course of the subsequent decade, more than one third are in free verse, e. g.:

> Kinder sind wir, rasch macht die Sonne uns müd,
> Die uns doch Ziel und heilige Zukunft ist,
> Und aufs neue an jedem Abend
> Fallen wir klein in der Mutter Schoß,
> Lallen Namen der Kindheit,
> Tasten den Weg zu den Quellen zurück.
> Auch der einsame Sucher,
> Der den Flug zur Sonne sich vorgesetzt,
> Taumelt, auch er, um die Mitternacht
> Rückwärts seiner fernen Herkunft entgegen,
> Und der Schläfer, wenn ihn ein Angsttraum weckt,
> Ahnt im Dunkeln mit irrer Seele
> Zögernde Wahrheit:
> Jeder Lauf, ob zur Sonne oder zur Nacht,
> Führt zum Tode, führt zu neuer Geburt,
> Deren Schmerzen die Seele scheut.
> Aber alle gehen den Weg,
> Alle sterben, alle werden geboren,
> Denn die ewige Mutter
> Gibt sie ewig dem Tag zurück.
> (*Die Nacht,* pp. 266–267)

In general this new representative form tends to be at least twice as long as the old with its three quatrains; stanza division, when retained, is very irregular, rime is continued, though quite without pattern, language becomes prosier, its syntax more complex and its vocabulary progressively less romantically evocative, more sober, and eventually quite common (*Krisis,* discussed below). Background imagery evidences just as decided a change. Rather than a mirror for mood, and a picturesque setting with only a brief afterthought, nature now prevalently becomes but a casual reference point for more prolonged reflection (*Auch die Blumen,* p. 270), and in accord with this shift of emphasis from description and feeling to a more dramatic thought process, these allusions to nature are now more commonly metaphorical or symbolical: as leaf upon leaf falls from Hesse's tree of life (*Vergänglichkeit,* p. 284), he longs passionately to experience all aspects of being—to die the death of a tree, a mountain, of sand and of grass, to be reborn a flower, a fish, a bird (*Alle Tode,* p. 289); night and its moon with its dreams of a lost *childhood-Heimat* are intimately associated with the sympathetic mother-principle, become symbols of *Natur* (*Herbstabend 1918,* p. 281), and burning day represents the stern father-principle, and its sun is *Geist* (*die Nacht,* p. 266).

During the first period of his career, Hesse is rarely given to metaphysical speculation. The painful facts of life (loneliness, transition, death) have impressed themselves upon his soul, but little effort is made to delve into the nature of *being* and the ultimate causes of suffering. Serious reflection upon this problem begins in 1917. In the ensuing free verse, the *malaise humain* is attributed to the very dichotomy of human existence and to the inherent flux of *being*. Immediately, Hesse acknowledges and accepts both aspects of life's duality, the very benign mother-principle (*Natur*), and the equally severe father-principle (*Geist*): in upward aspiration man will essay the conscious heights of the latter, and in fatigue will always return to the oblivious repose of the former (*Die Nacht*, p. 266). At moments of despondency, however, the father-principle of law, perception, and individuation, to which then all woes are ascribed, is caustically repudiated (*Rückkehr*, p. 278).

Just as distressing for Hesse as this suspension between life's two forces is the incessant *becoming* of life (*Die Nacht*, p. 266). Existence is to him a painful experiencing of endless deaths and rebirths. While this flux is not to be stayed, its pain may be alleviated in philosophical acceptance of the nature of things (*Auch die Blumen*, p. 270), or in the realization that the intensive experiencing of life in all its flux is a necessary concomitant of any desire to bring its poles into a more harmonious interplay (*Alle Tode*, p. 289). However, yet another resolution presents itself. Indulging in the Sankhya system of Hindu philosophy, Hesse envisages a new *Heimat*, the soul-nirvana transcending the realms of *Geist*, *Natur*, and their flux (*Media in Vita*, p. 311).[2] One had only to retire to one's innermost self–but Hesse was no oriental.

It is in this contained manner that Hesse continues for a number of years to ponder the lot of humanity. In ascetic retreat he seemed successfully to have reestablished himself. However, it was only a matter of time before these very circumstances were to occasion a new crisis, before the *Geist* and *Natur* dichotomy was to cease being an issue on a metaphysical plane, to become a psychological fact. By 1926, seclusion had become stifling and severe sublimation was beginning to take its toll. *Geist* is now dethroned and *Natur*, too long repressed, bursts forth, engulfing Hesse in a vengeful sensuality for almost

2 For the genesis of *Media in Vita* and a discussion of Sankhya philosophy see «Aus einem Tagebuch des Jahres 1920,» *Corona* III (1932–33), 207.

an entire year. It is this frantic interval which the poems of *Krisis* witness.[3]

This unique collection, consisting predominantly of free verse, is the outburst of an imagination inflamed by frustration, an obsession of inadequacy, and by fear. Feverish, with bloodshot eyes and aching head, Hesse flounders about in a mad vortex of dance halls, bars, and sex. Enviously he would be a naive *Naturkind*, play hot jazz and shimmy (*Neid*, p. 28), be a rakish young man about town (*Bei der Toilette*, p. 40), and experience sensual life in satiation (*Schweinerei*, p. 58). Possessed by these impossible desires and tormented by his conscience (*Ahnungen*, p. 67), Hesse sinks into sardonic despondency. The stench of life becomes unbearable (*Weinerlich*, p. 64), the smug bourgeois world of affluence and mediocrity is spared no invective (*Mißglückter Abend*, p. 15), and self-disparagement knows no bounds (*Sterbelied des Dichters*, p. 10). In this bitter frame of mind, cynical laughter is Hesse's ultimate recourse and death his only hope for release (*Fieber*, p. 53). However, the storm abates, equilibrium is regained, *Geist* and detached observation again prevail. And now, reconciling himself to this fitful vacillation between life's two poles, alternately saint and sinner, Hesse is prepared to experience and to exhaust whatever destiny may yet hold in store (*An den indischen Dichter Bhartrihari, p. 76*).

*Krisis* is not a collection of pleasant verse, nor is it poetically of much, if of any, significance. The substance is too crude, the language too common, the emotions are too turbulent and the thoughts too undistilled. It tries the very limits of poetry. However, much more vital to Hesse than poetic propriety, the aesthetic factor, and the reception by his public, was self-knowledge and sincerity with

3 *Krisis. Ein Stück Tagebuch*, Berlin, 1928, 85 pp. This very limited edition of forty-five poems is the poetic counterpart of *Steppenwolf*, 1927. Both works were written in the course of 1926.

their hope of rehabilitation.[4] *Krisis* was meant primarily to be therapeutic in function. In his critical plight, Hesse could not sincerely continue to write the *schöne Gedichte* expected by his public; he would not reduce his poetry to meaningless «Pralinés für das Publikum.»[5]

The excruciating catharsis of *Krisis* brings to an end Hesse's period of distress and quest. In *Selbsterkenntnis* he had come to terms with himself, in *Lebenserkenntnis* he was now to come to terms with life at large. Quitting his hermitage, he remarries, and in a more philosophical spirit allows the third and last phase of his life to take its more even course.

After years of painful growth Hesse now approaches that last vital turning point in life beyond which *Werden* becomes *Entwerden,* the self is slowly transcended and the unity of reality ultimately experienced.[6] In quiet retirement and ever closer communion with nature, struggle with himself and with the circumstances of life gradually subsides, emotions are subdued, and thought yields to contemplation. The schizophrenic *Steppenwolf,* with his somber seriousness and his desperate gospel of humor, becomes a serene *Glasperlenspieler,* who knows the value of playful observation *(Entgegenkommen,* p. 381) and for whom acceptance is that of faith and love.

A new way of life and a different attitude to its problems again bring with them corresponding changes in the general nature of Hesse's poetry. Turbulent intellectual-emotional experience had found its most ready ex-

4 «Nachwort an meine Freunde,» *Krisis,* p. 82.
5 «Schlechte Gedichte,» *Betrachtungen,* Berlin, 1928, p. 98.
6 «. . . so bedarf es für das Erlebnis, das ich meine, doch eben des hohen Alters, es bedarf einer unendlichen Summe von Gesehenem, Erfahrenem, Gedachtem, Empfundenem, Erlittenem, es bedarf einer gewissen Verdünnung der Lebenstriebe, einer gewissen Hinfälligkeit und Todesnähe, um in einer kleinen Offenbarung der Natur den Gott, den Geist, das Geheimnis wahrzunehmen, den Zusammenfall der Gegensätze, das große Eine» (Hermann Hesse, «Aprilbrief,» *Neue Züricher Zeitung,* April 29, 1952).

pression in dramatic free verse, calm contemplation was to find its most characteristic poetic form in reflective-narrative verse: longer poems consisting of irregular stanzas or dispensing with stanza division entirely, prevalently in iambic pentameter and with mixed rime patterns, e. g.:

Wie jede Blüte welkt und jede Jugend
Dem Alter weicht, blüht jede Lebensstufe,
Blüht jede Weisheit auch und jede Tugend
Zu ihrer Zeit und darf nicht ewig dauern.
Es muß das Herz bei jedem Lebensrufe
Bereit zum Abschied sein und Neubeginne,
Um sich in Tapferkeit und ohne Trauern
In andre, neue Bindungen zu geben.
Und jedem Anfang wohnt ein Zauber inne,
Der uns beschützt und der uns hilft, zu leben.

Wir sollen heiter Raum um Raum durchschreiten,
An keinem wie an einer Heimat hängen,
Der Weltgeist will nicht fesseln uns und engen,
Er will uns Stuf' um Stufe heben, weiten.
Kaum sind wir heimisch eingewohnt,
                              [so droht Erschlaffen;
Nur wer bereit zu Aufbruch ist und Reise,
Mag lähmender Gewöhnung sich entraffen.

Es wird vielleicht auch noch die Todesstunde
Uns neuen Räumen jung entgegen senden,
Des Lebens Ruf an uns wird niemals enden . . .
Wohlan, denn, Herz, nimm Abschied und gesunde!
(*Stufen*, p. 419)

Representation of nature, though now in the greater detail of detached observation (*Durchblick ins Seetal*, p. 403), has become relatively infrequent, dispassionate reflection with its more involved syntax, deliberate vocabulary, and halting rhythm, more common; and when, at the height of detachment, Hesse's thoughts soar to visions –to the world's creation and to the decline of that spirit which had found its ultimate expression in the Gothic cathedral and in the music of Bach–his poetry becomes as though transfigured: lofty narrative in studied simplicity (*Orgelspiel*, p. 395), a play of symbols in a slow impelling sweep of sound and suggestion (*Zu einer Toccata von Bach*, p. 383).

The more conventional quatrains of the last period evidence this same trend. Autumn, wilted gardens, empty fields, winds and rain continue to fascinate Hesse, but the once melancholy wanderer to whom nature had been little more than a mirror for mood, is now an impassive observer, has himself become but a mirror (*Gedenken an den Sommer Klingsors*, p. 352), and vague landscapes and silhouettes gradually give way to the more detailed descriptions of particular moments and situations (*Augenblick vor dem Gewitter*, p. 371). Just as detachment and observation climax in dispassionate, purely descriptive lyrical poetry, so does detachment and review of life's basic problems climax in dispassionate, purely reflective lyrical poetry (*Klage*, p. 380), and as Hesse's thoughts again spiral to visions, only symbol remains to give them expression (*Das Glasperlenspiel*, p. 391).

Following *Krisis*, Hesse's continued preoccupation with flux and dichotomy reverts to its earlier metaphysical plane. Man is again a child of *Natur* whose destiny is *Geist* (*Besinnung*, p. 376), a discordant composite (*Doch heimlich dürsten wir*, p. 381) prey to life's relentless flux (*Klage*, p. 380). However, Hesse no longer feels impelled to attempt in terms of philosophy to make these circumstances of life more tolerable. The acceptance he had long and vainly sought in philosophical speculation is now realized instead in religious experience: a faith in the ultimate meaningfulness of life. In this faith, that love is now made possible which can make harmony of chaos, alleviate anxious loneliness in humaneness, reconcile the principles of *Geist* and *Natur (Nachtgedanken,* p. 408), and acclaim life's flux *(Stufen,* p. 419).

Hesse's quest for the *Heimat* he had lost with his childhood and to which he had long clung in memory and dream, for which he had hoped in death and had sought in philosophical speculation, was ended. He had found not the oblivious harmony pursued, but the conscious harmony of man's second stage of innocence and grace[7]— life itself had become his refuge.

7 «Immer, zu allen Zeiten der Geschichte und in allen Religionen und Lebensformen, sind es dieselben typischen Erlebnisse, immer in derselben Stufung und Reihenfolge: Verlust der Unschuld, Bemühung um Gerechtigkeit unter dem Gesetz, daraus folgende Verzweiflung im vergeblichen Ringen um das Überwinden der Schuld durch Werke oder durch Erkenntnis und endlich Auftauchen aus der Hölle in eine veränderte Welt und in eine neue Art von Unschuld» (Hermann Hesse, «Ein Stückchen Theologie,» *Neue Rundschau,* XLIII, No. 1, 1932. 738–39).

# VOCABULARY AND GLOSSARY

Vocabulary and glossary are compiled to serve as reading aids.
For all nouns the plural is indicated. The genetive singular is
mentioned in parenthesis for strong nouns when it is not -(e)s,
and for all weak nouns.
All strong verbs are marked with an asterisk(*).
Only meanings required by the text are given.


## ABBREVIATIONS

| | | | |
|---|---|---|---|
| *bot.* | botany | *o. s.* | oneself |
| *coll.* | colloquial | *pl.* | plural |
| *Fr.* | French | *poet.* | poetic |
| *Ital.* | Italian | *s. o.* | someone |
| *Lat.* | Latin | *s. th.* | something |
| *obsol.* | obsolete | | |

**A**

Aare f  river in Switzerland

Aargau  Swiss canton

Abbé m (Fr.)  abbot; title of respect for a clergyman

abbesuchen  to visit systematically

Abendsonnenglast m -e radiance of the setting sun

Abendtrunk m ⁻e night-cap

abgebrannt (coll.)  ruined

Abgebrühtheit f (coll.)  callousness

abkämpfen  to obtain by fighting

in Abrede stellen  to deny

Abstecher m  side trip

Abstimmungsverfahren n procedure for voting

Abstinent m (-en), -en abstainer

achtfache Pfad m  the Noble Eightfold Path in Buddhism, leading to Nirvana

addio! (Ital.)  Goodbye!

Adept m (-en), -en  master

Adlige m (-n), -n  nobleman

Admiral m -e red-admiral butterfly

ad usum Germanorum (Lat.) for the use of the Germans

Affenbaum m ⁻e  baobab tree; monkey bread tree

Affenquadrille f -n  monkeys doing a quadrille (French square dance)

Aftermiete f -n  sub-lease

Agni (Sanskrit)  Hindu god of fire

Ahimsa f (Sanskrit)  Indian religious law forbidding the killing of animals

aimable (Fr.)  lovable

im Akkord arbeiten  to do piece-work

akrat (coll.)  accurately; exactly

Akribie f  scrupulous exactness

Alb pl. i. e. die Schwäbische Alb, a mountain range in Southern Germany

Albis m  mountain range in Switzerland

Albula  mountain pass in the Swiss canton of Graubünden

Alchemie f  alchemy

alea iacta est (Lat.)  the die is cast

Alemannisch  Alemannic

Alkermes  Greek wine

Alkoven m  recess

All-Eine m  all-embracing deity

Allerweltsmann m ⁻er  man of the world

Allokution f -en  hortatory address

Allotria pl.  fun

Alltagsnase f -n  everyday nose

Altane f -n  balcony

altbekannt  well-known

Altdorfer, Albrecht (1480–1538) German painter

Alten pl.  the ancients

Alterle n  (dear) old fellow

Altersbehinderung f  impediment of old age

**Altklugheit** f precociousness

**amice** (Ital.) friend

**Ammer** f name of a creek in Tübingen, university city in Swabia

**amön** (Lat.) lovely

**amor fati** (Lat.) the love of one's destiny

**Ämplein** n small hanging lamp

**Amselschlag** m blackbird's song

**amten** to perform the duties of one's office

**Amüsieren** n amusement

**Anabasis** f (military) advance

**Anathapindika** benefactor of Gotama

**anbequemen** to accommodate; to adapt

**ändlig** (coll.) = endlich finally

übel **angeschrieben** in bad repute

**angespannt** intense

**angestrengt** intent

**angezeigt sein** to be advisable

**Angstpeter** m (coll.) coward

**animula vagula blandula** (Lat.) pale little vagrant soul (from Aelius Spartianus, *Hadriani Vita*)

**anlachen** (fig.) to smile
mit sieben Himmeln anlachen to give a ‹come hither› look

**Anna Karenina** title of a novel by Leo Tolstoi (1817–1875)

**Anno** (Lat. ablative case of annus, year) in the year

**Anno Duback** (coll.) time immemorial

**anschiffen** (coll.) to piss

(gering) **anschlagen*** to think (little) of

**anschnauzen** to snap at

**Anstaltlichkeit** f institutionalization

**Anstandsvisite** f -n formal call

**antiquiert** antiquated

**Antonius** Saint Anthony of Egypt (251?–ca. 350), father of Christian Monasticism

**Äolus** (myth) Aeolus, god of the winds

**apage!** (Greek) Away!

**Apollinische** und Dionysische n the Apollonian and the Dionysian, antagonistic principles in Friedrich Nietzsche's philosophy

**apparuit iam beatitudo vestra** (Lat.) your blessedness has already appeared

**appellieren (an)** to appeal (to)

**Appenzell** Swiss canton

**Aquinat** m Saint Thomas Aquinas (1225–1274), Italian philosopher and Doctor of the Church

**Arabeske** f -n ornamentation of interlacing patterns; posture of a ballet dancer

**Araukarie** f -n (Bot.) small pine

**Arbeitsrausch** m intoxication of work

**Ariosto,** Ludovico (1474–1533) Italian poet

**a rivederci domani!** (Ital.) See you tomorrow!

**a rivederla!** (Ital.) Goodbye, see you again soon!

**Ärmelaufschlag** m ⸗e cuff

**Ärmelschoner** m - sleeve-protector or cuff

**Armhäuslerluft** f poorhouse atmosphere

**Arreststrafe** f -n punishment by confinement

**arriviert** successful

**ars longa, vita brevis; Seneca: vitam brevem esse, longam artem** (Lat.) life is short, but art endures

**ars moriendi** (Lat.) the art of dying

**Arve** f -n (Bot.) cembra-pine

**Äser** pl. of Aas (coll.) beast; louse

**Asklepios** Greek god of medical science

**Assisi,** Franz von (1182?–1226) Saint Francis of Assisi, originally Giovanni Bernardone

**assistono diversi santi** (Ital.) various saints are helping

**Assuan** city in Egypt

**Asti** capital of the Italian province Asti

**Astrild** m -e blue finch

**Ataraxie** f a state of tranquility

**Athanasius,** Saint (295–373) Greek patriarch of Alexandria

**Atharva-Veda** (Sanskrit) one of the four collections of prayers which are the basis of Vedic literature and religion

**Atlantis** legendary island in the Atlantic, west of Gibraltar, supposed to have sunk into the ocean

**Atman** (Sanskrit) individual soul; self; the life principle; breath

**au** (coll.) = auch also

**aufdröseln** to untwine

**aufgeräumt** jovial

**aufhebens machen** to make a fuss

**Aufnahmebereitschaft** f receptivity

**aufschüren** to stir up

**aufwerfen*** sich zum Ritter aufwerfen to be gallant

**Augapfel** m ⸗ apple of one's eye

**augurenhaft** foreboding

**Augustinus** (354–430) Saint Augustine, Doctor of the Church, one of the four Latin fathers

**Aurelian** (214–275) Roman Emperor

**auseinanderscherbende Masse** pl. mass of separate fragmentary pictures

**auseinanderspritzen** to separate into streams

**ausfressen*** (coll.) to eat up

**ausgehoben werden** to be drafted

ausgepfiffen haben (coll.) to be finished

ausgetreten to be worn down

auskneifen* (coll.) to escape

auspröbeln (coll.) to try

Auswürfling m -e outcast

aut Caesar aut nihil (Lat.) either King or nothing

Avancement n (Fr.) promotion

Azalee f -n (Bot.) azalea

## B

Bach, Johann Sebastian (1685–1750) German composer

Bäckerbubenschritt m -e the step of the baker's boy

Backfisch m -e (coll.) teenage girl

Backfischschwärmerei f teenage enthusiasm

Baden-Baden city and resort in Southern Germany

Baden on the Limmat famous spa near Zürich, Switzerland

Die Badereise des Doktor Katzenberger f novel by Jean Paul, pseud. Johann Paul Friedrich Richter (1763–1825), German novelist

Badwiese f -n meadow by a river where people swim

bagatellisieren to treat as a joke

Ball, Hugo (1886–1927) Swiss writer, actor, and one of the founders of Dadaism

Balte m (-n), -n man from the Baltic region

bambino (Ital.) child

Bambusgehölz n -e bamboo wood

Banause m (-n), -n Philistine

Bandelier n -e shoulder strap

Banyanenbaum m ⁀e banyan tree

Bärbele n - South German diminutive of Barbara

Barbiergehilfe m (-n), -n barber's helper

Barcarole f -n name given to a piece of music derived from songs sung by gondoliers in Venice

Bärenhäuter m - idler; lazybones

Barke f -n Mediterranean fishing-boat

Barmekiden pl. wealthy Persian family in the *Arabian Nights*

Bartscherer m (arch.) barber

Bast m -e plant fiber

Basta! (Ital.) That's that!

Batikstoff m -e batik cloth

Batuhöhle f Mongolian cave

Bauchgrimmen n griping stomach pains

Bayer m (-n), -n Bavarian

Beckei f name of an inn in Tübingen

beelenden to make miserable

Beerengesträuch n -e (Bot.) berry shrub

Beethoven, Ludwig van (1770–1827) German composer

Begnadung f state of grace or bliss

Begriffswelt f -en conceptual world

**Behältnis** n -se  container
**Beiklang** m ⸚e  admixture
**Beipferd** n -e  extra horse
**Beisel** n - (coll.)  pub
**Belial**  name of a devil
**Belletrist** m (-en), -en  man of
letters
**bemeistern**  to master
**Bemitleidetwerden** n  being
sympathized with
**bene vixit qui bene latuit.**
(Lat.) Ovid, *Tristia* 3, 4, 25;
Motto of the school of Epi-
curus; He has lived well who
has stayed well in hiding.
**Beobachtungswerkzeug** n -e
tool for observation
**Bereuung** f  repentance
**Bergamasker Wirt** m  the inn-
keeper of Bergamo
**Bergell**  Alpine valley between Switzerland and Italy
**Bergnest** n -er  remote village
in the mountains
**Berliner** m - (coll.)  large
knapsack
**Berner Oberland**  Highland
of the canton of Bern, Switzerland
**bescheidentlich**  humble
**Beschönigung** f  euphemistic
term
**besonnt**  sunny
**bespötteln**  to ridicule
**Betonwüstenei** f -n  concrete
desert
**Betriebmacherei** f  bustle
**Bettelgang** m ⸚e  begging cir-
cuit
**Bettstatt** f  bedstead

**Bevogtung** f  guardianship
**bewandern**  to travel through
**Bewillkommnung** f  welcome
**bewimpelt**  with pennons
**Bhagavad-Gita**  (Sanskrit)
poem incorporated into the
Mahabharata, great Sanskrit
epic of India
**bi -** (Lat.)  prefix, denoting
twice, double or two
**Bibamus!** (Lat.) Let us drink!
**Bibelwort** n  Bible readings
**Bienenkraut** n (Bot.)  thyme
**Bierhuhn** n ⸚er (coll.)  beer
drinker
**Bijou** n -s (Fr.)  jewel, darling
**Bildsplitterchen** n -  particle
of an image
**Bildstock** m ⸚e  wayside shrine
**Bimsstein** m  pumice-stone
**Birkendose** f -n  birch snuff-
box
**bisch** (coll.) = bist du  are you
**ein bissel** (coll.) = ein bißchen
a little
**Blagueur** m -e (Fr.)  joker;
teller of tall stories
**Blättergestiebe** n  drifting
leaves
**Blau** f  name of a river
**blauen**  to become or be blue;
(poet.) azure
**blaustählern**  steel-blue
**Blautopf** m  Blue Pot, a deep
well at Blaubeuren
**Blindschleiche** f -n  garter
snake
**Blumenstraußtapete** f  -n
wallpaper with floral bou-
quets

blumig flowery

Blust f (coll.) bloom

blutt (coll.) bare; poor

Bo-Baum m ¨e the sacred tree where Buddha received Enlightenment

Boccia-Bahn f outside track for playing Boccia

Bockleiter f -n stepladder

Böcklin, Arnold (1827–1901) Swiss painter

Bocksbart m ¨e (Bot.) goat's beard mushroom

bodenlos unfathomable

Bodensee m Lake Constance

Böhme, Jakob (1575–1624) German religious mystic

Bohrer m - drill

Bologneser m wine from Bologna, Italy

Bonne f -n (Fr.) maid

Born m -e (poet.) well

Börnlein n - (poet.) little spring

Borobudur Buddhist stupa in Java

Botticelli, Sandro (1447–1510) Italian painter

Bouteille f -s (Fr.) bottle

Boy m -s bell-boy

Brabant Brabant, former province of the Netherlands, now of Belgium

Brahman n (Sanskrit) i.e. essence of the universe

Brandmal n -e (fig.) stigma

Brandmarkung f stigmatization

Brausemut m mood of great gaiety

Brautleute pl. bride and bridegroom

Brautschau f wife-hunting

Brechung f -en refraction

breitschauflig with wide oars

Bremen city in Northern Germany

Bremgarten town in the canton Aargau, Switzerland

Brest f -en bodily weakness

Brombeere f -n blackberry

Bronzeguß m ¨sse bronze-cast

Brotwissenschaft f learning for the purpose of earning a livelihood

Brünig mountain pass in Switzerland

Brunnen village in the Swiss canton of Schwyz

sich brüsten to boast

brutto (Ital.) ugly

Büble n - (coll.) little fellow

buchen made of beech

Buchenlaub n beech foliage

Buchenstand m ¨e beech wood

Bücherschaft m ¨e book shelf

Bückling m -e bow

Buddha (Sanskrit) the Enlightened One, title given to the religious leader who founded Buddhism; believed to have lived from 563 B. C. to 483 B. C.

büffeln (coll.) to slave

Bundesgelübde n - vow to the league

buntscheckig spotted

Burano island in the lagoon of Venice

**Burckhardt,** Jacob (1818-1897) Swiss historian

**Bureauherr** m (-en), -en office manager

**Bürgenstock** m name of a Swiss mountain

**Bürgersmann** m (coll.) = Bürger citizen; bourgeois

**Bürgervereinsbibliothek** f -en public library

**Bürstenkopf** m "e crew cut

**Buschklepper** m - highwayman

**Buschnelkenrabatte** f -n bed of bush-carnations

**Busennadel** f -n brooch

**Butte** f -n tub

**Büttel** m - bailiff; beadle

**Butterteiggipfel** m - pastry

# C

**Cambrai** city in Northern France

**camposanto** (Ital.) cemetery

**caput mortuum** (Lat.) death's head moth

**Carmen** opera by Georges Bizet

**caro** (Ital.) dear

**caro amico** (Ital.) dear friend

**Causeur** m -e (Fr.) conversationalist

**cave frater!** (Lat.) Beware, brother!

**Cénacle** (Fr.) gathering of writers and artists

**censor morum** (Lat.) censor of morals

**chagrin d'amour** (Fr.) lover's grief

**Chargierte** m (-n), -n student in a fencing fraternity who has passed initiation

**charmieren** to charm

**Chasseur** m -e bell-boy

**Chattus Calvensis II;** Chattus of Calw Chattus was Hesse's nickname

**chemisette** f -s (Fr.) dicky

**Chimäre** f -n chimera

**Chioggia** a seaport town south of Venice

**Chopin,** Frédéric (1810–1849) Polish-French pianist and composer

**Christoffer** Saint Christopher, protector of travelers

**Chrysantheme** f -n (Bot.) chrysanthemum

**Chumm!** (coll.) = Komme!

**Chur** capital of the canton Graubünden, Switzerland

**Chymie** f chemistry

**Colleoni,** Bartolomeo (1400–1475) Italian soldier of fortune

**Comersee** m Lake Como

**con amore** (Ital.) with feeling

**consecutio temporum** (Lat.) sequence of tenses

**Couperin,** François (1668–1733) French composer

**Cremona** city in Northern Italy

**Cusanus** Nicholas of Cusa (1401–1464), German churchman and humanist

# D

**Dabeiseinwollen** n eagerness to participate

**Dachkammerberühmtheit** f hidden fame

**Dachrücken** m - roofridge

**Dachstock** m ¨e attic

**Dackel** m - dachshund; (coll.) fool, dunce

**Dagesch** forte (Hebrew) double period mark in consonant

**dahinfallen\*** to fall away, to disappear

**Dahlie** f -n (Bot.) dahlia

**Daimonion** (Greek) the inner voice; demonic inner mentor

**Dampfer** m - steamship

**dannen** (von dannen) away

**Darmkrampf** m ¨e intestinal cramp

**Däumling** m -e Tom Thumb

**deheim** (coll.) = daheim at home

**Dehmel,** Richard (1863–1920) German poet

**deliziös** delicious

**Demiurg** m demiurge, an inferior god who built the material world

**Demoiselle** (Fr.) Miss

**dengeln** to sharpen

**de rebus castaliensibus** (Lat.) about the affairs of Castalia

**derweil** (coll.) whilst

**despektierlich** disrespectful

**Desperado** m -s (Span.) desperado; outlaw

**Dessinateur** m -e designer

**de tentatione dormiendi** (Lat.) concerning the temptation to sleep

**Diabolus** m devil

**Diathermie** f (Greek) heating of tissues beneath the skin with an electrical apparatus

**Dickhäuter** m - thick-skinned fellow

**Dickkopf** m ¨e blockhead

**dickstämmig** thick-trunked

**Dierlammsch** of the Dierlamm family

**Distelfalter** m - painted lady

**Doge** m (-n), -n doge, chief magistrate in the former republics of Venice and Genova

**Dogenpalast** m doge's palace in Venice

**Dolde** f -n umbel; cluster

**dona ferens** (Lat.) bearing gifts

**Dorment** n dormitory in a monastery

**Dornenreif** m -e crown of thorns

**dörnicht** (coll.) thorny

**Dorpat** town on the Baltic Sea

**Douceur** n -e (Fr.) gratuity

**Drallewatsch** m (coll.) smartaleck

**Draperie** f -n drapery

**drauf** (coll.) = darauf

**dreckats** (coll.) = dreckig dirty

**zum Dreihenker** in the devil's name

**drüber** (coll.) = darüber above

Drücker m - doorknocker

Dryade f -n dryad; tree nymph

Dummelein n - dear «Dopey»

dumpfwohlig soporific

Dunder! (coll.) = Donnerwetter! Damn it!

Dundersfrau f damn woman

sich durchbringen* to make a living

durchdringend penetrating

Durchgangsstation f -en way station

Durchschnitts-Psychologe m (-n), -n mediocre psychologist

durchwalten to pervade

Duse, Eleonora (1859–1924) Italian actress

Düsseldorf city in Western Germany

düster gloomy

Duzbrüderschaft f -en familiarity (to the extent of saying ‹du›)

# E

e (coll.) = einer, eine, eines

ebbes (coll.) = etwas something

ebenbürtig equal

ebendas the very same

edelförmig (poet.) nobly shaped

Edelkastanie f -n edible chestnut

Ehrgefühl n sense of honor

Eichendorff, Joseph (1788–1857) German poet

Eichengestrüpp n oak underbrush

Eichmeister m - gauger

Eierrollen n game of eggrolling

zu eigen haben to possess

Eiger m mountain peak in central Switzerland

einbleuen to drill

sich etwas einbrocken (coll.) to get into trouble

eindachsen (coll.) to fall asleep

Eindunkeln n (coll.) = Dunkelwerden twilight

einen to unify

einfädeln (fig.) to contrive; to arrange

eingelegt inlaid

eingesargt entombed; put into caskets

Einkleidung f investiture

einkneifen* to squint (the eyes)

Einlage f -n deposit

Einmaleins n multiplication table

einschlagen* to be a hit
kalt einschlagen lightning strikes but there is no fire

einseifen to dupe; to get the best of s. o.

Einspänner m - one-horse carriage; (fig.) lonely man

sich einspinnen* to shut oneself in (like a spider)

einstreichen* to take in

einswerden* to become unified

eintrichtern (fig., coll.) to

hammer something into a person's head

**Einvernehmen** n agreement

**einziehen\*** to confiscate

**Eisbeutel** m - ice-bag

**Eisblume** f -n pattern of ice

**Eisenhandlung** f -en hardware store

**Eisumschlag** m ¨e ice-bag

**elbisch** elfin

**Elenderle** m nickname meaning ‹little misery›

**Elixier** n -e elixir

**Eloge** f -n eulogy

**Elsaß** Alsace

**emol** (coll.) = einmal once

**sich emporbäumen** to rear up; (fig.) rebel

**en effet** (Fr.) indeed

**Englischrot** n English red

**entfachen** to kindle

**Entgegenkömmling** m -e herald

**entgleisen** to derail

**enthäuten** to tear the skin off

**enthülsen** to shell; to uncover

**entleiden** to disgust s. o. with s. th.

**Entpersönlichung** f depersonalization

**Entrechtete** m (-n), -n outlaw

**entselbsten** to depersonalize

**Entselbstung** f self-abnegation

**Entsprechung** f analogy

**entstofflicht** abstract

**entwirklicht sein** to be unreal

**Ephorus** m -ren (Greek) overseer; supervisor

**erdarben** to save with difficulty

**erdhaft** earthy; terrestrial

**Erdreich** n earth; ground

**Eremitentum** n hermitism

**Erfahrungswurschtigkeit** f (coll.) indifference toward experience

**erfaßbar** comprehensible

**(er)feilschen** to bargain

**Erhabene** m (-n), -n sublime one

**erharren** to await

**Erika** f -ken heath

**Erinnerungsgut** n store of memories

**«Erkenne dich selbst!»** «Know thyself!» – basic sentence of Socrates' philosophy

**Erker** m - alcove; oriel

**erklecklich** substantial

**erklügeln** to devise; to concoct

**erlaben** to refresh

**erlaufen\*** to reach (by running)

**Erlebnisschicht** f level of experience

**erlöschen** to become extinguished

**erschauen** to behold

**erschoppeln** (coll.) to drink moderately

**ersiegen** to win

**ersoffen** (coll.) drowned

**ertasten** to reach by groping

**sich erwahren** to come true

**Estland** Estonia

**Euer Wohlgeboren** (arch.) Sir

**Euphorbie** f -n (Bot.) Euphorbia

**Exerzitium** n -tien (Lat.) exercise

**Extralektion** f -en extra lesson

**exzerpieren** to make an excerpt


**F**

**Fabrikantenmeinen** n manufacturer's way of thinking

**Fabrikler** m - (coll.) factory worker

**Fabriklerleben** n life of a factory worker

**fabulieren** to tell stories

**Fachblatt** n ⸚er professional periodical

**fackelbeglänzt** glistening in the torch light

**nicht fackeln** not hesitate to do

**fädig** threadbare

**Fahnenschwingen** n bannerswinging

**faillieren** to go bankrupt

**falb** pale yellow

**Falkenbeize** f hawking

**Falschmünzer** m - counterfeiter

**Familienüberlieferung** f family tradition

**Famos!** Great!

**Famulus** m -li (Lat.) servant

**Fanal** n -e signal beacon; (fig.) oriflamme

**fanatisieren** to make fanatical

**Farbenfolge** f sequence of colors

**Farbenschauer** m - shower of colors

**Farnwildnis** f -se wilderness of ferns

**faselnackend** naked

**in allen Fasern fiebern** to be in a state of nervous agitation

**Fassade** f -n outward appearance

**Faun** m -e faun; Roman rural deity

**Fechtbruder** m ⸚ (coll.) tramp

**Federputz** m feather headdress

**Fegefeuer** n - torment; purgatory

**Fehl** m -e fault

**Fehltritt** m -e tactless slip

**feldeinwärts** across the field

**Fell zu Markt bringen** n to sell the shirt off one's back

**Felsenkessel** m - rocky valley

**Felsentor** n -e passageway in the cliff

**Felsgestaltung** f rock formation

**Femgericht** n -e Vehmic tribunal

**ferneher** from faraway

**Ferngebliebensein** n staying away

**sich festbeißen*** to be obsessed with

**Festgemeinde** f -n group of celebrants

**Feurio!** Fire!

**Fichtenspargel** m - pine-sap

fidelitas (Lat.) conviviality; name of a glee-club

Fidelität f conviviality

Fiesole spa in the Italian province of Florence, Italy

Figurenwerk n statue

fix alert

flämischledern made of Flemish leather

flatterhaft fickle

Flaubert, Gustave (1821–1880) French novelist

Flebbe f -n (coll.) identification card

Die Fledermaus operetta by Johann Strauß

vom Fleisch fallen lose weight

jemandem am Zeug flicken to pick holes in s. o.

Fliederlaube f -n lilac bower

Die Fliegenden Blätter name of a magazine known for its humorous content

Fliesengang m ¨e paved passage

Fließblatt n ¨er blotting-paper

Flintenkugel f -n bullet

Flitter m - tinsel; false lustre

Flitterkleid n -er glittering garment

Florband n ¨er mourning crepe

Flügelknattern n wing-beat

flügeln to fly

Fluh f ¨e stratum; sheer face of a cliff

Flut f tide

Fortbestand m persistence

fortbewahren to maintain

Fra, frater (Lat.) brother; monk

Franken m Swiss franc

Fratz m -e rascal

Freinacht f ¨e (im Gasthaus) drinks on the house (at the inn)

Fremdenschar f -en horde of tourists

Fremdlingin f (poet.) stranger

freudefarb with the color of joy

Freundesrunde f -n circle of friends

Freundl n (coll.) dear friend

Freundschaftskündigung f severing of friendship

Friedrichshafen city in Southern Germany

Froberger, Johann Jakob (1616–1667) German composer

Frohmütigkeit f cheerfulness

frömmlerisch hypocritical

Frugivore m (-n), -n fruit eater; vegetarian

Frühlingskrone f -n spring crown

Frühlingspracht f splendor of spring

frumm (coll.) = fromm pious

Fuchs m ¨e tortoise-shell butterfly

Fuge f -n fugue

Fuggerei f a housing development for poor citizens of Augsburg, in Southern

Germany, built (1516–1519) by the Fuggers, a wealthy German banking family

Fuhrmann m -leute waggoner

Füllsel n - stopgap

Fünfer m - five Pfennig (piece); nickel

Fünfer und Weggli auf einmal have your cake and eat it too

Fünfuhrausgang m walk at 5 p. m.

Fürstentum n "er dukedom

Fußglas n "er wine glass with a base

Futtervogel m " pet bird

futurum exactum (Lat.) future tense

G

Gaienhofen village on Lake Constance

gaksen to cackle

Galgenvogel m " rascal

Ganesha Hindu god, Protector of scholarship

Gänsefeder f -n goose-quill

Gänsegeschwader n - flock of geese

Gant f (coll.) auction

Gasterei f banquet

gebären* to be in labor

Gebäu n -e (poet.) building

von sich geben vomit

gebündelt tied up in a bundle

Gedächtnisübung f -en memory exercise

Gefräßer pl (coll.) = Gefräßigen pl. gluttons

gefühlig (poet.) sensitive

Gegengabe f -n gift in return

gegoren fermented

gehäuft (fig.) copious

gehürnt horny; horned

geilen to be lascivious

geisten to be present in spirit

Geizkragen m - (coll.) miser

gekalkt whitewashed

Gekiese n (coll.) = Kies m gravel

Geklüft n cleaved rocks

Geknäuel n ball; tangle

Gekräute n (poet.) herbs

Geländerpfosten m - baluster

Geläut n ringing of bells

Gelöstheit f state of dissolution

Ha gelt! (coll.) Isn't that so?

Geltenlassen n tolerance

Gemach n "er (poet.) chamber

gemagert skinny

gemessen measured; reserved

Genf Geneva, Switzerland

Geniemäßige n ingenious

Geniereisle n (coll.) a genius' little trip

Gentildonnen pl. unmarried ladies of noble birth

Genua Genova, Italy

Geplärr n bawling

Gequake n quacking; croaking

Gerank n climbers; runners

Gerbersau fictitious name for a town in the Black Forest, answering to the description of Calw, Hesse's native town

Gerla f (Ital.) (funnel-shaped) basket

geründet (rare) rounded; (fig.) finished

gesalbt (fig.) unctuous

Geschätzte n (Schreiben) (arch.) (your) valued letter

Geschicklichkeitsprobe f -n test of skill or ability

Geschlechterfolge f -n succession of generations

geschleckt (coll.) overgroomed

geschnickelt, geschnackelt spic and span; dressed up

geschraubt stilted; stiff

gesittet well-mannered

gessa (coll.) = gegessen eaten

gestabte (Buchstaben) (letters) like upright posts

Gestühl pl. seats

Gestürme n (coll.) = Sturm m storm

Gestürzte m (-n), -n fallen person or thing

Getrabe n trotting

Getriebenheit f state of frenzy

getürmt piled up

Geuden n (coll.) = Vergeuden squandering

Gewalthaber m - despot

Gewilltheit f willingness

Gewitterdunst m ⁻e calm before the storm

Gewitterstimmung f stormy mood

gezähmt tamed

g'het (coll.) = gehabt had

Gichtiger m - arthritic person

Gignit autem artificiosam lusorum gentem Cella Silvestris. Waldzell has produced a skilfull race of players.

Gilet n -s vest

Giorgione (1478–1510) Venetian painter

Giotto (1266–1337) Florentine painter and architect

Gläsergeläut n clinking of glasses

glasig glassy

aufs Glatteis locken fool

glattgestrichen smoothed down

Glaubenssatz m ⁻e article of faith

Gleichbürtigkeit f equality of birth

Gleißen n glistening

sich ins Glied stellen to get in line

Glockenzug m ⁻e bell-rope

gloxig (Hesse's invention) pretentious

Gluck, Christoph Willibald von (1714–1787) German composer

Glücksvogel m ⁻ lucky fellow

Glutschrift f fiery writing

Gnadengabe f -n gift of grace

Gnocchi Italian dish of noodles with meat

gnostisch gnostic

Go Bang game played on boards

Gögö fictitious name of a hair-tonic

Gold(es)barren m - gold ingot

Goldlack m wallflower

Goldlazerte f -n golden lizard

Goldmacherküche f -n alchemist's kitchen or laboratory

Goldmachertiegel m - alchemist's crucible

Goldparmäne f -n golden pippin

Göppingen small town in Southern Germany

Gotama (Sanskrit Gautama) clan name of the Buddha in his last incarnation

Gottesbraut f "e nun

Gotthelf, Jeremias (1797–1854) Swiss writer and clergyman

goutieren to enjoy

Govinda Siddharta's friend, also one of the names of Krishna in the Bhagavad-Gita

grätig (coll.) irritable

Graubünden Swiss canton

greinen to cry

Grieche m (-n), -n Greek

Griffel m - stylus

Grillenzirpen n chirping of crickets

Grindelwald resort in the canton of Bern

Grobian m -e crude person

Groschen m - dime

Großtun n boasting

Grunderlebnis n -se fundamental experience

Grüßgott! Good day! (A south German greeting)

gucken (coll.) to peep

guet (coll.) = gut good

Gulden m - (arch.) coin

Gummizwinge f -n rubberring

Günsel m (Bot.) bugle

Gurgelton m "e guttural tone

Gustel short from of Gustav

Gymnasium n nine-year German secondary school

## H

Haber m (coll.) = Hafer oats

Habitué m -s (Fr.) one who frequents a place

haften bleiben to get stuck

halbgezogen half drawn

Halbgott m "er demigod

Hallelujazapfen m psalmsinger

Halma game played on boards

hämisch ironical; sardonic

Handorgel f -n accordion

das Handwerk legen put a stop to s. o.'s actions

Handwerksburschenpenne f -n hostel for journeymen

Hänselei f -en teasing

Hanswurst m clown; buffoon

Hanteln pl. dumbbells

hapern (coll.) to be unsatisfactory

happig (coll.) greedy

Hätschelei f pampering

Hat sich was! Nonsense!

Hauptkerl m splendid fellow

Hausdrache m -n vixen

Hausflur m -e entrance hall

Hausgang m ⏜e hallway

Hautgout m (Fr.) taste of meat that is not fresh

Heckenpfad m -e lane between hedges

Hefenkranz m ⏜e wreath shaped pastry made with yeast

Hegau m a hilly region in Southern Germany

Heidenkraft f great strength

Heidenmission f -en missionary service

Heilkunst f art of healing

Heiltrank m ⏜e medicine

heimchendünne Musik music like the tiny chirping of crickets

Heimtücker m - malicious person

heischen to ask for

Heißsporn m -e hotspur

hélas! (Fr.) Alas!

Heliopolis (Gr.) ‹City of the Sun,› now a suburb of Cairo, Egypt

heranfluten to swell up

herangedeihen* to thrive

heranzüchten to breed

Herausgehobenheit f state of exaltation

herbeistürzen to dash up

herbeiwinken to summon by waving

Herbsterstling m -e first (colored leaves) in autumn

Herbstzeitlose f -n (Bot.) autumn crocus

Herdenvieh n crowd

Herrensöhnchen n - gentleman's son

Herrschaftsgut n ⏜er estate

(hinter etwas) hertrotteln to (follow) with halting step

herumbosseln to muddle

Herumfingern n going through

herumschwätzen to gossip; to jabber

herunterspielen to play superficially

Herzensverhältnis n -se love affair

Hesperus a novel by Jean Paul Friedrich Richter

Hetäre f -n courtesan

heulen (coll.) to cry

Heumonat m July

e Hex (coll.) = eine Hexe a witch

Hexenschwindel m hocus-pocus

Hexenstaat m witches' habits

Hidalgo m -s (Span.) Spanish nobleman

hie (arch.) = hier here

hieratisch consecrated to sacred uses

Himmelsstürmer m - man reaching for the stars

hindämmern to dream away

hindehnen to extend; to stretch out

hindostanisch Hindustani

sich hineinversetzen to put oneself into a situation

**Hingenommensein** n rapture
**hinhauen** to cut down
**hinieden** on earth
**Hinleben** n wasted life
**hinnen** (poet.) away from
here
**hinschmeißen**\* to produce
**sich hinschmiegen** to nestle
up close
**hinsterben**\* to die out; to
waste away
**hinüberschwenken** to change
over
**Hirsau** little town in the
Black Forest
**Hirschhorngriff** m hartshorn
handle
**Historie** f -n story
**Historiograph** m (-en), -en
historian
**Hochbetagte** m (-n), -n very
old man
**Technische Hochschule** f Institute of Technology
**Hochwürden** ... The Very
Reverend ...
**hoffähig** presentable
**Hoffart** f inordinate pride
**Hoffmann,** Ernst Theodor
Amadeus (1776–1822) German romantic poet, musician, painter, lawyer
**Hofmannsthal,** Hugo von
(1874–1929) German poet
**Hofmeister** m - private tutor
**Hofzeremoniell** n court etiquette
**Hofzirkel** m social gathering
in the courtyard

**Hohenstaufen** m mountain
in Southern Germany
**Höhenwechsel** m - change of
altitude
**Holderbusch** m ¨e elderberry bush
**Holländer** m - Dutchman
**Holzstall** m ¨e woodshed
**homines bonae voluntatis**
(Lat.) men of good will
**honigtaubenetzt** sprinkled
with honey-dew
**Honoratiorenstube** f -n
room reserved for the people
of rank in a local restaurant
**Hopfenlesen** n hop-picking
**horsten** to nest
**Hospitant** m (-en), -en novice under the instruction
of a senior master
**Hotelzettel** m - hotel sticker
**Hügelflucht** f -en row of
hills
**Hügelkamm** m ¨e hill-crest
**hujus** (Lat.) of this month
**Huldigungsbrief** m -e letter
of admiration
**Humanistenhaltung** f humanistic behavior
**hünenhaft** like a giant
**Hü(st) und Hott!** (coll.)
Gee-up!
**Das Hutzelmännlein** story
by Eduard Mörike (1804–
1875)
**Hybris** f (Greek) wantonness
**Hygieniker** m - hygienist
**Hyperion** Friedrich Hölderlin's most famous novel

# I

**I bruch aigedlig nid, i wott numme-n-e gly schnaigge.** (coll.) Ich brauche eigentlich nichts, ich wollte nur einmal hereinschauen.

**Ifrit** m powerful demon in Arabic myth

**I han** (coll.) = ich habe

**Imme** f -n bee

**in artibus vivendi et amandi** (Lat.) in the arts of living and loving

**incipit vita nova** (Lat.) the new life begins; Dante, *Vita Nuova*

**in corpore** (Lat.) in person

**Indianer** m - American Indian

**Indisch** language of India

**ineinanderströmen** to merge

**ingenium felix et profectuum avidissimum, moribus placet officiosis** (Lat.) a most happy disposition, very eager for success, he ingratiates himself by his obliging manner

**ingenium valde capax, studia non angusta, mores probantur** (Lat.) a very open mind, his studies are not crabbed, his conduct is upright

**Initiant** m (-en), -en adept

**Inkunabel** f -n early printed book

**Innsbruck** city in Austria

**in saecula saeculorum** (Lat.) forever and ever

**Instanzenweg** m official channels

**insultieren** to insult

**Interessantheit** f capacity to interest

**Interlaken** city in the canton of Bern
causality

**irisieren** to be iridescent

**Irislicht** n -er iridescent light

**Irokese** m (-n), -n Iroquois

**Isar** f river in Bavaria

**isch** (coll.) = ist

**Ischiatiker** m - person suffering from sciatica

**Isis** Egyptian goddess

# J

**jach** (arch.) sudden; violent

**Jacobi,** Friedrich Heinrich (1743–1819) German writer and philosopher

**Jagdzeug** n hunting equipment

**jahraus, jahrein** year in, year out

**jeanpaulisch** pertaining to the poet Jean Paul

**Jegerle** Good gracious!

**Jena** university city in Thuringia

**Jerum!** (coll.) Dear me!

**Jeses!** Lord!

**jetz** (coll.) = jetzt now

**je vous assure** (Fr.) I assure you

**je vous remercie mille fois** (Fr.) I thank you a thousand times

**jo** (coll.) = ja

**jodlerartig** yodle-like

**Johanniskraut** n (Bot.) St. John's wort

**Jokel** m - fellow

**Juchhe!** Yip-pie!

**Julius** m July

**Jung, Carl Gustav** (1875–1961) Swiss psychologist

**Jüngerschaft** f discipleship

**Jünglingsjahr** n -e year of youth

**Jungmädchentum** n young girlhood

**Jura-Bergzüge** Jura mountain range

**Jux** m -e joke; fun

**K**

**Kabbala** f cabala, a system of esoteric theosophy

**Kainskinder** n pl. children of Cain

**Kainzeichen** n - brand of Cain

**Kalb, Frau von** patroness of Friedrich Schiller

**Kama** (Sanskrit) Hindu god of love

**Kamillentee** m camomile tea

**Kampanile** m -s (Ital.) bell tower

**Kampong** m Malayan village

**kanaresisch** Canarese, language spoken in South India

**bescheidenes Kaninchen** n modest fellow

**Kanzleischreiber** m - clerk

**Kanzone** f -n (Ital.) canzona, a term meaning lyric or song

**kapieren** to understand

**Kapuziner**(kresse) f (Bot.) nasturtium

**Karma** A basic creed of Brahmanism, Buddhism, Dschainism, according to which the fate of man after death depends on his earthly life

**Karzer** m - students' prison

**Kassiopeia** name of a constellation of stars

**Kastalien** Castalia in Greek mythology, a spring said to give poetic inspiration

**Kasteiung** f -en castigation

**Katalpe** f -n (Bot.) Catalpa tree

**Katechese** f -n catechizing

**Katzenbuckel** m - humped back

**Kausalitätsgesetz** n law of causality

**Kauz** m ̈e (coll.) strange fellow

**Kebse** f -n concubine

**keene** (coll.) = keine

**keilen** (Füchse) to win (new students for a fraternity)

**Keilrahmen** m - (typ.) quoinchase

**Kellerhals** m ̈e cellar door

**Kellerladen** m ̈ cellar window shutter

**Kilikien** Cilicia, Roman province in Asia Minor

**Kindermensch** m -en childlike person

**Kindlesbrunnen** m - baby well – in popular folktales, a well from which babies come

**Kirchenlicht** n -er (fig.) stupid person

**Kirchenvater** m " Church Father

**Kirchweihfest** n -e church festival

**klappen** to rattle

**klassizistisch** classical

**Kleiber** m - nuthatch

**kleinasiatisch** Near Eastern

**Kleinkampf** m "e small scale battle

**Klerus** m clergy

**klotzig reich** enormously rich

**Klüngel** m - clique

**Knabenpension** f -en boarding house for boys

**Knarre** f -n rattle; barker (coll.)

**kneipen** to go drinking

**Knisterlaut** m -e rustling sound

**knorzen** (coll.) to be stingy

**Knorzer** m - (coll.) little stumpy fellow; miser

**Knöterich** m (Bot.) knotgrass

**Kolik** f -en colic

**Kollation** f -en snack

**Kollektivgesicht** n -er common face

**in die Klemme kommen** (coll.) to get into a mess

**Kommerzienrat** m "e Councillor of Commerce (title)

**Kommilitone** m (-n) -n fellow student

**Kölnisches Wasser** toilet water with the trade name Eau-de-Cologne

**könnens** (coll.) = können Sie

**Konsistorialrat** m "e Councillor of Consistory (title)

**Konstanz** Constance, city in Southern Germany

**Konvent** m -e assembly

**Konventikel** n - conventicle (of dissenters)

**Korfu** Corfu, Ionic island

**Korinther** pl. people of (ancient) Corinth, Greece

**Korn** n grain (of paper)

**Kornnelke** f -n (Bot.) cornflower

**Kornrade** f -n (Bot.) corncockle

**Körperbau** m figure; shape

**Korrepetitor** m (-en) -en coach

**korrumpieren** to corrupt

**Koryphäe** f -n (Greek) master-mind; star

**Koseform** f -en term of endearment

**Kotau** m -e kow-tow

**Kotze** f -n coarse cloth; shaggy coverlet

**Kragenmantel** m " cape

**Krapplack** m reddish varnish

**Krawattensitz** m position of the tie

**krebsen** (coll.) to drudge

**Kredenz** f -en sideboard

**Kreislauf** m "e cycle (of incarnations)

**Kresser** m - a small fish

**zu Kreuze kriechen** to repent

**Kriegsgefangenenfürsorge** f Association to assist prisoners of war

**Kriegshetzepartei** f -en jingoist party

**Krischna** Krishna, a Hindu god

**kritteln** to find fault (with)

**Krone** f -n crown (a coin)
in die Krone steigen (coll.) to go to the head

**Krügelchen** n - little pitcher

**Krüppelschaft** f being crippled

**Krüppeltanne** f -n (Bot.) scrub pine

**Kufe** f -n tub; vat

**Kugelbüchse** f -n rifle

**Kugelfrucht** f "e round fruit

**Kuhdummheit** f blunder

**Kuhmist** m cow manure

**kumm!** (coll.) = komme!

**Kunkel** f -n (arch.) woman

**kuranzen** to scold

**Kustos**, Kustoden m custodian; curator

**Kutte** f -n cowl

**L**

**Lächelschein** m semblance of a smile

**Ladenglöcklein** n - shop bell

**Ladenmann** m "er merchant

**Ladenritze** f -n slit in a shutter

**Laios** father of Oedipus

**Lakschmi** Lakshmi, Hindu goddess of beauty and good fortune

**Lände** f -n landing-place

**Landjägerschaft** pl. rural policemen

**langröckig** long-skirted

**langschößig** with long coat-tails

**Lapislazuli** lapis lazuli, a blue stone containing sulphur

**lasziv** lascivious

**Läßlichkeit** f veniality

**Lateinschule** f -n school corresponding approximately to the American high school and the first two years of college

**Lattengerüst** n -e picture stand

**Lattenhaus** n "er lath hut

**Die schöne Lau** a story by E. Mörike

**Laubstreu** f litter of leaves

**Läufer** m - strip of carpeting

**Lautenschlagen** n lute-playing

**Lavazug** m "e lava flow

**Lebensfrühe** f early life

**Leberspatz** m (-en), -en liver dumpling

**Lebewelt** f society people

**Leckerli** n pl. (a type of Swiss) cookies

**Leerdenken** n method of emptying the mind by concentrating upon an object or goal in order to achieve liberation

**lehnen** (Geld) to lend (money)

**Lehrbub** m (-en), -en young apprentice

**Leibbinde** f -n flannel belt

**Leibwickel** m - compress

**Leichtfuß** m "e happy-go-lucky fellow

**Leilach** n -e (coll.) sheet

**Leim** m glue

aus dem Leim gehen fall apart

**Leinenmappe** f -n cloth writing pad

**Lenau,** Nikolaus (1802–1850) Austrian romantic poet

**Leopardi,** Giacomo, Conde (1798–1837) Italian poet

le ore passano e la morte è vicina. The hours pass and death is near.

**Levkoie** f -n (Bot.) stock

**Lichtenberg,** Georg Christoph (1742–1799) German physicist and writer

**Liderblinzeln** n eye-blinking

**Lido** m beach at Venice

**liebedienerisch** cringing

**Liebeslaube** f -en summerhouse (where lovers meet)

**Liebhaberaufnahme** f -n photograph taken by an amateur

**Liederfertige** m -n skilful minstrel

**Liedler** m - (poet.) minstrel

**liliputanisch** Lilliputian; dwarfed

**Linealästhetik** f linear aestheticism

**Linsengericht** n dish of lentils; «mess of pottage» – reference to Esau who sold his birthright to his younger brother Jacob. Gen. 25: 21–34, 27

**Literatendasein** n writer's existence

**Litzen** pl. braiding

**Livland** Livonia (comprising parts of Latvia and Estonia)

**Livorno** capital of the province Livorno, Italy

**Lockeglanz** m attractive splendor

**Loderkranz** m ⁓e flaming garland

**loderloh** blazing

**Lofoten** pl. islands off the coast of Norway

**Loggia** f loggia, arcaded or roofed gallery projecting from the side of a building

**Logis** n - lodgings

**logo-** (Greek logos) combining form meaning word or thought

**loh** (arch.) blazing

**Lohboden** m ⁓ tanning ground

**Lohengrin** nickname of the preceptor Lohe, allusion to the knight of the Holy Grail

**Longwy** town in Northeastern France

**Lortzing,** Albert (1801–1851) German composer of operas

**loshämmern** to hammer away

**losreden** to start talking wildly

**Losung** f -en slogan

**Louis der Grausame** (also Ludovicus Crudelis and Luigi) (1880–1962) Louis Moillet, painter

**Löwe,** Karl (1796–1869) German composer, mainly of songs

**Lucca** city in central Italy

**Ludendorff,** Erich (1865-1937) Prussian general

**Luder** n - rogue

**Lueg!** (coll.) Sieh!

**Luftikus** m -se (coll.) windbag

**Lug** f (coll.) lie

**Lugano** town in Switzerland near Montagnola, where Hesse lived from 1919

**Lügenbeutel** m - liar

**Lumpenkram** m ¨e stupid rubbish

**lüpfen** (coll.) to lift

**Lusores** (Lat. pl.) players

**lustgestachelt** spurred by lust

**Lusthain** m -e pleasure grove

**lustrum** n -ren or -ra (Lat.) period of five years

**lustverklärt** radiant with delight

**Lüttich** city in Eastern Belgium

**Luzern** Lucerne, city in Switzerland

**Luzifer** Lucifer, leader of the angels' revolt

**Lykien** Lycia, Roman province in Asia Minor

# M

**mädchenzier** girlishly graceful

**Mädele** n - South German diminutive for girl

**Madhawa** one of the names of the Hindu god Krishna

**Magadha** ancient kingdom in India

**magari!** (Ital.) I surely hope so!

**Mägdegezänk** n maid's quarrel

**Mägdetrab** m scurrying of maids

**Magnetberg** m legendary mountain which attracts objects like a magnet

**Makrönchen** n - macaroon

**Malaiin** f -nen Malayan girl or woman

**Malakka-Rohrstock** m ¨e Malacca cane

**Maloya** mountain pass in the Swiss canton of Graubünden

**Malve** f -n (Bot.) mallow

**Mammutbaum** m ¨e (Bot.) sequoia

**Manderl** n - (coll.) little man

**Männeken** n (coll.) = Männchen n little fellow

**Männergeschäft** n -e man's business

**Mannheit** f manliness; maturity

**Mantiker** m - (Greek) soothsayer; prophet

**Mara** (Sanskrit) spirit of evil

**Marguerite** f -n (Bot.) marguerite

**markten** to haggle; to bargain

**Markusflagge** f -n standard of St. Mark, patron saint of Venice

**Martini,** Simone (1284–1344) Italian painter

**Massenwürgen** n mass slaughter

**Matte** f -n mat

**Matthison,** Friedrich von (1761–1831) German lyrical poet

**Maturitätsprüfung** f final examination (at a secondary school)

**maudern** (coll.) to be tired

**Mauervorsprung** m ⸚e projecting of wall

**Maulaffen feilhalten** to stand gaping

**Maulbronn** town in Southern Germany

**Maya** (Sanskrit Maja) energy that creates the world of appearances

**media in vita** (in morte sumus) (Lat.) In the midst of life, (we are in death)

**Meisterdrucker** m - master printer

**Meistersingervorspiel** n overture to the opera *The Master-singers* by Richard Wagner

**memento mori!** (Lat.) Remember death!

**Memnon** (Greek Myth.) King of the Ethiopians, made immortal by Zeus

**Memphis** ancient city in Egypt

**Menschensatzung** f man made law

**Menschenwert** m -e human value

**Menschenwesen** n- human being

**Meriten** pl. merits

**Merkur** m Mercury

**Mesmer,** Franz Anton (1734–1815) physician, founder of the theory of animal magnetism

**Meßbub** m (-en), -en acolyte

**Metier** n -s (Fr.) profession

**Metzger** m - (coll.) butcher

**Miesmacher** m - (coll.) defeatist; pessimist

**Milchwecke** f -n roll

**mille fiori ... a te, Santa Maria** (Ital.) a thousand flowers to you, Saint Mary

**minister verbi divini** (Lat.) teacher of God's word

**Misere** f wretchedness

**Mistfink** m (-en), -en (coll.) filthy person

**mitbetroffen** to be personally affected

**Mitgrieche** m (-n), -n fellow student of Greek

**Mittagsbrand** m noonday heat

**Modekanone** f -n fashionable author

**mogeln** (coll.) to cheat

**Mohikaner** m - Mohican

**Mohrenkopf** m ⸚e pastry

**molo** m (Ital.) pier

**Molosser** Molossus, ancient metrical foot

**Mondregenbogen** m moon rainbow

**Mon rêve familier** (Fr.) *My*

*Familiar Dream,* poem by Paul Verlaine

**Monteverdi,** Claudio (1567–1643) Italian composer

**Montreux** resort on Lake Geneva

**Moos** n (coll.) cash

**Morbio Inferiore** pleasant glen near Montagnola

**Mordent** m -e (Mus.) a grace made by alternation of a principal tone with an auxiliary tone

**Mordsknaller** m - terrible crack

**Morgenlandfahrer** m - traveler to the East – a reference to Hesse's *The Journey to the East,* meaning people who believe in spiritual values beyond everyday reality

**Mörike,** Eduard (1804–1875) German poet

**Moritat** f -en long popular ballad

**Morris,** William (1834–1896) English poet and craftsman

**Mosel** f Moselle

**Moskite** f -n mosquito

**Mostkelter** f -n cider-press

**Mucius Scaevola** a Roman hero who demonstrated his courage by putting his hand on burning coals

**Mühleziehen** n mill (game)

**Murano** island in the lagoon of Venice

**muskelstrotzend** muscular

**müssens** (coll.) = müssen Sie

**Mützentroddel** f -n tuft

**beide Mythen** pl. two mountains in Switzerland

N

**Nabelbeschauung** f navel contemplation

**Nachgefühl** n -e aftertaste

**Nachhall** m resonance

**nach neune** (coll.) = nach neun Uhr

**Nachreife** f late maturing

**nachskandieren** to scan verses

**sich jemandem nachwerfen** to throw o. s. at s. o.

**nachzeichnen** to copy

**Nagold** f river in Southern Germany

**Narzisse** f -n (Bot.) daffodil

**Nashornvogel** m " rhinoceros hornbill (bird)

**Naue** f -n boat

**Neapel** Naples, Italy

**Nebelspalter** Swiss newspaper

**nebendraußen** (coll.) = draußen outside

**Nebenfunktion** f -en secondary function

**Nebengelüst** n -e secondary desires

**Nebenperson** f -en person of no consequence

**Neckar** m river in Southern Germany

**net** (coll.) = nicht

**Netzbügel** m - butterfly-net

**Nichtkonvertit** m (-en), -en nonconvert

Nichtseiende n the nonexistent

Nidelzeltli Swiss candy

Nikolaus von Kues (1401–1464) philosopher and theologian

nit (coll.) = nicht

no (coll.) = nur

Noachide m (-en), -en Noachian

Noblesse f (Fr.) nobility

nonno (Ital.) grandfather

Notenpult n music stand

Novalis pen name of Friedrich von Hardenberg (1772–1801), German poet

novellino m (Ital.) book of novellas

Novize m (-n), -n novice

Nüd Schöiners as wäns dimmered = Nichts Schöneres als wenn es dämmert

Äs schöins wildgwachses Liedli (coll.) = Als ein schönes wildgewachsenes Liedlein

Numinose n noumenon, a nonempirical concept


O

obenhin superficially

Oberstaatsanwalt m ¨e attorney general

Obliegenheit f duty

Obstbude f -n fruit stand

Ochsenkarren m - oxcart

Ochsentreiber m - oxherd

Odenwald m Oden Forest

Odeur m (Fr.) fragrance

offerieren to offer

Öhrn m hallway

Okarina f -s (Ital.) wind instrument producing soft whistlelike sounds

Om symbol of the lord of creation

ontisch ontic

opuscula pl. (Lat.) little works

Original n -e original; (quite a) character

Orlando Roland, legendary hero of the Charlemagne cycle

Ornamentgewirke n ornamental designs

Orplid E. Mörike's poetic dream island

Öse f -n loop

Osterberg m hill overlooking Tübingen

Osteria f (Ital.) inn

Outsiderwurschtigkeit f (coll.) the outsider's apathy


P

Pack n mob

Padua Padova, city in Italy

Pamphilien Pamphylia, Roman province in Asia Minor

Pan (Greek) god of forests and herds

Papi Daddy

paradelang as long as the parade lasts

Patisserie f -n (Fr.) pastry

Patron m -e (coll.) fellow

Jean Paul pseud. for Johann Paul Friedrich Richter (1763–1825), German novelist

**Pauli** Latin genitive of Paulus

**paululum appropinquant** (Lat.) they come a little nearer

**Paulum** Latin accusative of Paulus

**Pechschwitzer** m - pitchmaker

**pêle-mêle** (Fr.) in confusion

**Pendüle** f -n chimney clock

**Pennbruder** m " homeless tramp

**Penne** f -n tramps' lodging house

**Pentateuch** m (Greek) the first five books of the Old Testament

**Peregrina** (fictitious) name of a girl in a group of E. Mörike's most famous poems

**Perron** m -s platform (train)

**Perückenbaum** m "e (Bot.) smoke tree

**Pfarrverweser** m - church administrator

**Pfeifenstrunk** m "e short pipe

**Pfennigklauberin** f -nen penny pincher

**Pferdebahn** f -en tramway

**Pfiffikus** m -se cunning fellow

**Pfründhaus** n "er old people's home

**Phäake** m (-n), -n Phaeacian – seafaring island people fond of joyous living

**Philip Neri**, Saint (1515–1595) Italian reformer

**Philomele** (Greek) poetic name of the nightingale

**Piazzetta** f (Ital.) small plaza

**Pierrot und Pierette** (Fr.) Male and female white-faced clowns in French pantomime

**die Alte Pinakothek** famous art gallery in Munich

**Pindar** (c. 518–446 B. C.) Greek poet

**Pinte** f -n tavern

**Pisangfrucht** f "e banana

**Pisidien** Pisodia, Roman province in Asia Minor

**Plafond** m -s (Fr.) ceiling

**Plaid** n -s traveling rug, blanket

**Plaisir d'amour ne dure qu'un moment, chagrin d'amour dure toute la vie** (Fr.) «Pleasure of love lasts only a moment, grief of love is life-long»

**polakisch** (coll.) = polnisch

**Politeia** Plato's book about the ideal state

**Pönitenz** f atonement; penance

**Popanz** m -e scarecrow

**Pordenone,** Giovanni (c. 1484–1538) Italian painter

**Post** f -en stagecoach

**auf dem Posten sein** to mount watch

**post exitum** (Lat.) after death

**Posthalter** m - keeper of post horses; (coll.) commonplace chatter

**Postlawine** f -n avalanche of mail

**povera me!** (Ital.) Poor me!

**Poverello** (Ital.) ‹The Poor›, one of the names Saint Francis called himself

**poverino!** (Ital.) Poor little darling!

**Prätendent** m (-en), -en pretender

**Prajapati** (Sanskrit) supreme deity, often identified with Brahma

**Prälatenmehl** n flour for the prelates (high quality flour)

**präpotent** predominant

**Prato** town in Tuscany

**Prauw** f (Malay prao) a double-ended outrigger canoe with large sail

**Präzeptor** m -en preceptor

**pressieren** (coll.) to hurry

**preziös** precious; dainty

**Primgeiger** m - first violinist

**Primus** m (Lat.) best student

**Privatdruck** m -e private printing

**Privatissimum de rebus castaliensibus** (Lat.) closed lecture on the affairs of Castalia

**Prunksessel** m - honorary chair

**Psychokratie** f psychocracy

**den Pudel machen** (coll.) to drudge

**Purcell,** Henry (1659–1695) English composer

**pythagoreisch** Pythagorean

**Q**

**Quadratur** f (Geom.) squaring (the circle)

**quäken** to squeak

**Quart** n -e (typ.) (in) quarto

**ein guter Quartierzettel** a good recommendation

**Querfalte** f -n horizontal facial line

**quirlen** to twirl

**Quodlibet** n -s medley

**R**

**Raabe,** Wilhelm (1831–1910) German novelist

**Räderung** f (arch.) breaking on the wheel

**Raisonnement** n (Fr.) reasoning

**Ranküne** f -n (Fr.) grudge

**Raptus** m -se fury

**Rasenplan** m lawn

**Raubzeug** n beasts of prey

**Rauhbein** n -e (coll.) ruffian; bully

**Raupen- und Puppenstand** m metamorphic stage

**Ravenna** city in Italy

**Rebhang** m ‥e vine-covered slope

**Reblaube** f -n grape-bower

**Rechen** m - rake

**recherchieren** to request

**Rechnerseele** f -n mercenary person

**Redensart** f -en phrase; expression

**Redentore** (Ital.) m Redeemer

**Redestehenmüssen** n being forced to speak

**Refugium** n (Lat.) refuge

**regengepeitscht** lashed by the rain

Reifezeugnis n -se (secondary) school leaving certificate
reinbaden to purify
Reinette f -n pippin
Reiselast f -en traveler's burden
Reisemaschine f -n portable typewriter
über (den Haufen) rennen* (coll.) to run over
Renommistentum n bragging
Renommisterei f (coll.) = Renommiererei boasting
Rentenverzehrer m - man of private means
reservatio mentalis (Lat.) mental reservation
Reutlingen town in Southern Germany
Reval town on the Baltic Sea
Rheinfall m waterfall on the Rhine near Schaffhausen, Switzerland
Richtblock m ⸚e executioner's block
Riedgewächs n -e marsh plants
Riesenkarton m -s large box
Riesenmetzelei f -en (general) massacre
Rigi mountain in Switzerland
Rig-Veda f oldest sacred book of Hinduism
Rindvieh n -viecher ( coll.) blockhead
Ringelnatz, Joachim pen name of author, Hans Bötticher, (1883–1934)

ringer (coll.) sooner
Ritterspiel n -e tournament
Rittersporn m (Bot.) larkspur
Riva spa in Northern Italy
Rockschöße pl. coat-tails
Rohrsessel m - wicker chair
Roigel m famous fraternity known for heavy drinking
Rolladen m - Venetian blind
Rösselsprung m (Chess) ⸚e knight's move
Roßberg m summit in the Swabian Alps
Rößlein n - (dear) little horse
Rotbrüstchen n – robin
Rötel m red chalk; ruddle
Rottang m cane
Rübliland n (coll.) = Rübenland beet country
Ruch m (Geruch) smell
Rückert, Friedrich (1788–1866) German poet and Orientalist
Ruderpartie f -n boat trip
ruhmredig boastful
Rundschriftfeder f -n pen for cursive writing
Rune f -n rune
Ruskin, John (1819–1900) English author and social reformer

S

Saaltochter f ⸚ waitress
Sachverwalter m - counsel; attorney
Sackgeld n -er pocket money
Sackmesser n - pocket-knife

301

**sakrisch** (fein) (coll.) damned (good)!

**Sakya** clan name of Siddharta

**Sakyamuni** m (Sanskrit) «wise man of the Sakya clan»

**Salamanca** university town in Spain

**Salwald** m ¨er Sala Grove

**Samana** m -s (Sanskrit sramana) Samana, an ascetic

**Samaveda** one of the four collections of Vedic literature

**Sam(me)t** m -e velvet

**Sandsteinboden** m ¨ sandstone floor

**Sandsteinfliese** f -n sandstone tile

**Sankt Moritz** resort in Switzerland

**Sansara** (Sanskrit samsara) chain of finite existences without salvation

**Säntis** m summit in the Alps of Appenzell, Switzerland

**santo cielo!** (Ital.) Good heavens!

**Sarasate,** Pablo Martin Meliton de (1844–1908) Spanish violinist

**satis!** (Lat.) Enough!

**Satyam** (Sanskrit) Supreme Reality, an appellation of Brahma

**Satyr** m (Greek) a lecherous woodland deity

**Saufbold** m -e drunkard

**Säule** n (coll.) little pig

**Savoyische** n area in Northwestern Italy

**Schabernack** m -e practical joke

**Schachtelhalm** m -e (Bot.) horse-tail

**schaffeln** to work sluggishly

**Schaffensmöglichkeit** f -en possibility for creation

**Schaffhausen** city in Switzerland

**Schafgarbe** f -n (Bot.) common yarrow

**Schaft** m ¨e bookshelf

**Schall,** Franz (1877–1943) Classical scholar

**Schamane** m (-n), -n shaman, magician or healer among primitive peoples

**Schambinde** f -n loincloth

**Schamtuch** n ¨er loincloth

**Schanzer** m - (coll.) a person who crams

**scharmieren** to charm

**Schattenhut** m ¨e sun hat

**Schattenstreifen** m - strip of shadow

**Schatz** m ¨e treasure; (coll.) sweetheart

**Schatzi** n (coll.) little darling

**Schaukelbrett** n -er swing

**schaumbefeuchtet** sprayed with froth

**Schauung** f vision

**scheen** (coll.) = schön

**Scheibenschütze** m -n target-shooter

**über den Schellenkönig loben** to flatter

**Schelling,** Friedrich Wilhelm Joseph (1775–1854) German philosopher of the Romantic Era

**Scherben** m - (coll.) pot

**Scherzname** m -n nickname

**sich ineinander schicken** to become reconciled to each other

**Schieber** m - (coll.) racketeer

**Schieblade** f -n drawer

**Schiebung** f -en (coll.) racket

**Schierling** m -e (Bot.) hemlock

**Schifflände** f -n landing-place

**Schikane** f -n ruse

**Schildwache** f -n sentinel

**Schilfufer** n – reedy shore

**Schinken** m - (coll.) buttock

**Schiwa** Shiva, the destroyer, third member of the Hindu Trinity or Trimurti

**Schlafmansarde** f -n attic bedroom

**Schlägerklappern** n sabre rattling

**schlankbeinig** slender legged

**Schlaraffia** fool's paradise

**Schleifer** m - slow waltz

**schleirig** veiled; hushed

**Schlemmerei** f gluttony

**Schleppnetz** n -e trawl net

**‹Schlotzer›** m - sucker (nickname)

**(arme) Schlucker** m - (poor) wretch

**Schlund** m ⸚e abyss

**Schmarren** m - (fig.) rubbish; (Lit.) ‹penny dreadful›

**schmuck** neat

**Schnapphahn** m ⸚e highwayman

**(an)schnauzen** to snap

**Schnecke** f -n snail or coil (hair style)

**Schnitzbrot** n -e bread containing pieces of dried fruit

**schnobern** (coll.) = schnuppern to smell; to snuffle

**Schnurrpfeifereien** pl. trifles; odds and ends

**Scholarenlied** n -er (medieval) scholar's song

**Schonhülle** f -n protective cover

**schöppeln** steady (moderate) drinking

**Schoppen** m - half a pint (of beer)

**Schorschel** f Georgie

**Schrägwand** f ⸚e inclined plane or wall

**Schreiertum** n hullabaloo; clamor

**Schrempf,** Christoph (1860–1944) Protestant theologian

**Schubart,** Christian Friedrich Daniel (1739–1791) Swabian poet

**Schuhnestel** n -n (coll.) shoe lace

**Schülerpensionat** n -e boarding-school

**Schulvorsteher** m - school principal

**Schulzenknecht** m -e servant of the village mayor

**Schütz,** Heinrich (1585–1672) German composer

**in dero Schutz** (arch.) under whose protection

**Schützenmatte** f -n rifle range

**Schwab,** Gustav (1792–1850) German poet

**Schwabenland** n Swabia

**Schwabenstreich** m -e tomfoolery

**Schwabing** artist quarter in Munich

**schwadronieren** (coll.) to chat

**Schwarmgeist** m enthusiastic mind

**Schwärze** f darkness

**Schwarzwald** m Black Forest

**Schwatz** m chatter

**Schweinsblase** f -n hog's bladder

**schwerbodig** heavy

**schwergeprüft** sorely tried

**schwerlebig** to take life too seriously

**se** (coll.) = sie

**Seebucht** f -en lake bay

**Seelenhaltung** f -en attitude of mind or soul

**Seifenblase** f -n soap bubble

**Seifenblasenschillern** n scintillating of soap bubbles

**Seilgeflecht** n -e plaited rope

**sich auf die leichte Seite legen** to make it easy for oneself

**Selbsterhaltungsdrang** m drive of self-preservation

**selbstgefertigt** homemade

**Selbstprüfung** f -en self-examination

**Selbstverwirklichung** f self-realization

**Seminarist** m (-en), -en student at the seminary or preparatory school

**Sennalpstock** Swiss mountain

**Sennentracht** f -en local Alpine costume

**Sensengeläute** n sound of scything

**Sentenz** f -en maxim

**Serenata** f (Ital.) serenade

**Siebensachen** f pl. (coll.) belongings

**Signorelli,** Luca (1441–1523) Italian painter

**s'il vous plaît** (Fr.) please

**simplificateurs** m pl. (Fr.) simplifiers

**Simplizissimus** satirical weekly magazine (1896–1944)

**sinnieren** to brood

**Sirach,** das Buch the book of Sirach, i.e. Ecclesiasticus, also called the Wisdom of Jesus, the Son of Sirach

**sitzen*** (coll.) to be in prison

**Skandalgerücht** n -e scandalous rumor

**Smyrna** harbor city in Asia Minor

**socios habere malorum** (Lat.) to have company in one's misery

**der verlorene Sohn** the Prodigal Son

**Solingen** town in West Germany

**Solitär** m -e individualist; lone-wolf

**Sondererscheinung** f -en special phenomenon

**sonnenstill** motionless in the sunshine

**Sophia** f (Greek) wisdom

**Sortiererin** f -nen sorter

**Spalenquartier** n quarter near Spalenringweg in Basel

**Spalenring** m street in Basel, Switzerland

**Spargroschen** m - savings

**Spatz** m (-en), -en sparrow; dumpling

**spektakeln** to kick up a fuss

**Spekulantenhäuslein** n - house built to sell at a profit

**Sperber** m - sparrow hawk

**sperren** to block; to oppose

**La Spezia** city in Northwestern Italy

**Sphärenharmonie** f (Pythagorean) harmony of the spheres

**Spielmarke** f -n playmoney

**Spintisieren** n (coll.) philosophizing (meant ironically)

**Spiräe** f -n (Bot.) spiraea

**Spittel** m (coll.) - hospital

**Spitz** m -e Pomeranian dog

**Spitzeltum** n police spying

**Sporengeläut** n clinking of spurs

**sprachempfänglich** sensitive to language

**Sprengwagen** m " watering-cart

**Sprich deutsch!** (Swabian usage) Speak clearly and without rhetorical embellishments!

**Springquelle** f -n fountain

**spritzig** snippy

**sprödeln** to act coy

**spürig** perceptive

**Stabelle** f -n (coll.) wooden stool

**Stachelschwein** n -e porcupine

**Stadtmusik** f town band

**Stadtschultheiß** m (-en), -en mayor

**Staffel** f -n step; stair

**stählen** to harden; (fig.) to fortify

**stake(l)n** (coll.) to stalk along

**Staketenzaun** m "e picket fence

**standen** (mit) covered (with)

**Standesgefühl** n class consciousness

**standhalten*** to stand firm

**stangenhaft** polelike

**Stänkerei** f (coll.) squabble

**sich aus dem Staub machen** (coll.) to decamp

**staubzart** fine as dust

**aus dem Stegreif** improvised

**Steiermark** f Styria, province of Austria

**Steilfläche** f -n steep cliff walls

**steinicht** (coll.) stony (ground)

**Steinklopfer** m - stone-breaker

**Stellfalle** f -n regulating gate

**Sterngestiebe** n flurry of stars

**Stift** m -e (coll.) apprentice

**Stifter**, Adalbert (1805–1868) Austrian writer, born in Bohemia

**Stiftler** m - student in the

theological seminary in Tübingen

**Stilsünde** f -n transgression against the style

**Stimmengänge** pl. voices

**Stimmenwirrnis** f babel of voices

**Stoa** f (Greek) stoicism

wie **(ge)stochen** as engraved

**Stockscherbe** f -n flowerpot

**Storchschnabel** m ⸗ stork's bill

**Stradivari** f violin made by Antonio Stradivari

**stramingestickt** done in needlepoint

**Straßenkehle** f -n crooked path

**Strauß,** Emil (1886–1960) German novelist

dumpf **streben** to vaguely strive

**Streber** m - (coll.) (professional) climber

**Streifenmuster** n - striped design

**Stresemann,** Gustav (1878–1929) German statesman

**Strich** m -e bowing

**Strichlagen** pl. design

**striegeln** to curry

**Stubenmagd** f ⸗e housemaid

**Stübli** n (coll.) drawing room

**Stuegert** (coll.) = Stuttgart city in Southwestern Germany

**Stuhlherr** m (-en), -en President; Chairman

**Stundenbruder** m ⸗ member of a pietistic sect

**Stundenwesen** n discussions and worshipping in pietistic circles

**Sturzbad** n ⸗er shower

**Stuttgart** city in Southwestern Germany

**Suada** f (Lat.) flow of words

**Südhang** m ⸗e southern slope

**Sühnebad** n ⸗er bath of atonement

**Summa contra Gentiles** by Saint Thomas Aquinas (1225–1274), Italian philosopher and Doctor of the Church

**Summa theologica** by Saint Thomas Aquinas (1225–1274), an exposition of theology on philosophical principles

**Summentempel** m *Summa theologica* by Saint Thomas Aquinas

**surren** to buzz

**Sutra** (Sanskrit) an Indian literary form resembling ‹aphorisms›

**Swinehund** m -e filthy fellow

**Synedrion** n (Greek) High Council

**Syringe** f -n (Bot.) lilac

# T

**Tafelklavier** n -e grand piano

**Taine,** Hippolyte (1828–1893) French historian and writer

**Taktmäßigkeit** f well-timed beat

**Tamil** Dravidian language of India

**tannen** made of fir

tannenforstbekränzt
wreathed with forests of fir

**Tannenschlag** m "e fir-grove

**Tantras** sacred books of Tantrism, a secret cult of Hinduism

**tappig** clumsy; awkward

**Tarock** n -s taroc (card game)

**Tasso,** Torquato (1544–1595) Italian poet

**Tätscheln** n fondling

**Tat Twam Asi** (Sanskrit) meaning ‹You are it› which refers to the unity of the world and all creatures

**Taubenschwarm** m "e flock of pigeons

**Taufschmaus** m "e christening feast

**taumelbunt** abundantly colorful

**Taurus** m mountain range in Asia Minor

**tempelhaft** templelike

**Teppichklopfständer** m - crossbar on which to hang rugs to be beaten

**Terrassenbrüstung** f -en terrace balustrade

**Terzine** f terza rima, an Italian form of iambic verse

**Tessin** canton of Switzerland

**Teufelsbraten** m - rake

**Thebais,** die Wüste desert of Thebes

**Theodizee** f theodicy, vindication of God's justice in permitting evil

**Theokrit** (c. 300–260 B. C.) Theocritus, Greek poet

**Theophanie** f theophany, visible manifestation of God

**Theophrast** (c. 372–287 B. C.) Greek philosopher

**Theosophie** theosophy, doctrine of a modern sect founded mainly by H. P. Blavatsky (1875), which proposes to establish direct contact with divine principle through contemplation

**Thu Fu** (712–770) Tu fu, Chinese poet

**tibi** (Lat.) to you

**Tingeltangel** m - (low) music-hall

**Tirol** Tyrol

**Tobak** (coll.) i.e. Tabak m tobacco

**Toccata** f (Ital.) composition, usually for harpsichord or organ, in free style

**todesfahl** deathly pale

**todeswichtig** deadly important

**Tollerei** f fooling about

**tonig** claylike

**Der goldene Topf** tales by the German romantic novelist and composer Ernst Theodor Amadeus Hoffmann (1776–1822)

**Torbogen** m " archway

**Torre** resort near Naples, Italy

**Tort** m -s (Fr.) vexation

**Torwart** m -e gatekeeper

tota pulchra es (Lat.) you are entirely beautiful

Trägersack m ⁏e haversack

Traktat n -e treatise

Trasimeno Lake Trasimeno (now Lake Perugia), Italy

Trauerwedel m - crêpe streamer

Treber pl. husks (of grapes)

Treppenspindel f -n newel post of a spiral staircase

Treppenstiege f -n flight of stairs

Treppenweg m -e path with steps

très bien (Fr.) very well

Tretmühle f -n treadmill

Triktrak n backgammon

trist(e) (Fr.) sad

Tristan opera by Richard Wagner

Trockenschuppen m - drying shed

Troddelmütze f -n tasseled cap

Trödler m - secondhand dealer

Tropf m ⁏e dunce

Trüsche f -n burbot

Trutzkopf m ⁏e obstinate fellow

Tübingen university town in Southern Germany

Tuerei f (coll.) much ado

sich tummeln (coll.) hurry

Turmfalke m (-n), -n kestrel

Tuskulum Tusculum, town in ancient Latium

Typologie f classification of types

U

überbeschäftigt overly occupied

überflort covered with crêpe

Überfülltheit f surfeit; excess stock

übermochte overwhelmed

Übername m (-ns), -en nickname

übersternen (poet.) to outshine

überwach overly alert

überzeitlich super-temporal

Uhland, Ludwig (1787–1862) Swabian poet

Uhrschlag m ⁏e clock chime

Ulk m -e fun

Ulkname m (-ns), -en nickname

Ulmon, König king in E. Mörike's fictitious Orplid

Umbrien Umbria, province in Central Italy

umdrängen to surround; to swarm around

umdunkeln to surround with darkness

umfahn (coll.) = umfassen to embrace

Umgänger m - (poet.) haunting ghost

umgelitzt turned up

Umsassen pl. neighbours

umtaumeln to flit around

unangetastet unaffected

Unausschöpfbarkeit f inexhaustibility

unbekömmlich unwholesome

un bon graveur sur cuivre

(Fr.) a good engraver on copper

**unerhört** unheard of; scandalous

**ungattig** naughty

**ungehemmt** unrestrained

**ungemildert** unmitigated

**Nichts für ungut!** No harm meant!

**unio mystica** (Lat.) mystic union

**Universitas litterarum et artium** (Lat.) Republic of letters and arts

**Unsrigen** pl. our people

**Untergehölz** n -e undergrowth

**unterschwellig** subconscious

**unverhehlt** unconcealed

**unverschmelzbar** incompatible

**Unwert** m worthlessness

**Upanishaden** pl. (Sanskrit) treatises on man and the universe

**Urbrief** m e original text

**urhaft** primeval

**Urirotstock** m mountain in the Swiss canton of Uri

**urmäßig** primal

**Urmutter** f " mother of mankind

**urplötzlich** very suddenly

**Urschlamm** m primeval slime

**Urtrieb** m -e primal instinct

**Urvolkstümliche** n the genuine characteristics of the people

**Urzauber** m primal mystery

**V**

**Valenciennes** city in Northern France

**Valentin,** Karl (1882–1948) Bavarian comedian

**Valet** n -s farewell

**Valuta** f -ten value; currency

**Vedas** pl. (Sanskrit) sacred Hindu books

**Vedute** f -n view

**Veitstanz** m St. Vitus' dance

**V.j.A.d.H.** = Verein jüngerer Angehöriger des Handelsstandes (fictitious) association of younger members of the business classes

**Venedig** Venice

**Verästelung** f -en network of branches

**veratmen** to breathe

sich **verbeißen**\* to be set on s. th.

**Verbindungsbruder** m " fraternity brother

**verblassen** to die away

**verblättern** to shed leaves; to strip of leaves

**verbleichen**\* to pass away

**verdichten** to thicken; (fig.) to take shape

**verdöseln** (coll.) to daydream

**verdubeln** (coll.) to waste

**verdudeln** (coll.) to play badly

**verflackern** to flicker away

sich **verfratzen** to become distorted

**Lärm verführen** to make great noise

vergeistigt refined; spiritualized

vergrauen (poet.) to grow grey

verhangen overcast

verheeren to devastate

verhetzt rushed

verhunzen to spoil

Verinnerlichungsrummel m vogue about introspection, «turning on soul»

verknäult tangled

verkrümeln to crumble; to fritter away

verlechen to lick

verlohen to burn out

verludern to dissipate; to fritter away

verlüdert (coll.) squandered

Vermöglichkeit f wealth

vermoosen to become moss covered

vermoost moss-covered; antiquated

verrinnen* to run out

verschnitten clipped

verschrien be in ill repute

jemanden verschwatzen to tell tales about s. o.

Verschweigung f concealment

verschweinigeln (coll.) to defile

verschwellen* to swell shut

Versenkung f immersion in thought

versorgt (-es Gesicht) worried (look)

Versponnenheit f being wrapped up (in an idea)

verstiegen extravagant

verstürmt squally; storm-swept

vertrödeln to idle away (the hours)

vertrotteln to trudge along

vertrübt darkened

Veruneinigung f disunity

Verwachsenheit f fusion

verwölkt clouded

ist verwundet is hurt

sich verzanken (coll.) to quarrel

verzeichnen to draw badly

Vicus Lusorum (Lat.) village of the players

Viechereien pl. foolish pranks

Vigilie f -n (Lat.) vigil

Vikarius m vicar

mediceische Villen villas of the Medici

Virtuosenzuschnitt m cut of a virtuoso

Vishnu (Sanskrit) second in the trinity of Hindu gods

vita contemplativa (Lat.) contemplative life

vitae patrum (Lat.) biography of the early fathers of Christianity

Vita nuova title of a book by Dante Alighieri

Vitznau town in Central Switzerland

Vivarium n -ien vivarium, enclosure for keeping indoors plants or animals

Vogeldreck m bird droppings

**Vogelschlag** m   singing of birds

**Vogelschluck** m -e   tiny sip

**Volapük**   invented language intended to be universal

**Völkerkrieg** m -e   world war

**Völkerverbrüderungsunternehmung** f   international brotherhood movement

**vollsinnig**   normal minded

**voltigieren**   to perform equestrian acrobatics

**von dannen**   thence

**Vorarlberg**   Austrian province

**vorbeitreffen***   to miss

**Vorderstube** f -en   front room

**Vorfrühlingsahnung** f -en   feeling of early spring

**vorrecken**   to project

**Vorstadtkneipe** f -n   pub in the suburbs

**Vortreppe** f -n   front steps

**vorüberschlendern**   to wander past

**vorübertapern**   to stagger along

**votre Altesse** (Fr.)   Your Highness

**votre très humble serviteur** (Fr.)   your most obedient servant

**vous comprenez?** (Fr.)   do you understand?


# W

**Wachsfutteral** n -e   oil-cloth case

**Wachstuchmäpplein** n-   little portfolio made of oil-cloth

**Wagentritt** m -e   carriage step

**Waiblinger,** Wilhelm (1804–1830)   German poet

**Waldgötze** m (-n), -n   woodland deity

**Waldgürtel** m   belt of forest

**Walstatt** f ̈en   battlefield

**walzen** (coll.)   to march

**Wams** n ̈er   jacket

**die Wankelmutter überkommt ihn**   he becomes dizzy

**wann's** (coll.) = wenn es

**Wappenvogel** m ̈   heraldic bird

**Wasen** m -   lawn; turf

**Wasserwirbel** m -   whirl pool

**Wegerich** m (Bot.)   plantain

**Weggli** n (coll.)   roll

**wehbeklommen**   oppressed with misery

**weiben**   to court

**ob allen Weiben** (coll.) — unter allen Frauen

**«Weiberkutschiererei»** f   «Women drivers!»

**Weidenwuchs** m   willow growth

**Weiderich** m -e   willow-herb

**Weidling** m   small boat

**Weimar**   city in Central Germany

**Weinmut** m   crying mood

**Weinwärtel** m -   student-butler (in a fraternity)

**Weißenstein**   town on the Baltic Sea

weißgegipst  covered with white plaster

Weißgerber m - tanner

weiträumig extensive

Welschschweizer m - French-speaking Swiss

Weltfertigkeit f knowledge of the world

Welti, Albert (1862–1912) Swiss painter

Weltläufte pl.  ways of the world

Weltleute pl.  worldly people

Werte n (Schreiben)  (your) esteemed letter (old-fashioned business style)

Werte-Dämmerung f depreciation of values

Wicke f -n (Bot.)  vetch

Widerhaken m - barb

wiederkäuen  to ruminate

Wiedertäufer m - anabaptist

Wiesengatter n - fence railing

Wildheuer m - man who mows grass on mountain ridges

Wildwuchs m natural growth

willfährig compliant

Winde f -n (Bot.)  bindweed

Wingert m (coll.)  vineyard

Winkelgottheit f -en  petty god

Winterthur city in the canton of Zurich, Switzerland

wirklichkeitslos unrealistic

Wispel name of one of E. Mörike's fictitious figures

wittern  to scent

wohlgeborgen well protected

Wohlgestalt f  handsome figure

Wohnlichkeit f comfort

Wolf, Hugo (1860–1903) German composer, mainly of songs

Wolfram Wolfram von Eschenbach (c. 1170–1220), medieval poet

wölken to become cloudy

Wolkenfetzen m - bit of cloud

Wolkengewimmel n mass of clouds

Wolkenschlange f -n serpentine cloud

Wollenschal m -e wool scarf

Wollspinnerei - Aktiengesellschaft f joint stock company of a wool spinning mill

Wortgeklimper n word jingle

Wotan Woden, supreme god in Germanic religion

Wunderwesen - n miraculous creature

das ist doch Wurst! (coll.) never mind!

es ist wurst und egal (coll.) it doesn't matter

Wüstenei f -en  barren wilderness


X

Xenie f -n epigram


Y

Yogin m yogi

**Z**

Zänkerei f bickering

Zapfenzieher m - corkscrew

Zappetta f (Ital.) pickaxe

Zarathustra Zoroaster, (628–551 B. C.), religious teacher of ancient Persia, founder of Zoroastrianism

Zarge f -n rib (of a violin)

Die Zauberflöte a fairy opera by Wolfgang Amadeus Mozart (1756–1791), Austrian composer

Zauberkram m magic paraphernalia

Zaungast m ⸚e one who looks on without paying

Zeilenabstand m ⸚e interval between lines

Zeisig m -e greenfinch

lange Zeit nach jemandem haben to miss s. o.

Zeitgötze m (-n), -n temporary idol

Zelot m (-en), -en fanatic

Zenon Zeno of Citium (c. 334–c. 262 B. C.), Greek philosopher, founder of Stoicism

zephirhaft like a gentle breeze

Zerfallenheit f ruin; (fig.) decadence

Zerknirschung f contrition

zerknüllen to crush

zerlüdert dissipated

Zerrform f caricature

Zerrspiegel m (fig.) distortion

zerschmeißen* to smash

zerschwatzen to talk s. th. to death

zerstieben* to scatter

zerstücken to mangle

zerwühlen to dishevel

Zeugnisheft n -e report card

Ziehharfe f -n accordion

Zierbau m -ten decorative building

Zimmermannsgeselle m (-n), -n journeyman carpenter

zimmetfarben cinnamon-colored

Zinnoberinitialen pl. vermilion initials

Zirkelquadratur f squaring of the circle

Ziselierarbeit f -en chased work

Zisterzienser m - Cistercian monk

Zote f -n dirty joke

Zotenflüstern n whispering of dirty stories

Zuckung f -en twitch

Zug m ⸚e disposition; trend

Zugängerin f -nen cleaning woman

zulaufend pointed

Zulukaffer m (-n), -n Zulu

Zunachten n saying goodnight

Zündkraft f (fig.) stirring power

Zunft f ⸚e guild

Zürich Zurich, city in Switzerland

zusagendenfalls in case of acceptance

**Zusammenhausen** n living together

**zusammenkriechen\*** to crouch

**Zuschauertum** n state of being an onlooker

**Zuwarten** n waiting

**Zuwenig** n deficiency

**Zweig,** Stefan (1881–1942) Austrian poet, novelist and biographer

**Zweigwerk** n boughs

**Zwergobstbaum** m ¨e dwarf fruit tree

**zwiegestalt** dimorphous

**zwischenein** at times

# SELECTED BIBLIOGRAPHY

Andrews, R. C. "The Poetry of Hermann Hesse: A Birthday Tribute (1877–1952)." *German Life and Letters* 29(1952):117–27.

Anselm, Felix. "Hermann Hesse." *Poet Lore* 53(1947):353–60.

Artiss, David. "Key Symbols in Hesse's *Steppenwolf.*" *Seminar* (Toronto) 7(1971):85–101

Bandy, Steven C. "Hermann Hesse's *Das Glasperlenspiel* in Search of Joseph Knecht." *Modern Language Quarterly* 33(1972):299–311.

Baumer, Franz. *Hermann Hesse.* Translated by John Conway. New York: Frederick Ungar Publishing Co., Modern Literature Monographs Series, 1969.

Beerman, Hans. "Hermann Hesse and the Bhagavad-Gita." *Midwest Quarterly* 1(1959):27–40.

Benn, Maurice. "An Interpretation of the Work of Hermann Hesse." *Life and Letters* (Oxford)3(1950):202–11.

Boa, Elizabeth, and Reid, J. H. *Critical Strategies: German Fiction in the Twentieth Century.* Montreal: McGill-Queen's University Press, 1972.

Bonwit, Marianne. "Der leidende Dritte." *University of California Publications in Modern Philology* 36(1952):91–111.

Boulby, Mark. *Hermann Hesse: His Mind and Art.* Ithaca, N.Y.: Cornell University Press, 1967.

———. "Der vierte Lebenslauf, as a Key to *Das Glasperlenspiel.*" *Modern Language Review* 59(1966):635–46.

Bretenskey, Dennis F. *Siddhartha:* A Casebook on Teaching Methods." *English Journal* 62(1973):379–82.

Brink, A. W. "Hermann Hesse and the Oedipal Quest." *Literature and Psychology* 24(1974):66–79.

Brownjohn, A. "German Protestant in Guru's Clothing." *Encounter* 41(1973):103–7.

Brunner, John W. "The *Natur-Geist* Polarity in Hermann Hesse." In *Helen Adolf Festschrift,* edited by Sheema Z. Buehne, James L. Hodge, and Lucille B. Pinto, pp. 268–84. New York: Frederick Ungar Publishing Co., 1968.

Buchanan, Harvey. "Hermann Hesse's Pilgrimage." *Shenandoah* 9(1958): 18–22.

Butler, Colin. "Defective Art of Hermann Hesse." *Journal of European Studies* 5(1975):41–54.

———. "Hermann Hesse's *Siddhartha:* Some Critical Objections." *Monatshefte* 63(1971):117–24.

———. "Literary Malpractice in Some Works of Hermann Hesse." *University of Toronto Quarterly* 40(1971):168–82.

Casebeer, Edwin F. *Hermann Hesse.* New York: Warner Paperback Library, Writers for the Seventies Series, 1972.

Cast, Gottlob C. "Hermann Hesse als Erzieher." *Monatshefte* 43(1951): 207–20.

Clement, Samuel. "An Act of Mental Synthesis." *The Gazette* (Montreal), January 17, 1970.

Cohn, D. "Narration of Consciousness in *Der Steppenwolf.*" *Germanic Review* 44(1969):121–31.

Cohn, Hilde D. "The Symbolic End of Hermann Hesse's *Glasperlenspiel.*" *Modern Language Quarterly* 2(1950):347–57.

Colby, Thomas E. "The Impenitent Prodigal: Hermann Hesse's Hero." *German Quarterly* 40(1967):14–23.

Crenshaw, Karen O., and Lawson, Richard H. "Technique and Function of Time in Hesse's *Morgenlandfahrt:* A Culmination." *Mosaic* (Winnipeg)5(1972):53–59.

Crosby, Donald H. "Goethe's *Wiederfinden* and Hesse's *Zu einer Tokkata von Bach.*" *German Quarterly* 39(1966):140–47.

Dehorn, W. "Psychoanalyse und neuere Dichtung." *Germanic Review* 7(1932):245–62, 330–58.

Deml, Ferdinand. "Hermann Hesse—the Opponent of Violence." *Central Europe Journal* (Bonn) (July–August 1972):278–82.

Diamond, William. "Hermann Hesses Weltanschauung." *Monatshefte* 22(1930):39–44, 65–71.

Digan, Kathleen E. *Hermann Hesse's Narcissus and Goldmund: A Phenomenological Study.* New York: Revisionist Press, 1975.

Domino, Ruth. "The Hunchback and Wings (*Steppenwolf*)." *Approach* 2(1957):20–28.

Engle, Eva J. "Hermann Hesse." *German Men of Letters* 48(1964):251–74.

von Faber du Faur, Curt. "Zu Hermann Hesses *Glasperlenspiel.*" *Monatshefte* 40(1948):177–94.

Farquharson, Robert H. *An Outline of the Works of Hermann Hesse.* Toronto: Forum House Publishing Co., 1973.

———. "The Identity and Significance of Leo in Hesse's *Morgenlandfahrt.*" *Monatshefte* 55(1963):122–28.

Fickert, Kurt J. "The Development of the Outsider Concept in Hesse's Novels." *Monatshefte* 52(1960):171–78.

———. "The Friendship Theme in Hesse's Novels." *University of Dayton Review* 10(1973):47–56.

———. "Symbolism in Hesse's *Heumond.*" *German Quarterly* 34(1961): 118–22.

Field, George Wallis. "On the Genesis of the *Glasperlenspiel.*" *German Quarterly* 41(1968):673–88.

———. *Das Glasperlenspiel:* Concerning the Date of Its Einleitung." *German Quarterly* 43(1970):538–39.

———. *Hermann Hesse.* Boston: Twayne's World Authors, 1970.

———. *Hermann Hesse.* New York: Hippocrene Books, 1972.

———. "Hermann Hesse as Critic of English and American Literature." *Monatshefte* 53(1961):147–58.

———. "Hermann Hesse: A Neglected Nobel Prize Novelist." *Queen's Quarterly* (Kingston)65(1961):514–20.

———. "Music and Morality in Thomas Mann and Hermann Hesse." *University of Toronto Quarterly* 24(1955):175–90.

Flaxman, Seymour L. *"Der Steppenwolf:* Hesse's Portrait of the Intellectual." *Modern Language Quarterly* 40(1954):349–58.

Foran, Marion N. "Hermann Hesse." *Queen's Quarterly* (Kingston)40 (1948):180–89.

Ford, Richard J. "Hermann Hesse: Prophet of the Pot Generation." *Catholic World* 212(1970):15–19.

Freedman, Ralph. "Hermann Hesse." *Contemporary Literature* 10(1969): 421–26.

———. *The Lyrical Novel: Studies in Hermann Hesse, André Gide, and Virginia Woolf.* Princeton, N.J.: Princeton University Press, 1963.

———. "Romantic Imagination: Hermann Hesse as a Modern Novelist." *PMLA* 73(1958):275–84.

Friedrichsmeyer, E. "Bertram Episode in Hesse's *Glass Bead Game.*" *Germanic Review* 49(1974):284–97.

Goldgar, Harry. "Hesse's *Glasperlenspiel* and the Game of Go." *German Life and Letters* 20(1966):132–37.

Gontrum, Peter B. "Hermann Hesse as a Critic of French Literature." *Symposium* 19(1965):226–35..

———. "Oracle and Shrine: Hesse's *Lebensbaum.*" *Monatshefte* 56(1964): 183–90.

Gowan, Birdeena L. *"Demian,* by Hermann Hesse." *Monatshefte* 20(1928): 225–28.

Gropper, Esther C. "The Disenchanted Turn to Hesse." *English Journal* 61(1972):979–84.

Gross, Harvey. "Hermann Hesse." *Western Review* 17(1953):132–40.

Hallamore, Joyce. "Paul Klee, Hermann Hesse, and *Die Morgenlandfahrt.*" *Seminar* (New South Wales)1(1965):17–24.

Halpert, Inge D. "The 'Alt-Musikmeister' and Goethe." *Monatshefte* 52(1960):19–24.

———. *"Vita activa* and *Vita contemplativa."* *Monatshefte* 53(1961):159–66.

———. "Wilhelm Meister and Joseph Knecht." *German Quarterly* 34(1961):11–20.

Heilbut, Ivan; Jacobson, Anna; and Shuster, George N. *Die Sendung Hermann Hesses. Drei Beiträge zur Würdigung des Dichters.* New York, 1947.

Heller, Peter. "The Creative Unconscious and the Spirit: A Study of Polarities in Hesse's Image of the Writer." *Modern Language Forum* 38(1953):28–40.

———. "The Masochistic Rebel in Recent German Literature." *Journal of Aesthetics and Art Criticism* 2(1953):198–213.

———. "The Writer in Conflict with His Age: A Study in the Ideology of Hermann Hesse." *Monatshefte* 46(1954):137–47.

Hertz, Peter D. *"Steppenwolf* as a Bible." *Georgia Review* 25(1971):439–49.

317

Herzog, Peter Heinz. "Hermann Hesse and China: Chinese Influence in the Earlier Works of the German Poet." *United College Journal* (Hong Kong)9(1971):231–39.

Hill, Claude. "Hermann Hesse als Kritiker der bürgerlichen Zivilisation." *Monatshefte* 40(1948):241–53.

————. "Hermann Hesse and Germany." *German Quarterly* 21(1948):9–15.

Hirschback, Frank D. "Traum und Vision bei Hesse." *Monatshefte* 51(1959):157–68.

Hughes, Kenneth. "Hermann Hesse's Use of Gilgamesh Motifs in the Humanization of Siddhartha and Harry Haller." *Seminar: A Journal of Germanic Studies* 5(1969):129–40.

Iben, Icko. "Hesse's Humor." *Scripta Humanica Kentuckiensia* 3(1957). (Supplement to *Kentucky Foreign Language Quarterly*.)

Jacobson, Anna. "Hermann Hesse: Anlässlich der Auszeichnung durch den Nobelpreis." *Monatshefte* 39(1947):1–8.

Jaeger, Hans. "Heidegger's Existential Philosophy and German Modern Literature." *PMLA* 67(1952):635.

Jehle, Mimi. "Das moderne deutsche Kunstmärchen." *Journal of English and German Philology* 33(1934):452–61, 475–78.

————. "The Garden in the Works of Hermann Hesse." *German Quarterly* 24(1951):42–50.

Johnson, Sidney M. "The Autobiographies in Herman Hesse's *Glasperlenspiel.*" *German Quarterly* 29(1956):160–71.

Jonas, Klaus W. "Additions to the Bibliography of Hermann Hesse." *Papers of the Bibliographical Society of America* 49(1955):358–60.

————. "Hermann Hesse in Amerika: Bibliographie 1914–1952." *Monatshefte* 44(1952):95–99.

Joyce, Robert E. "Toward the Resolution of Polarities in Hermann Hesse's *Steppenwolf.*" *American Benedictine Review* 17(1966):336–41.

Kilchenmann, Ruth J. "Hermann Hesse und die Dinge: Unter Bezugnahme auf Rainer Maria Rilke." *German Quarterly* 30(1957):238–46.

————. "Der Stil Hesses als Ausdruck seiner Persönlichkeit." *Kentucky Foreign Language Quarterly* 5(1958):95–99.

Klaiber, P. H. "Hermann Hesse." *Monatsblätter für deutsche Literatur* 8(1903):11–13.

Klawiter, Randolf J. "The Artist-Intellectual In or Versus Society?: A Dilemma." In *Studies in German Literature of the Nineteenth and Twentieth Centuries* (Festschrift for Frederic E. Coenen), pp. 236–50. Chapel Hill: University of North Carolina Press, Studies in Germanic Languages and Literature, 67, 1970.

Koch, S., "Prophet of Youth." *New Republic,* July 13, 1968, pp. 23–26.

Koester, Rudolf. "Hesse's Music Master: In Search of a Prototype." *Forum for Modern Language Studies* (St. Andrews)3(1967):135–41.

————. "Hesse and the Problem of Aging." *Texas Studies in Literature and Language* 7(1966):362–69.

————. "The Portrayal of Age in Hesse's Narrative Prose." *Germanic Review* 41(1966):111–19.

318

————. "Self-Realization: Hesse's Reflection on Youth." *Monatshefte* 57(1965):181–86.

————. "Terminal Sanctity or Benign Banality: The Critical Controversy surrounding Hermann Hesse." *Bulletin of the Rocky Mountain Modern Language Association* 27(1973):59–63.

Lange, Marga. " 'Daseinproblematik' in Hermann Hesse's *Steppenwolf*: An Existential Interpretation." *Queensland Studies in German Language and Literature* (Brisbane)1(1970):85.

Lesser, J. "Nobel Prize Winner." *Contemporary Review* 171(1947):31–34.

Leuchter, Johanna. "Sex Roles in Three of Herman Hesse's Novels." In *Images of Women in Fiction: Feminist Perspectives*, pp. 175–80. Bowling Green, O.: Bowling Green University Popular Press, 1972.

Malthaner, Johannes. "Hermann Hesse's *Siddhartha*." *German Quarterly* 25(1952):103–9.

Mann, Thomas. "Hermann Hesse: Liberator of a Stifling Provincialism." *Saturday Review of Literature*, January 3, 1948, pp. 5–7.

Maurer, Warren R. "Some Aspects of the Jean Paul–Hermann Hesse Relationship with Special Reference to *Katzenberger* and *Kurgast*." *Seminar: A Journal of Germanic Studies* 4(1968):113–28.

Michels, Volker, ed. *Hermann Hesse: A Pictorial Biography*. Translated by Yetta and Theodore Ziolkowski. New York: Farrar, Straus, and Giroux, 1975.

————. "Hesse in den U.S.A.—Hesse bei uns." *Westermanns Monatshefte* 5(1971):52–59.

Middleton, J. C. "An Enigma Transformed in Hermann Hesse's *Glasperlenspiel*." *German Life and Letters* 10(1957):298–302.

————. "Hermann Hesse's *Morgenlandfahrt*." *Germanic Review* 32(1957): 299–310.

Mileck, Joseph. "*Das Glasperlenspiel*: Concerning the Date of Its Einleitung." *German Quarterly* 43(1970):539–41.

————. "*Das Glasperlenspiel*: Genesis, Manuscripts, and History of Publication." *German Quarterly* 43(1970):55–83.

————. *Hermann Hesse and His Critics: The Criticism and Bibliography of Half a Century*. Chapel Hill: University of North Carolina Press, 1958.

————. "Hermann Hesse as an Editor." In *Studies in German Literature of the Nineteenth and Twentieth Centuries* (Festschrift for Frederic E. Coenen), pp. 210–22. Chapel Hill: University of North Carolina Press, Studies in Germanic Languages and Literature, 67, 1970.

von Molnár, Geza. "The Ideological Framework of Hermann Hesse's *Siddhartha*." *Die Unterrichtspraxis* 4(1971):82–87.

Pachter, Henry M. "On Re-reading Hermann Hesse." *Salmagundi* 12(1970):83–89.

Parry, Idris. "*The Glass Bead Game*." In I. Parry, *Animals of Silence: Essays on Art, Nature, and Folk-Tale*. London: Oxford University Press, 1972.

Paslick, R. H. "Dialectic and Non-Attachment: The Structure of Hermann Hesse's *Siddhartha*." *Symposium* 27(1973):64–75.

Peer, Larry H. "The Glass Beads in Hesse's *Glasperlenspiel.*" *Notes on Contemporary Literature* 2(1972):7–8.

Pevert, Krystyna. "Hermann Hesse: Apostle of the Apolitical Revolution." *Tri-Quarterly* 23–24(1972):302–17.

Ranly, Ernest W. *"Journey to the East." Commonweal* 97(1973):465–69.

Reichert, H. W., et al. "Discussion of Herbert W. Reichert: Nietzsche's Impact on the Prose Writings of Hermann Hesse." *Symposium* 28(1974):52–57.

Ritchie, Gisela F. "Stifter und *Der Steppenwolf:* Ein Beitrag zu den geistigen Beziehungen grosser Dichter." In *Husbanding the Golden Grain: Studies in Honor of Henry W. Nordmeyer,* pp. 265–78. Ann Arbor: University of Michigan Press, 1973.

Rose, Ernst A. "The Beauty from Pao: Heine-Bierbaum-Hesse." *Germanic Review* 32(1957):5–18.

———. *Faith from the Abyss: Hermann Hesse's Way from Romanticism to Modernity.* New York: New York University Press, 1965.

Schludermann, Brigitte, and Finlay, Rosemarie. "Mythical Reflections of the East in Hermann Hesse." *Mosaic: A Journal for the Comparative Study of Literature and Ideas* 2(1969):97–111.

Schneider, Christian I. *Hermann Hesse's "Betrachtung des Krieges."* Proceedings of the Pacific Northwest Conference on Foreign Languages, Twentieth Annual Meeting, April 11–12, 1969. Vol. 20. Edited by Jerrold L. Mordaunt. Victoria, B.C.: University of Victoria.

Schwarz, Egon. "Hermann Hesse, the American Youth Movement, and Problems of Literary Evaluation." *PMLA* 85(1970):977–87.

———. "Zur Erklärung von Hesses *Steppenwolf.*" *Monatshefte* 53(1961): 191–98.

Seidlin, Oskar. "Hermann Hesse's *Glasperlenspiel.*" *Germanic Review* 23(1948):263–73.

———. "Hermann Hesse: The Exorcism of the Demon." *Symposium* 4(1950):325–48.

Serrano, Miguel. *C. G. Jung and Hermann Hesse: A Record of Two Friendships.* New York: Schocken Books, 1965.

Shaw, Leroy R. "Time and Structure of Hermann Hesse's *Siddhartha.*" *Symposium* 2(1957):204–24.

Sorrell, Walter. *Hermann Hesse: The Man Who Sought and Found Himself.* Atlantic Highlands, N.J.: Humanities Press, Modern German Authors Series, 2, 1975.

Spector, Robert Donald. "Artist Against Himself: Hesse's *Siddhartha.*" *History of Ideas Newsletter* 4(1958):55–58.

Spivack, C. "The Journey to Hell, Satan, the Shadow, and the Self." *Centennial Review* 9(1965):420–37.

Spivey, Ted R. "The Reintegration of Modern Man: An Essay on James Joyce and Hermann Hesse." *Studies in the Literary Imagination* (Georgia State College)3(1970):49–64.

Stein, Gisela. "Earlier Versions of Two Hesse Poems 'Einst vor tausend Jahren,' 'Nachst in April notiert.' " *Germanic Review* 39(1964):300–304.

Steiner, Georg. "Eastward Ho!" *New Yorker,* January 18, 1969, pp. 87–97.

Taylor, Harley U. "The Death Wish and Suicide in the Novels of Hermann Hesse." *West Virginia University Philological Papers* 13(1961):50–64.

———. "Hermann Hesse's Berthold: Probable Source of *Narziss and Goldmund." West Virginia University Philological Papers* 20(1973):43–46.

———. "Homoerotic Elements in the Novels of Hermann Hesse." *West Virginia University Philological Papers* 16(1967):63–71.

Taylor, Rachel Annand. "Fiction. Forms of Personality: *Steppenwolf." Spectator,* May 18, 1929, pp. 790–93.

*Times Literary Supplement.* "Cultivating Hesse." (London), August 31, 1973, pp. 989–91.

Timpe, Eugene F. "Hermann Hesse in the United States." *Symposium* 23(1969):73–78.

———. 'Hesse's Siddhartha and the Bhagavad-Gita." *Comparative Literature* 22(1970):346–57.

Townsend, Stanley R. "The German Humanist Hermann Hesse: Nobel Prize Winner in 1946." *Modern Language Forum* 23(1947):1–12.

Toynbee, Philip. "Hermann Hesse: The Prodigy." *The Observer* (London), April 28, 1957.

Vordtriede, Werner. "Hermann Hesse: *Das Glasperlenspiel." German Quarterly* 19(1946):291–94.

Webb, Eugene. "Hermine and the Problem of Harry's Failure in Hesse's *Steppenwolf." Modern Fiction Studies* 17(1971):115–24.

Weimar, Karl S. "*Siddhartha,* translated by Hilda Rosner." *German Quarterly* 26(1953):301–2.

Willecke, Frederic H. "Style and Form of Hesse's *Unterm Rad." Kentucky Foreign Language Quarterly* 8(1961):147–56.

Willson, A. Leslie. "Hesse's Veil of Isis." *Monatshefte* 55(1963):313–21.

Wood, Ralph Charles. "Hermann Hesse." *American-German Review* 23(1956):3–5, 38.

Zeller, Bernhard, ed. *Portrait of Hesse: An Illustrated Biography.* New York: McGraw-Hill Book Co., 1971.

Ziolkowski, Theodore, *Fictional Transfigurations of Jesus,* pp. 151–61. Princeton, N.J.: Princeton University Press, 1972.

———. *Hermann Hesse.* New York: Columbia University Press, 1966.

———. "Hermann Hesse's Chiliastic Vision." *Monatshefte* 53(1961): 199–210.

———. *Hesse: A Collection of Critical Essays.* Los Angeles: Phoenix House, Twentieth Century Views Series, 1973.

———. "Hermann Hesse: *Der vierte Lebenslauf." Germanic Review* 42(1967):124–43.

———. "Hermann Hesse's *Steppenwolf:* A Sonata in Prose." *Modern Language Quarterly* 19(1958):115–33.

———. "Hesse's Sudden Popularity with Today's Students." *University* (Princeton, N.J.)45(1970):19–25.

———. *The Novels of Hermann Hesse: A Study in Theme and Structure.* Princeton, N.J.: Princeton University Press, 1965.

————. "Saint Hesse Among the Hippies." *American-German Review* 35(1969):19–23.

————. "Quest for the Grail in Hesse's *Demian.*" *Germanic Review* 49(1974):44–59.

————. *Zur Aktualität des Glasperlenspiels.* aus seinem Vorwort zu amerikanischen Ausgabe des Glasperlenspiels. New York: Holt, Rinehart and Winston, 1969.

Zweig, Stefan. "*Demian.*" *New York Times Book Review*, April 8, 1923, p. 14.

# SELECTED DISSERTATIONS ON HESSE

Boarsma, Clarence. "The Educational Ideal of the Major Works of Hermann Hesse." (University of Michigan, 1949).

Bruechner, Werner. "The Discovery and Integration of Evil in the Fiction of Joseph Conrad and Hermann Hesse." (University of Arizona, 1972).

Colby, Thomas E. "Hermann Hesse's Attitude Toward Authority: A Study." (Princeton University, 1959).

Donovan, Joseph C. "Gnosticism in Modern Literature: A Study of Selected Works of Camus, Sartre, Hesse and Kafka." (University of Wisconsin, 1971).

Dow, James R. "Hermann Hesse's Märchen: A Study of Sources, Themes, and Importance of Hesse's Märchen and Other Works of Fantasy." (University of Iowa, 1966).

Farrar, Edward A. "The Quest for Being: D. H. Lawrence and Hermann Hesse." (Purdue University, 1975).

Fickert, Kurt J. "The Problem of the Artist and the Philistine in the Work of Hermann Hesse." (New York University, 1952).

Grimes, James M. "The Nature of Hesse's Glass Bead Game and Its Function in the Novel." (Vanderbilt University, 1972).

Gould, Loyal N. "Romantic Traits in the Main Characters of Hermann Hesse." (University of North Carolina, 1955).

Gouvens, Marjorie. "Hermann Hesse in America (and England): A Bibliography and Commentary." (Indiana University, 1975).

Halpert, Inge D. "Hermann Hesse and Goethe, with Particular Reference to the Relationship of *Wilhelm Meister* and *Das Glasperlenspiel.*" (Columbia University, 1957).

Heller, Peter. "The Writer's Image of the Writer. A Study in the Ideologies of Six German Authors, 1918–1933 (Thomas Mann, Hermann Hesse, Toller, Grimm, Brecht, Jünger)." (Columbia University, 1951).

Karr, Susan Elisabeth. "Hermann Hesse's Fairy Tales." (University of Washington, 1972).

Kilchenmann, Ruth J. "Wandel in der Gestaltung der Natur in den Werken Hermann Hesses." (University of Southern California, 1956).

Leaman, Ellen A. "Self-affirmation and Self-abnegation as Limiting Factors in the Work of Hermann Hesse." (Tulane University, 1966–67).

Maier, Emanuel. "The Psychology of C. G. Jung in the Works of Hermann Hesse." (New York University, 1952).

McCormick, John O. "Thomas Wolfe, André Malraux, and Hermann Hesse. A Study in Creative Vitality." (Harvard University, 1951).

Middleton, J. C. "Hermann Hesse as Humanist." (Oxford University, 1954).

Mileck, Joseph. "Hermann Hesse. A Study." (Harvard University, 1950).

Miller, Jean Sawyer. "The Search for Identity in Selected Novels of

Hermann Hesse: A Thematic Study for the Secondary Schools."
(University of Georgia, 1972).

Remys, Edmund. "Hermann Hesse's *Das Glasperlenspiel.* A Concealed
Defense of the Mother World." (University of Cincinnati, 1975).

Rich, Doris E. "Der deutsche Entwicklungsroman am Ende der bürgerlichen Kultur 1892–1924." (Radcliffe College, 1940).

Rudebusch, Verne A. "A Thematic Analysis of Hermann Hesse's *Narcissus and Goldmund.*" (University of Cincinnati, 1973).

Schneider, Christian I. "Der Tod als dichterisches Grundmotiv und
Existenzproblem bei Hermann Hesse." (University of California,
Santa Barbara, 1968).

Talafous, Don Francis. "The Theological Anthropology of Hermann
Hesse's Novels." (Graduate Theological Union, 1972).

Willecke, Frederick Henry. "The Style and Form of Hermann Hesse's
Gaienhofer Novellen." (New York University, 1960).

Woerner, Robert Frederick. "D. H. Lawrence and Hermann Hesse: A
Comparative Study of Two Critics of Modern Culture." (Indiana
University, 1962).

Ziolkowski, Theodore Joseph. "Hermann Hesse and Novalis." (Yale
University, 1956).